MW01244147

When the
SMOKE
Cleared

A MURDER MYSTERY IN MALDEN

A True Crime procedural by
the lead police investigator

BILL POWERS

POWERSCOURT
PRESS

When the Smoke Cleared: A Murder Mystery in Malden
A PowersOnPolicing True Crime Thriller
by Bill Powers

Copyright © 2023 by Bill Powers

No part of this book may be reproduced, stored in a retrieval system, or transmitted in any form by any means, electric, mechanical, including photocopying and recording, or by any information storage and retrieval system, without prior written permission from the publisher other than the inclusion of brief quotations embodied in articles and reviews.

This is a work of non-fiction and depicts actual events in the life of the author as truthfully as recollection and research permits. None of the events or their locations have been altered or fabricated. All persons mentioned within are actual individuals; there are no composite characters. However, several participant's names have been changed to respect their privacy and safety. On occasion, dialogue consistent with the character or nature of the person has been supplemented.

Published by

PC POWERSCOURT
PRESS
www.powersonpolicing.com

ISBN: 979-8-9866824-0-2
LCCN: data on file

Editing by Cynde Christie, WritingCoachCynde.com
Cover and Interior Design by Nick Zelinger, NZGraphics.com

First Edition

Printed in the United States of America

I dedicate this book to my Dad who taught me
what "right" looked like.
He was my counsel, guiding light and mentor:
A giant among men: Big Bill Powers

"I never will forget him
For he made me "what I am"
Though he may be gone
Memories linger on
And I miss him, the old man"
Phil Coulter

"It is not the critic who counts; not the man who points out how the strong man stumbles, or where the doer of deeds could have done them better. The credit belongs to the man who is actually in the arena, whose face is marred by dust and sweat and blood; who strives valiantly; who errs, who comes short again and again, because there is no effort without error and shortcoming; but who does actually strive to do the deeds; who knows great enthusiasms, the great devotions; who spends himself in a worthy cause; who at the best knows in the end the triumph of high achievement, and who at the worst, if he fails, at least fails while daring greatly, so that his place shall never be with those cold and timid souls who neither know victory nor defeat."

Teddy Roosevelt

Table of Contents

Prologue

The Kelly Hancock case is a story of the vicious murder of a vulnerable young runaway by a ruthless predator, but I believe it is also a love story—maybe not in the conventional way we think about love, but in some ways, at an even higher level. That's a judgment call I will leave for you to consider when you close the cover to this book.

On July 18, 2000, I responded to a call from Sgt. Jimmy Connolly for a possible homicide in Malden, MA. In the midmorning on a hot and muggy day when I maneuvered my Crown Vic around an idling fire engine and into a parking space in the lot of the midsized condo complex. I spotted Malden Sergeant Steve Ruelle, and Inspector Johnny Rivers talking with Connolly and two Troopers assigned to our office, Eddie Forster and Duke Donoghue. They seemed nonchalant in their conversation outside the building's front entrance as people walked in and out without anyone stopping and questioning them, which surprised me a bit.

My first impression was that they were acting this way because they had a handle on things and maybe the facts did not support the reason for the callout. That hasty thought disappeared as a worst-case scenario one crept in: that perhaps this wasn't a classic scene where someone was dead, someone was under arrest, the murder weapon bagged and tagged, and we were just waiting for the death wagon from the morgue to show up. Unfortunately, history said my gut feeling was most likely the correct one.

My name is Bill Powers and after more than two decades as an investigator, supervisor, and detective unit commander, I've learned a bit about homicide cops and prosecutors. Experienced homicide cops, male and female, have a way about them. It isn't arrogance, ego, or swagger but a subtle reveal of self-assurance and confidence often referred to as a command presence, the ability to exhibit self-control while in the midst of chaos. Hard to define in a few words, and maybe it takes one to know one, but I can spot a detective that "does bodies" a mile away.

I also know a little something about reading body language, and collectively, they weren't giving off any encouraging vibes. No one looked in my direction or acknowledged my arrival. No one had a notebook or pen in hand. No one was on their cell phone or running around with their hair on fire like something important was happening or developing. A lack of urgency or intensity was never a good sign.

"What have we got?" I asked.

"Honestly, Dlt, we don't know," said John Rivers. "We are just getting started and you can bet we will get to the bottom of it, and when we do, you just know it's going to be a pissah of a story."

That, we would learn, was the understatement of the day.

Our relentless investigation over the next several months developed a person of interest and a fistful of potentially damning evidence but no victim or unidentified corpse. Even with some local media attention, we didn't receive one call or lead to send us off in any direction. The case remained active, and there was never a thought by any one of us that the file would find its way to the cold case cabinet. As days turned into months and many new and old death investigations required attention, the heat on this case reduced to a simmer but never was it moved to the back burner.

This event happened two decades ago, yet for my unit and myself, and all who worked on the investigation, the memories are as fresh as if it happened this year. I had never fashioned myself as an author, but I do believe I can compose a compelling story. This recounting of the factual events of this case, from the crime scene through to the jury verdict, is fascinating and absorbing but also educational. By personalizing this story, I trust you will see victims of crime and their surviving family members through a broader and brighter lens: one focused on compassion, empathy, and understanding about the pain and grief of others. Likewise, I hope you will gain a better understanding and a more positive view of the people who have dedicated their professional lives to keeping all of us a little safer and more secure.

. . . .

Homicide detectives differ from other professionals. The most important thing to know is we are neither special nor heroes because of what we do. We may be your neighbors or someone you recognize from church, or youth sporting events, or someone you wave to while you are getting rid of your trash at the town transfer station on Saturday morning.

We do not wear five hundred dollar business suits or eat in expensive restaurants. We buy our clothes at bargain marts and wholesale clubs. When we find time to eat while working we generally grab a sandwich at a neighborhood market or we sit in the parking lot of a McDonald's wolfing down a burger and fries from the $2 menu while going over witness interview reports. We are this way because history tells us it is likely we will be spending part of the day searching through a bloody crime scene with a rapidly decomposing body or climbing into a putrid dumpster, fending off rats and seagulls while ripping through bags of fetid garbage to search for discarded evidence. Through experience, we know that if the setting becomes a little overwhelming to the senses and we puke on our partners or ourselves, it is better the stuff we just spent five dollars on ends up on a pullover purchased at Walmart for twenty bucks. It is gross, and it sucks, but you can't run from it—and you better be fighting to be the first one in or you will hear about it from the others.

The professional life of homicide investigators and prosecutors is one of fits and starts. The pace is not only uneven and unpredictable but can sway from monotonous to intense in a quick minute. The upbeat and pleasant tempo of the office can change considerably moments after someone answers an urgent call from a local police department (PD) or a medical examiner's office (OCME). For others, all of the reasons for not wanting to take on the mission are understandable and reasonable. Thankfully, we homicide cops thrive on the lifestyle, the unpredictable pressures, and the challenges that the position demands. We look forward to the sound of the ringing phone and the call to saddle up.

Our mission is to examine how and why someone died. Our goal is to conduct an extensive and meticulous investigation through the collection of evidence and information with the prospect that the medical examiner can match our information with their medical findings and determine the cause and manner of death. If it is ruled a homicide, then our primary objective is to bring those responsible to justice.

In every homicide investigation, detectives and prosecutors share one common goal: to fully investigate the case and ultimately bring the person or persons responsible for the death(s) before a judge and jury. Oftentimes we inch along a narrow legal tightrope as we conduct searches and interrogate "people of interest," fully aware that one ill-considered move or poor decision could send us into a free fall with the potential of a disastrous ending. In order to avoid those missteps, we build a series of safety nets to prevent fatal mistakes and unnecessary damage to the case. We work collaboratively, meet often, and value and encourage differing opinions and insight, as well as discussions about our various experiences. When done right, the ending is as hoped, an arrest and conviction. There is no high fiving and fist pumping in the courtroom. There is only a smile and shared nods acknowledging that we did our job well and the judge and jury validated the combined efforts of the police, the crime lab, the Medical Examiner, and the prosecutor.

Over time, I've come to believe that being a homicide investigator is not a job but a unique calling that requires a total commitment of the heart, brain, and soul. As heartbreaking and depressing as the job is at times, I have never done anything more important or rewarding in my professional life. As one of my peers sighed one evening after a heartbreaking death notification, "I love what I do; I just don't always love what I have to do." It is a saying I repeat in my head on an almost daily basis.

• • • •

In 2000, the year Kelly Hancock was murdered, I was a detective lieutenant and, by title, the commanding officer of the detective unit in the Middlesex County District Attorney's Office. I'd had twenty-six years of service with a handful of previous detective assignments in every rank. I had been in Middlesex as a sergeant in the early 1990s before my promotion and transfer as detective lieutenant to the Suffolk County District Attorney's Office. My heart was always in Middlesex, though, and when Martha Coakley secured the election as district attorney (DA), I applied for the leadership position. She selected me to return home; it was perhaps the happiest day in my career.

At Middlesex, I was a member of an extraordinary team. We were a cadre of state police officers acting as the DA's designees to investigate significant felony crimes, including all sudden, unattended deaths reported in any of the fifty-four cities and towns and twenty-one college campuses that fall inside the county borders. Middlesex is one of eleven District Attorney's Offices (DAOs) in the Commonwealth. The jurisdiction is the largest with one-fifth of the real estate and a population that is more than double that of any other county.

Our unit had an overall "station strength" of twenty-four, but that number could fluctuate up or down depending on the department's assets and needs at the time. Several officers worked the Narcotic and Public Protection Unit, while the rest of the unit "did bodies," or, as others would call it "working the dark side." In 2000, there were four homicide teams, each with a sergeant and two troopers. In addition, there was an executive officer—a lieutenant—with oversight over some cases. We are a small, intimate group of men and women who thrive on loyalty, camaraderie, and the mission of investigating deaths and solving murders. There are no alpha dogs or lone wolves. We do not work independent of our colleagues. We are faithful to one another and our investigations to a fault.

• • • •

The usual office routine was to dispatch one officer to a scene where the cause of death was not apparent but probably not a homicide. If the call was for a homicide, the team responded. Because death doesn't work on a timetable or occur during normal working hours, an officer and team had the off-hours call every weekday and/or the weekend. We always posted the schedule a month in advance so everyone could plan his or her lives accordingly. Assignment swapping happened frequently based on family needs and court responsibilities. Someone was always willing to step up and fill in the void.

Massachusetts has a unique system that determines how we investigate deaths. The law dictates that the DA in each county has direct oversight of all death cases. They also have the discretion to nominate whom they want as their investigators. In all but four major cities, their designees are the state police.

Additionally, the law requires that the state troopers work in partnership with the PD of jurisdiction on all death investigations. Sounds a bit convoluted and problematic, but with the right people in place, it works perfectly. In general, we bring a lot of knowledge and experience to the table, as well as all of the department's resources, like the Crime Lab Unit, the Air Wing Unit, and the Underwater Recovery Unit. The local detectives may not have had a homicide in their city or town in decades, so they lack experience, but they know and understand the geography and the demographics of their community, and they usually know the "players" as well. Most often, the arrangement works perfectly.

• • • •

The trip from my home on the south side of Boston to the office at the Middlesex County Courthouse on the north side of the city was a mere ten and a half miles, but in the morning rush hour that could take anywhere from forty-five minutes to an hour and a half, door to door. Thankfully, I had a CD player with a five-tray carousal and half dozen Bose speakers along for the ride. My musical choices were important because they typically stimulated my brain and set the mood for the day ahead. I might have relied on the invigorating music of Faith Hill or the percussion drumbeats of Phil Collins, but more than likely, the festive Irish tribal music from the Wolf Tones or the Saw Doctors energized the start of my day.

Getting from the breakfast counter at home to my desk at work was a four-step ritual. The drive was the first step; finding a parking place in a neighborhood full of private homes and small businesses was the second. Anything within a quarter of a mile was a victory.

The third was the approach to the entrance into the Middlesex County Courthouse. At quarter to nine every weekday, a crowd arrived for work or a court appearance. They came from all directions and merged on the sidewalk out front. They pushed toward the one and only doorway. They bumped and jostled one another before surging inside and up a few stairs to the security checkpoint. The intense anxiety that comes with a court appearance was already coursing through the nervous systems of most in the crowd. Jurors, victims, and witnesses might have found themselves standing a few feet from defendants or their attorneys, squished together like sardines in a can. They inched forward, trying hard not to make eye contact or hear their name spoken. Once through the security checkpoint, they bolted toward the bank of elevators and took a quick trip upstairs to the offices and courtrooms.

Surviving the entrance ritual brings me to the final, but critical, step in the process: the coffee run. Failure to make that call from the lobby was something you did at your own peril. It didn't matter that you didn't drink coffee or weren't in the mood for a cup; it only mattered others might. The reasoning was simple: we were family, and we took care of one another. We extended this courtesy to everyone in the office, including visitors and assistant district attorneys (ADAs). To skip that call was an affront to all, and the shame and humiliation you would suffer for not calling wasn't worth deviating from the family norm. Failure to call would present the opening everyone was looking for to pound away at your thoughtlessness. While they might not remember the great cases you solved, they would never forget the day you failed to make a coffee call. You could count on an anecdotal comment or two about your "alligator arms" by a speaker at your retirement party.

On a mid-July morning, I thought my call was going to cost me a sawbuck for six coffees until a voice chimed in for a Mountain Dew. With tip, I got five back from my twenty and a lesson on being in on time so someone else had to make that call.

Despite the daily chaos, having our office in the same building as the courtrooms, the DAO, and the county jail was a huge plus. It was efficient, and there would always be troopers nearby if there were issues or outbreaks in a courtroom that required increased security. On occasion, if an ADA or local detective wanted to interview or "park" a witness away from a defendant or their friends there was a conference room to accommodate them.

You couldn't enter the office for the state police unit by mistake. The massive grey metal doors bore the same distinctive blue and white circular door seals affixed to the front doors of all state police marked cruisers. They sprung open for business every weekday morning at eight a.m. and never closed before five p.m.

I walked up the two flights of stairs, and after passing through the small outer office stepped into the massive main office. I put down the two trays onto the countertop that fronted the desk of our office administrative assistant, Lana, and paused for a second to catch my breath, and then in a slow, measured, wheezing voice announced that the coffee had arrived.

• • • •

I retired after thirty-three years of service, and it is safe to say I have forgotten a lot more about most investigations than I remember. The case that I am about to share though, like a few others, always holds a special place in my memory and my heart. It was never part of any plan, but along the way, I developed a passionate urge to tell this story. It is complete, fair, remarkable, and every word factual.

CHAPTER 1

The Crime Scene

Few things can piss off a cop or firefighter quicker than an unexpected, surprise callout at the end of a shift. Just ask any one of us and watch for the narrowing of the eyes and the scowl or wince that crosses our face remembering times when it happened. The recall is usually negative because it caused the cancelation or alteration of premade plans. On occasion, though, you might hear, "Except there was this one time when something seemingly small and inconsequential turned into something big and far-reaching, and we later found out we were standing on the tip of an iceberg—and I'm glad I was there and that we got it right."

Tuesday, July 18, 2000, was a warm, muggy summer morning in Malden, MA. The rising sun was barely visible as it strained to bore a hole through the overcast sky and shine its blinding orange light onto the awakening land below. It's what guys on the mid-shift referred to as God's searchlight, making an opening to brighten the day. For those rolling out of their beds it was a welcome sight, but for those up all night it meant squinting through some tired eyes, as the glare made for difficult driving at the end of a shift.

An unremarkable twenty-four-hour tour of duty was winding down for the firefighters assigned to the trucks at the Salem Street Fire Headquarters. They were packing their ditty bags and watching the clock. At seven a.m., they would be out the door and heading home to get breakfast for their kids or off to their second job in one of the trades. However, at precisely 6:21 a.m., the blare of the stationhouse alarm signaling a report of fire disrupted their getaway plans. The call came from Master Box 3121 at the Malden Mills Condo Complex at the corner of Eastern Avenue and Linwood Street, a building less than a half mile away.

"Shit, shit, shit! I swear to Christ this happens every freaking time we are ready to go and I have family plans!" one of the guys bellowed out. It was what everyone else was thinking. "You know it is some dipshit who burned his bagel while he played in the shower and it tripped the freaking alarm," he added.

But it wasn't a call they could ignore or a decision they had to make. Like it or not, they had just moments to gear up and jump onto the truck as the huge white overhead doors rolled up, the red lights flared to life, and the high-pitched scream of the siren announced to the neighborhood that they were pulling out and needed clear passage.

The deputy chief led the way in the company car, and both Engine 1 and Ladder 1 followed as they rolled across Salem Street. They screamed down Holden Street past Malden High School on the right before taking a left onto Eastern Avenue, and after a few hundred yards, they took a quick right and immediate left into the parking lot for the condo complex. The entire trip took less than a minute and a half.

As they jumped from the apparatus, the firefighters could hear the alarms blaring inside and watched as the residents slowly streamed into the parking lot in their nightclothes or business attire. There was a noticeable but faint smell of smoke with no visible flame. This was certainly more than the burnt toast they had groused about as they dressed for the call.

They went about the business of coupling and pulling hose from the truck, attaching it to the nearby hydrant, dragging it into the building, and once the nozzle man was poised and ready to enter the fire scene, they would charge the line with water and ready for the attack.

The deputy ran up the front stairs, entering through the glass doors and located the fire alarm annunciator panel on the wall. A flashing icon indicated the alarm was coming from the basement level in the function room located down a flight of stairs from the atrium-style entrance. He detected a light haze of smoke wafting up from the stairwell.

Captain Trimble from Engine 1 hooked a nozzle onto a hose neatly tucked into the wall beside the first floor standpipe and stretched it out.

This would be a backup to the larger hose and would draw its water from inside of the building. They descended the stairs to the basement level and headed toward the function room in the familiar attack formation firefighters trained on for decades. There were two doors to the function room and the deputy, with a key handed him by a trustee, unlocked the nearest, and apparently safest, one.

There was light smoke coming from the edges of that door, but the firefighter's eyes focused on the other door about thirty feet further down the hallway. They noted smoke and soot marks at the top of the door and smoke and water pouring out the bottom and into the hallway rug, a clear sign to them that was the hotspot or the place where the fire was concentrated.

Trimble opened the door cautiously, and saw the billowing smoke gather and rush into his direction. He slammed it shut and told the other firefighters to mask up before they pushed their way in.

Dan Thoman, an eighteen-year veteran, was the nozzle man from Engine 1 and the first to enter the room in front of the captain. The big hose was perched on his shoulder, the activating lever at his fingertips ready to set in motion at the first sight of flame. The open doorway now provided a natural exit route for the thick, acrid smoke that had been building inside. It charged toward the firefighters with fury, turning the visibility to zero. The stench from the smoke had the unmistakable odor and taste of a petroleum product, probably gasoline. Trimble put his hand onto Thoman's back, and they inched deeper into the room with their right shoulders rubbing along the wall, grasping the hose like a lifeline that would allow them to back out of the room if it became treacherous or unbearable inside.

After twenty feet, the wall ended and the room opened on the right side to a living room setting. The second wave of firefighters entered from behind, and using their halligan tools, smashed the four ceiling level windows to vent the smoke and then shut down the sprinkler system. After the heaviest smoke made a hasty escape, their view became a lot clearer. They pushed up their masks and quickly surveyed the scene. They extinguished what remained of the smoldering fire, which appeared limited to the living room section. The flood of water that poured from the ceiling sprinklers suppressed the spread of flame, so the fire damage was minimal and limited to the rug and furniture, but the damage from the smoke and water was extensive. The room was in disarray, and a love seat and chair lay tipped over, as did a glass table. There were several inches of water on the floor streaked with an iridescent sheen, and a strong odor of gasoline remained in the air, all unmistakable signs of an arson—and based on what they saw, maybe other crimes as well.

Seventeen years of training and experience told the captain this was likely an arson case and a criminal police matter.

"Hey, guys!" Captain Trimble bellowed over the commotion, "I think this room is definitely a crime scene, so treat it accordingly. Continue to search for victims and hotspots, and vent the smoke and water, but don't, under any circumstances, touch, or move anything, or you'll be in court explaining to the judge why you did."

He called into the dispatch center and requested they summon Malden PD detectives to the scene. Sergeant Steve Ruelle and Inspector Johnny Rivers from the criminal bureau were heading in for the day shift when they heard the call and rerouted their approach to the fire scene at the occupied condo complex.

Ruelle and Rivers had a long, cooperative history with the deputy and the captain. Rivers had been the department's Arson Investigator for years and responded to virtually every suspicious fire scene. The four met outside the building, and the deputy got right to the point.

"This is a weird set of circumstances," he started, "the sprinklers knocked the fire down before we got here, but there was a huge mass of thick black smoke and it reeked of gasoline, so I obviously thought it might be an arson. When we got to the source, though, there were chairs and a table knocked over, and it didn't come from us. I'm no expert, but it looks like there may be some blood on the furniture and maybe the walls, but it could be soot from the fire. I'm just not sure. But you guys taught me that it is your call and always better to be safe than sorry; that's why I called for you."

They all went inside, and after a few minutes of looking around and smelling the obvious accelerant, Rivers said he wanted to reach out to the State Fire Marshal's office for added expertise. When he called, he specifically asked that they bring Lucy, their arson-sniffing dog, along for the ride.

The detectives were sloshing around the function room in their rubber boots, rough sketching the scene, and documenting their initial observations when Lucy poked her head into the room. She announced her presence with a series of excited whines and she was straining on her leash and panting to get to work. Lucy was a highly trained and decorated accelerant detection canine. At the other end of her tether was Paul Horgan, a state police sergeant attached to the Fire Marshal's office. Lucy and Paul had met more than seven years earlier at a training in Connecticut, and they were inseparable from that moment on. They trained together every step of the way, always receiving their certifications as a team.

There were still a couple of inches of water flowing out the door and into the building's drainage pipe when Lucy first put her nose to the water. She alerted on four distinct stain areas, sitting and wagging her tail each time, looking up to Horgan for approval and a couple of kibbles from his pocket. When she wasn't signifying an alert, normally Lucy would stand and wait for the next command. This day, however, she bent her head down and lapped at the water around the stains in the carpet. No matter how many times Horgan tugged at the leash to keep her focused, Lucy kept going back to the water.

He turned to Rivers and said, "John, I know this sounds crazy, but the only time I have to pull her away from drinking water at a fire scene is when there is blood or "deco" (body decomposition) in the mix. I think we have a lot more than an arson here."

• • • •

Pat Silva, another investigator from the Fire Marshal's office, arrived shortly after Horgan to help with the investigation. Pat began his professional career as a full-time firefighter a few miles up the road in Salem, MA, where he worked for eight years before switching gears and careers when he joined the ranks of the state police. It was safe to say he knew his way around both a fire scene and an investigation. The responsibility of determining the cause and origin of the fire would fall to him. After some introductory conversation about what they knew and what they were learning, Pat thought it was critical to reach out to Crime Scene Services for a trained specialist to photograph, fingerprint, and document the entire room.

When the water level was near zero and the smoke had cleared, a couple of large pinkish-colored stains appeared on the rug and there were similar noticeable spots and blotches on the furniture. Deeper and closer inspection of the wall by the door showed what appeared to be reddish-brown smears and possible blood spatter. Lucy's instincts were right on the money, and she earned a bonus cookie or two for her efforts.

Silva then called the crime lab and requested assistance from a chemist to collect the arson evidence for further analysis and to test and collect any of the apparent bloodstains that were starting to show through the saturated surfaces.

In an unconventional and unscientific way, Lucy confirmed what Ruelle and Rivers were already thinking. Her instinctive behavior changed the focus and concern from the original call for an arson to a more intense investigation of a potentially violent crime.

Johnny Rivers made the call to the state police office in the Middlesex DAO to request assistance. He thought it might not turn out to be a homicide, but there was no sense waiting for a victim before they activated the full team. Ruelle and Rivers preferred to be proactive in cases like this where the need for a death investigation was apparent. They wanted a full team in place advancing the case together from the beginning. Experience told them things always went better that way.

• • • •

I was at my desk when the phone rang at around eleven a.m. Lana fielded the call. Her seat was located a few steps from my office and within easy hearing range. I wasn't eavesdropping, but I caught her friendly voice, "Hi, Jimmy, where are you guys? With Rivers and Ruelle? That must be good for a few laughs."

For a few seconds, she was quiet and a small gasp seeped out while she listened, and then, in a much different tone, she commented, "Oh wow, really? Oh my God! Seriously?" and then a pause, followed by, "Yeah, he's right here. I'll put him on."

Lana had a cheerful disposition, and her delightful laughter usually filled her conversations, but not this time. I sensed trouble when she turned in her seat and simply said, "Billy, I have Jimmy Connolly on the phone, and he needs to talk to you."

Lana transferred the call, I answered and listened as Jimmy said, "Good morning Boss. I don't know if you got the heads-up on this, but I'm with Duke and Eddie, and we are over in Malden at a fire in a condo building. It's an interesting situation: it looks as though someone started a fire in the function room to try to cover up a crime scene. There's a couple of big pinkish stains on the floor and what looks like blood spatter on the walls. So far, the firefighters have pumped out about a foot of water that poured out of the sprinkler system and smothered the fire before it could do any heavy damage. They cleared the residents to return, but most of them are just grabbing some stuff and leaving or going to work.

"It might be a good idea if you filled the DA in and then headed this way. We are at the Malden Mills Condo building on Linwood Street where it intersects with Eastern Avenue."

My first thoughts were that it had all the indicators of a major crime scene that could gain a great deal of media attention and we would need to prepare for that eventuality. More importantly, and because of the complexity of issues, particularly the potential legal ones around search and seizure as well as evidence collection, we needed to have someone from the DAO on-scene to guide us through the maze. I asked Jimmy if Adrienne Lynch, the chief of the Malden division of the Middlesex DAO was aware of the situation. He reminded me that she was in Columbia, SC, lecturing at a DA's conference and wouldn't be back until Monday. Gerard Butler, a senior ADA, was filling in for her, and he expected him to arrive shortly.

The distance from our office in the Cambridge Courthouse to the scene in Malden was a little less than six miles, and with regular congestion and traffic it could be a half an hour ride. Flashing blue lights and a blaring siren could open the pathway and shorten the travel time, but as the crime scene was secure and under control, my arriving a few minutes sooner wasn't going to help solve anything and would only piss off every commuter I passed. The slower trip also gave me plenty of time to think through the facts, as I knew them, and start to formulate a game plan to make sure all our bases were covered. It was a great comfort knowing that the best-trained crime scene specialists were either on-scene or would be in short order and that the detectives from both the Malden PD and the state police were experienced and knowledgeable. Most importantly, we had worked together in the past on other homicides with very successful outcomes.

My fundamental role as the detective lieutenant throughout a death investigation was one of oversight and direction. Experience and guidance mattered most: the institutional memory gained from literally hundreds of past investigations coupled with the battle scars and remembrances of both screw-ups and successes. My goal was always to diminish the former and accentuate the latter.

The detectives working on the case did the bulk of the work. In this instance, as in most others in my office, my detectives had a history of working together and great investigative instincts, a passion to solve the case, and most importantly, relied on one another to prevent mistakes. We all worked as a team and had no tolerance for lone wolves who wandered off and followed their impulses rather than the plan. When working with competent detectives and ADAs, it often reminds me of a quote from Mahatma Gandhi, "There go my people. I must follow them, for I am their leader."

When I arrived at the scene, firefighters were washing down the equipment and returning it to their trucks. Strands of dark smoke were still streaming out of the broken windows on the building's ground level, and there was a noticeable stench of gasoline in the air. There were several people milling around in the lot that I presumed were residents and neighbors.

Jimmy Connolly and Johnny Rivers walked to me as I approached the buildings entrance. A few moments later, Steve, Duke, and Ed Forster broke away from what they were doing and joined the conversation.

They were gathering information from personal observations and conversations with firefighters, and were in the beginning stages of interviewing residents, neighbors, and people working in nearby businesses. Canvassing is a long and tedious part of any investigation and perhaps the second least favorite, just ahead of diving into putrid dumpsters looking through garbage bags for hidden evidence.

We talked for a few minutes about the uniqueness of what they discovered, and then they brought me in to look at the crime scene first-hand. After a quick familiarization with the room and the scene as the firefighters first encountered it, I spoke with Pat Silva. Although a trooper now, Pat still spoke in firefighter's jargon. He talked of the "fire load" and said it was limited to the furnishings in the living room section of the function room. He said there were no accidental heat sources that could have caused a fire. He went on to describe what he considered a pour pattern (the manner of distribution of the accelerant prior to ignition). He pointed out a trail of burn areas and soot marks that supported his comments and mentioned that Lucy's "hits" for accelerants were consistent with what the physical evidence showed. Lastly, Silva pointed to the six sprinkler heads in the living room section and noted that the fire activated four of them, which poured down with enough pressure and volume to drown the fire shortly after it began. He noted the four open heads centered in the area where the fire occurred. There was still a lot of work to do, but he said he was confident that he would be able to establish the cause and origin of the fire.

In addition to the two pinkish blotches in the rug by the furniture, there were also areas of reddish-brown stains on lower parts of the wall nearest to the unlocked door. John Drugan, the crime lab chemist, joined the conversation. "Guys, I think these preliminary tests are affirming what we thought. They have all been positive for blood, and the quick reaction to the chemicals has been dramatic."

Silva's experienced eyes allowed him to offer an initial opinion that someone caused the fire by spreading an ignitable liquid over the love seat, chair, and flooring and then introducing an open flame to the accelerant. The fire spread laterally across the floor and onto the chair and love seat. As the fire progressed, the increasing heat set off the sprinkler heads, which consumed and extinguished the flames. It was the collective opinion of all present that someone had set the fire intentionally and deliberately to cover up and contaminate the scene of a violent crime.

A quick study of the visual evidence, including the bloodstains, suggested there had been a chaotic fight in the room prior to setting it ablaze.

While the specialists continued to comb the crime scene for signs of trace and physical evidence, my team wandered away to pick up where they left off, interviewing anyone and everyone in the area who might have seen or witnessed something unusual or remarkable before, during, or after the fire alarm sounded.

Perhaps the most difficult circumstance at the start of every case is that detectives come in blind and work backward to gain information and learn. Initial observations of a crime scene are important, but what we see is the aftermath of the event. We need to find witnesses with information that supports and/or explains what we, the detectives, saw. As the saying goes, "We don't know what we don't know," and the only way to learn is by talking with people and learning from them. Eyewitnesses are the best sources, but unfortunately, like all gems, they are rarely easy to find. In many instances, they have left the scene to go about their business, thinking someone else will be there to fill in the blanks for the police. At other times, they are afraid of real or imagined consequences and leave hoping to remain anonymous. In yet other circumstances, they are in the wrong place at the wrong time and have a fear of discovery because their presence could put their marriage or employment in jeopardy. On occasion, they just don't like or trust the police or the criminal justice system. Regardless of the reason, locating honest cooperating witnesses can be a difficult task.

The canvassing spread out in two directions: first with the condo residents and then with the people working at the neighboring businesses. Most of the initial resident interviews were quick because many had left after the fire alarms went off, and those who remained had mostly been asleep at the time and had nothing to offer in the way of observations or personal thoughts. To be thorough, my investigators would return later that evening and for several days afterward to ensure they spoke with every resident. This gave everyone the opportunity to share information about not only the fire but also any suspicions they may have about people they had seen in the building or scuttlebutt they had picked up from neighbors about possible suspects or persons of interest. There didn't appear to be any forced entry into the building, so there was every reason to believe the assailant was either a resident or a guest of one.

Just as important as the gathering of information, the opportunity to create some face time between the police and residents is valuable. First impressions are lasting and can go a long way in building trust. Knowing there is a police presence and an active investigation helps to calm some of their fears. A simple handshake and exchange of a business card can be the opening to a positive dialogue that might not take place at that moment or for weeks, months, or even a year. Then, if that person either learns more information or has prior information they were initially unwilling to share, they have a number to call, and the person on the other end will be a detective with whom they have already met and shared a conversation.

It was evident from speaking with several residents that they were understandably scared and concerned for their safety and security. From our initial dialogues, we learned that they were not all cut from the same bolt of cloth. Most of the units were owner occupied, but several were sublets. Many residents worked at white and blue-collar mid-wage professions, while others were, for any number of different reasons, without work and around the property most days. This was by no means a homogeneous community. This wasn't the setting the writer's considered when they created Melrose Place. None of the residents shared that there was a big, happy family feeling atmosphere throughout the building. It was a decent place to live but not one with smiley face welcome mats lying beneath unlocked doors.

There were pockets or small groups that knew one another in a superficial but friendly way. They might share some Chinese food from the restaurant across the street, watch a movie together, or even go halves on the cost of some recreational drugs, but that was about it. Most stayed to themselves and, at least while they were there, walked softly and wore blinders and earplugs.

With the outside interviews completed and the function room in the competent hands of the crime scene and arson specialists, my onsite detectives ventured into the management office on the first floor to learn a bit more about the building and the people who called it home. They got a list of the residents and a floor plan showing fifty-five housing units that corresponded with those names. The manager was cooperative and knowledgeable, answering questions as best he could. He also provided a little insight regarding a few of the residents, and why they might or might not be willing to speak with us. The manager told them that the function room was not a gathering spot, and rarely did anyone use it at night. The doors remained locked, and the only way to access it, was with a key. Keys were few, and they were in the sole possession of the trustees or in the management office. He only loaned out the keys for planned, preapproved events and always got them back from the renters.

Steve Ruelle was combing through the manifest when he noted the name Lester Morovitz in Condo Number 115. "Isn't he the guy who owns the taxi company across the street?" he asked.

"Yes," was the reply, "but he doesn't live here. He's on the deed, but his kid lives there with a woman and two kids. His name is Tommy Crouse. He is an odd duck, coming and going all hours of the day and night, but he doesn't cause problems. I think he works for his old man. He would be a good person to speak with, but I don't think he was around this morning. I didn't see his Chevy Blazer out there."

The taxi service operated twenty-four hours a day, so there was always someone fielding calls in the office's dispatch center. Eddie, Duke, and Ruelle took a walk across the street to see if Morovitz was in his office. Fortunately, he was, and he invited them in. After introductions and small talk about the fire and the weather, they asked him what he knew about Tommy Crouse.

"Oh, Tommy's my stepson; I'm married to his mother. When they fixed up the building and turned it into condos a few years ago, I bought one of them so Tommy; his girlfriend, Esther Fournier and their kids would have a place to live and I could keep an eye on him. He works here for me. He's an unreliable employee, but what am I going to do? He's family."

They asked if he knew where Tommy was, and he said the whole family had gone to visit with Esther's family in New Hampshire earlier in the morning.

"They were fortunate," he recalled, "they left a few minutes before the fire alarm went off. Tommy called me early this morning and told me

Esther had the 'itches' really bad and she had to go to a doctor but her medical insurance was in New Hampshire and she had no coverage in Massachusetts."

Morovitz reached for his cell phone and quickly scanned through it to see what time he had spoken with Crouse in the morning. "Here, he called to tell me at five forty-five a.m." Eddie Forster asked him if he thought five forty-five a.m. was a little early for a wake-up phone call from his stepson to say he wouldn't be in for work. Lester told them he had thought it was a bit odd at the time, but so were many weird things about Tommy Crouse. He said he thought it would be best if they talked directly to him about the fire and his early departure. He added that he spoke with Crouse several times during the day and he got the impression that Tommy wasn't planning on coming back tonight. Morovitz gave them Crouse's home and cell phone numbers as well as an address in Candia, NH, for Esther's parents.

As the day wore on, our team made telephone calls to area hospitals asking about emergency room visits with unexplained, serious injuries. We alerted the OCME to the situation, and they promised to notify us if they received a call to any death scenes with unexplained injuries.

The canvass wore on, and my detectives approached people on the street, at the bus stop in front of the building, and in the parking lot of the condo complex and questioned them about anything they may have seen that seemed unusual or out of the ordinary as they headed out earlier in the day. Most shrugged their shoulders and had little or nothing to offer. The condo owners were just glad the sprinklers suppressed the fire with minor damage and they were able to return to their homes. The check marks next to the names on the building's roster grew by the hour, but there was little information gained.

A tenant who lived in a unit on the third floor that overlooked the parking lot and Eastern Avenue was different. He turned out to be the guy who inaugurated the flow of relevant information that the officers were waiting to hear. Duke and Pat Silva spoke with him as he arrived home from work. Duke opened the conversation and told him they were investigating a small fire in the function room. Duke only referred to the fire and not their suspicions of violence. The tenant said he had wanted to speak to the police all day about his early morning observations.

"I have a regular daily routine I follow on workdays," he said. "Today was no different. At around five thirty a.m., I took the elevator down to the first floor and was heading toward the front door and out to my car to for the short drive to where I work in Cambridge. I remember when I stepped out of the elevator; I heard voices coming from the doorway of the condo to my immediate right. The guy who lives there is Tommy Crouse; he lives there with his girlfriend, and they have two kids. When I walk through the lobby toward the front door I pass by an open area, and I can see right down to the floor below where the function room is located. I don't remember seeing or smelling anything unusual."

He continued, saying that normally he never saw anyone in the parking lot that early in the morning but that day had been different.

"Once I stepped outside, I noticed Tommy Crouse walking away from his blue Chevy Blazer, pulling an empty child's wagon behind him. He has his own parking spot, but he'd parked in a space reserved for visitors and close to the handicap ramp that led into the building. We never said anything to each other, and I don't know if Crouse even saw me."

The tenant asked a few questions, focusing on whether or not the fire was deliberately set. Pat simply replied, "That is what we are trying to determine, and the information you are sharing is very helpful to us reaching a conclusion." The tenant went on to tell Pat and Duke that he first learned of the fire when his girlfriend called him at work with the news around seven a.m.

"I've been thinking about it all day and how odd it was to see Crouse pulling a kid's wagon in the parking lot at the crack of dawn." He said he was relieved that the officer's spoke with him and gave him a chance to share what little he knew. Neither the tenant nor the investigators realized it at that moment, but they had just begun to pry the lid off Pandora's Box.

After talking with the tenant and Morovitz, everyone started to feel and believe that the slow, painstaking, but logical march toward the truth had begun. We knew we had a crime scene with bloodstains and blood spatter on the walls, obvious signs of a brutal fight, and an accelerant-rich fire that was apparently set to destroy any physical evidence. That was a good start, but we still had no victim, no known eyewitnesses, no weapon, no talk on the street, and no missing person report. We were officially nowhere, but we were starting to head somewhere.

The initial crime scene processing was completed by late afternoon, and until everything inside dried and the smoke completely cleared, there was little more that could be done. Before the troopers, crime lab chemists, and the Fire Marshal's officers left, they briefed Connolly on what they were able to do and what still needed completing. They collected several pieces of possible evidence, including blood and water samples from the floor, walls, and furniture and burnt areas of cloth from the furniture and the rug. The seized samples would go to the state police crime laboratory for testing. The crime scene officers would be back in a day or so when the room had dried and the smoke had completely cleared to finish their work. The Fire Marshal's officers would be back as well to further inspect and test the fire suppression system and seek out other evidence and witnesses. We planned to be back very early in the morning to pick up where we left off. Canvassing and the search for witnesses and evidence would come first for us.

An issue that arises at the start of all investigations is the urgency of getting the primary work done and then prioritizing the next steps. Everyone involved has an already open and burgeoning caseload that requires him or her to break away for days at a time to complete a myriad of responsibilities surrounding their other cases. The big advantage to the team concept is that members can drop from sight for a day or a week to attend to other business and the investigation will continue seamlessly with the other team members filling in as and where needed.

It is also the reason that team members meet or speak daily, either in person or on the telephone. They share and review the information gathered from new interviews, talk about potential leads that require follow-up, and discuss lab results that trickle in from evidence seized at the crime scene, autopsy findings, and questions from the medical examiner. The meetings keep everyone engaged and updated so there is no disruption or need to reeducate later.

• • • •

Darkness was settling in, and the summer air was cooling off after the rain had passed. It had been a miserable day punctuated at several points with drenching downpours. The early momentum was waning, and fatigue was growing. Everyone was physically and emotionally exhausted and very, very hungry. The initial adrenaline rush for all of us had long since passed. Everyone had sweated through their clothes more than once that day, and we all smelled of the oily, acrid smoke that had settled into our shirts and pants from the time spent mucking around in the function room. There was a feeling in all of us that this was probably a good time to hit the pause button and stop for the day. Go home, throw the grungy clothes into a plastic bag, shower, grab a beer and some food, and get a good night's rest. We could gather at the Malden PD early in the morning, review what we had learned, discuss any new information that might come in overnight, and formulate a game plan for the day. There were always things to do, but we also had to follow the evidence and be prepared to adjust the plans when more relevant and important information became available. Adapting to a changing environment causing redirection happens in every case; following a predetermined template never works.

As we stood in the condo parking lot and discussed our next steps, the one piece of information we couldn't get away from was that Tommy

Crouse had left at the break of dawn to go to New Hampshire with his family—and they had fortuitously left moments before the alarms went off.

"Seriously," Jimmy Connolly said, "Who does that? Think about it. At five thirty in the morning, you wake up two little kids and your girlfriend from a sound sleep, get them dressed, pile them into a car, and drive an hour plus to New Hampshire. The only urgency to the trip is your girlfriend has the itches and wants to see a doctor in New Hampshire. It makes no sense at all."

There was concern that waiting overnight wasn't the right answer. Johnny Rivers spoke up and said, "Look, Crouse is Morovitz's stepson, and whether he likes him or not, we know he's already been on the phone telling him we were there and asking questions about him and his early departure and we were looking to talk with him. Crouse and his girlfriend are probably already trying to create an alibi and get their story straight."

There was a unified and, at least for this group of detectives, obvious reaction. Duke said what everyone else was thinking.

"Look, we don't think they are returning tonight. We know what we want to do and really must do: blitz them with questions now. Let's jump in a cruiser, head up to New Hampshire, and catch them by surprise. They will never expect that we would be knocking on their door tonight. They will be shocked and disorganized when they see us. Let's go and catch them off guard."

We all agreed. With a new shot of adrenaline to the system, there was a noticeable and collective rise in the energy level. Steve, Johnny, Eddie, and Duke piled into Eddie's unmarked Crown Vic and headed north at "state police speed," which normally cuts fifteen minutes off an hour and a half ride. On the way up Route 93 to New Hampshire, they talked over what they had learned, and what they didn't yet know, and what they hoped to learn from the interviews. They came up with a few common questions for both Crouse and Fournier so they could compare their memories and answers. They also wanted to speak with her parents and see what they knew and what they had observed during the day.

Earlier in the evening, a couple of Malden's night detectives dropped by for a briefing on the case and to offer their help. Once the cruiser headed off to Candia, they headed back to their station to continue the search for a victim. With no information other than a blood-soaked crime scene, it was going to be a difficult task.

Even though we made calls earlier in the day to try to locate a possible victim, there had been shift changes and new personnel manning emergency rooms and the OCME. The detectives started by re-contacting more than a dozen hospital emergency rooms in the Greater Boston area. Malden's only hospital closed the previous year, so by then, most ambulance transports brought the victims to Massachusetts General Hospital or one of several other outstanding Boston trauma centers. The steady answer was, "No, not here, sorry. We will call you if anyone comes in reporting they were the victim of an assault."

After an hour or so of nothing but no, they turned their attention to checking the teletype files for recent missing persons or unidentified victims of a violent assault, both dead and alive. They started locally but then spread the area of concern throughout New England and eventually nationally. They constructed a message about an apparent arson scene in their town with signs that it was possibly a cover-up for a violent crime. They electronically distributed the message throughout New England hoping the other departments would post it on detective bulletin boards and in dispatch centers and speak about it at shift roll calls. The midnight shifts would be coming on-duty shortly, and they would most likely be the ones to take note of any strange encounters from the previous night.

Jimmy Connolly and I remained at the complex for a bit longer, tying up loose ends and making sure to secure the function room doors. At our request, the building manager had the locks replaced by a locksmith earlier in the day, and the only set of keys was in our possession. The room was still an active crime scene, and just in case a defense counsel raised the issue of evidence contamination or tampering during a trial, we could respond that we closed, locked, and secured the room for the day. Jimmy and I headed home just as the other team members were rolling up on the Fournier home.

My trip home, although punctuated with a lot of uneasiness about unanswered concerns and questions, was more relaxed than the drive to Malden earlier in the day. While we had no known victim, we did have sufficient evidence that had the appearance of a homicide scene. Until we learned otherwise, we would proceed on that premise and not specifically consider it an arson scene. If we waited for a dead body to turn up critical evidence would be lost, altered, or destroyed and rendered useless. Likewise, memories would fade or change as residents shared information with one another, and eyewitnesses might go quiet.

Massachusetts law only requires the local police contact the DAO when they learn of a death, not if, or when they suspect one. There was great comfort knowing that our office, the state police, and the DA had worked with the Malden detectives on a number of past homicide cases. The combined detective units shared a genuine respect and camaraderie that allowed us to work together as a harmonious and unified team. I was grateful that they brought us in on the case right away.

From my perspective, we were in a very advantageous situation. Bringing the investigative units together at the beginning of the day eliminated any friction, distrust, or finger pointing about lost or damaged evidence. Likewise, having an ADA working alongside lessened the chances of legal missteps during interviews, searches, or identifications. Gerard Butler was one of the most knowledgeable ADAs, and there was nobody more discerning and thorough than his supervisor, Adrienne Lynch. We were off to a very promising start.

As was always the case in these kinds of mysteries, we had no idea how long it would take to solve and prove. None of us realized we were just a few steps down a long, dirty road with more twists and turns and highs and lows than an amusement park roller coaster. This case could turn out to be the most challenging ride of our careers, but we all buckled in and prepared for whatever lay ahead.

CHAPTER 2

The Investigation

The first day of any investigation is always frenzied and reactive with everyone scrambling to get a handle on things and making sure evidence and witnesses aren't lost or forgotten. There is only one opportunity to get it right, and there is no excuse for laziness or lack of attention to detail. Once the scene is processed, the evidence removed, and known eyewitness statements are in the book, there is an opportunity to slow down, gain control, and be more proactive. At that point, there is a lot less scrambling, more purposeful and targeted moves, and usually a more comfortable night's rest. I think of it as throwing a tent over a multiple ring circus and securing it against potential storms.

My unit and I gathered at the Malden Detective Unit at nine thirty the following morning, but Gerard called to say he was running a few minutes late. Like the rest of us, his work plate was overflowing with open cases, trial preparations, and court appearances. He had to off-load that morning's work onto another ADA who would reschedule his appointments and court appearances due to the unforeseen circumstances.

His situation was not unlike all of ours. Sudden, unattended death cases don't follow a published schedule, and when reported, regardless of the time of day or day of the week, they demand an immediate response. We put everything else on hold, or someone else in the office picks it up.

We sat around the conference table, the conversation flowed easily, and the banter was light. Talk was of the magnificent Parade of the Tall Ships that had sailed from Boston Harbor on Sunday morning after more than a week at dockage. The event had consumed the city as hundreds of thousands of people took advantage of the summer weather and, for most, a once in a lifetime opportunity to walk the docks and board the largest sailing ships from a time long past. Ruelle said he had hoped to bring his family into town but the crowds were huge and the sun was hot, so they had elected to pass.

Duke smiled and said, "Let me tell you, Steve, as beautiful as the scene was to onlookers, it was even more spectacular standing on the sidelines in uniform and taking it all in on the event organizer's dime. I spent most of my time posing for pictures with people from all over the world. My face hurt from smiling so much. Everyone was there for a good time, so there were no real issues except traffic and a few nuisance calls about unauthorized vendors."

The overtime opportunities had been fabulous, and many of us took advantage and worked double shifts from six in the morning, until ten at night. The extra money helped pay some bills and, for some, covered the cost of a family vacation on the Cape, but our bodies were tired and not fully recovered before Tuesday morning when we caught this case. It was fair to say our brains were functioning but our asses were dragging.

Everyone but Connolly sipped from cups of hot coffee, looking for that morning energy boost. Jimmy always opted for a Mountain Dew regardless of the hour of day.

Before we sat, each of us plunked down our field interview notebooks onto the conference room table. Next to our badge, firearm, and a pair of handcuffs, our spiral notepads are the most essential piece of equipment for any detective. The pages and pages of handwritten scribbling is culled from interviews, crime scene processing, and personal observations along with random information about the case that may play a key role at some later date. They become the roadmaps detailing where we'd been, where we were, and where we needed to head. They were indispensable crutches for recall, especially when writing reports. Names, phone numbers, addresses, dates, and times of all statements are recorded in the chrono-logical order they were taken. They are invaluable during later interviews as well because you can flip back and fact-check a witness's comments or memories against the things you know to be true or see if they conflicted with comments or memories of other witnesses. We purchase the slim three-by-six-inch pads by the gross, and we always have packs in reserve in our cruiser trunks.

When Gerard slipped into the room, he took an open seat in the middle of the oversized table. "Thanks for indulging me this morning, guys. Since my phone didn't ring last night and my beeper never went off, I'm supposing that we aren't much further ahead than we were last evening when you guys headed to New Hampshire."

"Our trip to Candia last night was kinda productive, but we didn't come home with a boatload of new information or anyone in custody," said Duke. "They were cooperative and answered our questions, but they definitely had rehearsed a script and tried their best to stick to it. We have a lot of work to do looking into their alibis, and undoubtedly, we will be talking with them some more as we go forward and learn more. No one lawyered up, so we left the door wide open for a return visit or two."

Gerard turned to Steve Ruelle and asked what, if any, information had come into the detective unit or dispatch center on the overnight shift.

"I guess it depends how you look at it," he replied. "The simple answer is we learned nothing new. We checked the area hospital's emergency rooms again with negative results. There were no missing reports filed at our station and no responses to a teletype message that we sent out to all area PDs detailing the arson as well as the blood evidence found in the room, but we didn't hear a peep from any of them. On the other hand, we have done and will continue to do our due diligence and follow-up to make sure nothing has slipped past us and through the cracks. It is very worrisome that with so much blood loss we don't have a known victim yet. It's starting to look like we have a homicide on our hands, and we are on a search and recovery mission and not a rescue one."

It looked like someone dropped a box of bobble head dolls onto the table, with everyone nodding in agreement.

"Why don't we start by going over yesterday's events, talk about the trip to New Hampshire and what you learned, and then let's make a game plan for what we want to accomplish today. I have been speaking with Adrienne," Gerard continued. "She is still on her teaching assignment in South Carolina, but she'll be back on Monday and will be taking over for me. I have a trial coming up and have motions to respond to, people to re-interview, and experts to interview. She wanted me to make sure to cover our legal bases as far as the evidence collection and preservation for testing. She also wanted your input on starting the grand jury subpoena process for any records that may hold some critical information to help us move the case further. Suffice it to say, she is revved up and eager to get back and immerse herself in the case."

"From a legal point of view, I think we are in good shape," I offered. "The function room is a common area with no singular ownership, so nobody has an expectant right of privacy claim. No need for a search warrant, the consent from office management will cover us. Aside from a strong suspicion of arson, we don't have anyone in custody, nor are we yet in a position to accuse anyone of setting the fire, so at least for now; there is no reason to Mirandize anyone. We can talk it out later, but it would be helpful to start the subpoena process for telephone records from Crouse and Morovitz. We know the two spoke yesterday, but how often, when, and to whom else could widen the list of people we will want to contact. After we do some follow-up legwork today, we may have a few more requests for other types of records."

"Are you guys comfortable with the thoroughness of the work done by the Fire Marshal's investigators and the crime scene analysts as far as the documentation of the scene as they found it and the collection of accelerant and blood samples they took to analyze at the lab?" Gerard asked.

"Yes, but they aren't finished," said Connolly, "the room is secured with a new lock, and Stevie Ruelle has the only keys to it, so that should prevent admittance by anyone else and negate anyone saying the scene was contaminated after we left. Trooper Karol Setalsingh from Crime Scene Services told us he would be back either today or tomorrow to start processing for fingerprints. He needs the room to dry out before he can start dusting with fingerprint powder, otherwise the powder just forms clumps. Paul Horgan said he, or someone from his office, would be back to look at the sprinkler system and finalize a determination of cause and manner of the fire. They will follow through with a detailed report of their work and their findings."

Rivers chimed in, "I've collected the reports from the firefighters regarding their response and observations at the scene, and I'll be getting the logs and the fire alarm records as well. I'll start a three-ring binder for them. Once I get all of the info, we can review and check it against what we've learned from witnesses. It can also help us when we are fact-checking statements and alibis."

"Eddie, did you have any luck with the trash search yesterday?" asked Butler.

"No, nothing really," Eddie replied. "They have an outside dumpster for the condo's rubbish that had been removed before we got there yesterday. They took it to the transfer station in Everett and dumped it out. We took a ride over there, and the guys who work there were helpful. They knew exactly where the stuff from that truck was, and they grabbed it and spread it out on the ground so we could inspect it. It smelled awful, but we didn't see anything that looked like a person or anything bloody. I requested a cadaver dog from the state police this morning, and I'm waiting to hear back."

"Anything more on the canvassing?" inquired Gerard.

Duke answered up, "We still have a way to go, but between all of us, we spoke to about thirty of the residents and some folks from the building management office. The management people sent us across the street to Malden Taxi and Lester Morovitz, and that was huge for us. He was upfront about being Crouse's stepfather and told us he talked with him earlier that morning before and after the fire and several more times during the day. He opened the path that took us to Candia and Crouse. He showed us his phone's call log, and it appeared the original call from Crouse came in at 5:49 a.m. Morovitz also gave us Crouse's cell phone number and the address in Candia where he was staying."

Duke continued, "We also spoke with a guy later in the afternoon who lives up on the third floor. He was anxious to talk, and he told us he saw Crouse pulling a kid's wagon in the parking lot around five thirty that morning and that he'd parked his truck in a visitor's space, not in his designated spot. The guy said he left at the same time every workday and he has never seen Crouse or anyone else in the parking lot at that time. It was really his comments about Crouse's movements that sealed the deal and convinced us to interview Crouse last night."

"Why don't we talk about last night then? Who went to the Fournier house to interview them?" Gerard asked, looking around the room.

Ruelle answered up, "Honestly, none of us even knew where Candia was, so we looked up the phone number for the PD and called before we headed there. It is a small town just north of Manchester and just south of Hookset. They have about four thousand residents and a PD with maybe one patrol on the street at night. We asked for assistance and a uniform presence to make the introduction at the Fournier home, and they were very helpful."

After taking a sip of his coffee, Ruelle continued, "On the drive up, we decided to break into teams so we could do the interviews simultaneously. When we arrived, Crouse and Esther were there, as were her parents. They appeared surprised and a bit nervous to see us, but they were courteous and invited us in. We had the uniform officer from Candia meet us there, and he knocked on the door. We didn't want them freaking out wondering why four guys they didn't recognize were knocking on their door late at night."

"Eddie and I spoke with Crouse on the porch while Johnny and Duke were talking with Esther in the kitchen," Ruelle continued. "Eddie, do you want to talk about what Crouse had to say?"

Eddie was a very good interviewer with the patience of a saint, but when it came to talking about a case in a room full of others, he would rather not.

"Johnny, why don't you go first? Then I won't have to say as much," was Eddie's answer.

Johnny Rivers flicked through his notebook before stopping on the page with the comments from Esther's interview. "I think Duke would agree that she was cooperative," Johnny started, "but she also seemed confused and nervous, and at times, she either repeated the questions or answered them somewhat hesitantly. She was very sure and particular about some things, but her memory was vague about things that mattered. It was clear to us that she and Crouse had already talked and rehearsed the outline of her statement. She told us that she and Crouse are not married, nor engaged, and that she has two kids but only the younger one is hers with Crouse. They are together a lot, but she retains the Candia home as her official residence because of health care opportunities." Johnny continued, "She knew about the fire and how they left shortly before it started, but she didn't indicate she spoke with anyone from the building to learn more about it. We asked her about how they spent Monday evening, and she told us that all four of them were home. After dinner, around eight o'clock Crouse left to rent a video but returned later and said they didn't have what he wanted. She didn't know if he stopped anywhere else before coming home.

"She said all four of them always sleep in the living room together. I asked her about the rest of the evening, and she said she fell asleep around ten o'clock and Crouse was home, but she didn't know whether he stayed in or went out after that. She told us she had a bad night sleeping because of her poison ivy and needed to go to her parent's house so she could get treatment.

"They woke at five o'clock, and the two of them went to their storage bin, removed some bags of clothing, and put them into the truck. She insisted they never left each other's sight all morning. She said after they loaded up the truck they put the kids into the back seat, and she added that as they were leaving around six, they saw another resident in the parking lot and said hi to him.

Johnny checked his notes, and continued, "We asked her about Crouse's work schedule, and she told us he works for his stepfather at the cab company across the street and never has a problem getting time off. Did I forget anything, Duke?"

Duke answered, "No, you pretty much covered it. The only other thing was we asked her about the function room and whether or not they ever used it."

"That's right," Johnny continued. "She said they had only been in there once, back in April for their daughter's birthday party. She said they never had a key to the room and that the door was opened for them by some guy named Pat."

Eddie flipped through the pages of his notebook as if it was an unwelcome chore, finally settling on the section that had notes from the interview with Tommy Crouse.

"Steve and I took him out onto the front porch to talk so the others couldn't listen to our conversation. We identified ourselves and told him we were there to talk about the fire in his condo building that morning and that we had information he left before the fire started. We asked him about what he did on Monday, the day before the fire. Basically, he said he worked at Malden Taxi for his stepfather until early afternoon and then he headed over to his mother's house to clean out her garage and move some stuff because they were moving. He said his mother told him he could take whatever he wanted. He then said he stayed there until about two thirty or so and came back home and stayed there until about six o'clock.

"We asked him about dinner, and he said they weren't sit-down eaters, so he couldn't recall when and what they ate. He said around six o'clock he went to the Eagles Club, where he basically stayed to himself, left, and went home sometime around eight to eight thirty. He remembered that he left again to rent a movie, but they didn't have what he wanted so he came back home and stayed there for the rest of the night. He said they all got up early because Esther had a rash or something and needed to go to New Hampshire for treatment. He said before they left, he and Esther went into the storage unit and removed some bags of clothes for the kids and he threw them into the back of his truck. We asked what time they left for New Hampshire, and he said, 'Around quarter of six.' Steve and I also asked him about the function room, and he said he had only been in it twice. He said they used it back in April for their kid's birthday party on a Saturday and they went back in the next day to clean it up. He said they never had a key to it.

"That's mostly what he had to say," Eddie said, closing his notebook. "I mean, he was clearly nervous and agitated, and he was really vague on his memory of stuff that just happened the day before and earlier that day. I wouldn't say he was confrontational, but he wasn't being passive either."

As Gerard started to talk, Eddie piped up, "Oh yeah, and we asked if he minded if we took a quick look in the back of his truck. He didn't object, but he was fidgety about allowing us anything more than that. It was dark, and all we had was a flashlight I borrowed from Duke. Crouse opened the rear glass lid, and we looked inside. There was a bunch of junk back there, but we weren't looking for anything in particular, just looking for anything that stuck out. We didn't see anything that looked like obvious evidentiary stuff, so we didn't ask to take anything or go inside to the truck bed."

Gerard asked how long they had spent at the house, and everyone agreed they had finished up and got back onto the road home in around forty minutes. The conversation about the status of the investigation completed, the guys were growing antsy to head back to the complex to get started.

"As we head out of here this morning, what is it you all think we should be focusing on? I mean, instinctively, what do you think we are looking at?" Gerard asked no one in particular.

"I think I can speak for everyone here," Johnny Rivers responded. "Based on what we have learned from the crime scene and the limited interviews we have been able to conduct, I would say there is a consensus that we are working on an arson for sure, with the real possibility of a homicide," said Rivers. "I wouldn't say we have a suspect in Tommy Crouse, more like what the feds like to refer to as a person of interest. We need to follow the evidence and the comments and see where they take us. My sense is either we clear him through his statements and alibi or, if he fabricated them, we will bury him with them. It is too early to tell, but we have a lot of untapped sources and resources right now, and that's what we want to get started on."

"Okay then," Gerard offered, "let's wrap it up and drift over to Malden Mills. We can continue to knock on doors, even those of residents we have already seen. I'm guessing there was a lot of chatter amongst them last night, and we don't want to squander an opportunity to scoop that up and sift through it. Let's plan on grabbing lunch around one and see what develops in the meantime."

Rivers stayed behind. He wanted to start a profile workup on Crouse. Who was he, did he have a past criminal record, did his name appear in the Malden PD archives for any reason, did he have an active driver's license, and did he own the truck he was driving, etc.? His preliminary search would extend far beyond Malden to include state and national criminal databases to find out a little about him and maybe gather information that would help in the interview process. With any luck, there could be some significant information that could open new avenues to travel and doors to knock on.

An unwritten, but well understood rule in any investigation is to do your background homework as soon as possible and preferably, before you start interviewing people who may be principles in the case. It's not always possible because of the way events transpire, particularly on the first day of the case, but when you have a planned interview, there is no excuse for not scouting out, at the minimum, some basic, easily available information about the person. A deeper dive is in order when the person may have had some direct contact with the scene or a person of interest in the case.

As we headed to our cars, Duke called out that he was stopping first at the Mobil gas station next door to the condos. The day before at the fire scene, the deputy fire chief had remarked that the place didn't open until seven, but the previous night, someone else had thought it opened at six. That one-hour window could be a big difference. If the deputy was right, the place had not yet opened when the fire broke out, but if it was six, then there could be a treasure trove of information if they had video recordings or cash register receipts that could lead them to potential witnesses or a suspect.

Kathy Barrett, a trooper from the state police canine unit and the handler of one of the human remains recovery specialist dogs (Cadaver dogs), returned Eddie's call while we were in the meeting and left a message that she would join us in the midafternoon because she already had a scheduled search for the morning.

Thus, the second day of our hunt for answers and investigative leads was underway. Cases always develop their own pace and rhythm. In this case, my team of detectives were already a proven, harmonious group that had played well together in past cases—maybe not an orchestra with everyone playing different instruments but more of an a capella group with each bringing their own distinctive voice to the performance.

Duke's visit to the gas station/convenience store got the day off to a good start. The store *did* open at six a.m. each morning, and the clerk on duty was the same man who had opened the store the day before. He told Duke there was a surveillance camera system that captured four different views on one screen, including the food section, the area around the cash register, the front door, and the outside gas pumps. He also said the cash register camera recorded the time, date, and transaction of all purchases. At Duke's request, the store clerk turned over two videotapes that held the recordings of Tuesday's events. He also agreed to retrieve the transaction records from the previous day and make a copy for Duke. The tape wasn't viewable with a conventional VCR, but there was sophisticated video equipment and a media specialist back at the DAO, and there would be time to go through it with him later. We didn't know if the tape might bear any fruit, but to have it in our possession was a positive step as we built our case. Most stores with video monitoring systems recycled the tapes every couple of days and covered over anything taped previously. Fortunately, no one had yet recorded over the tapes from the day before.

Door-to-door canvassing is monotonous, mind numbing, and crucial. Most people aren't used to speaking to the police and can be nervous about giving any information that they feel might jeopardize their safety. We ask the same questions to everybody with maybe one or two additional ones based on newer information or the response a person offers. Most often, the results are the same, with seemingly nothing gained. Like sifting for gold, though, you don't always collect big nuggets, but you stay at it because even tiny flecks can have some value when added with others. For example, it is common for a friend or colleague of a suspect to tell you he knows nothing about the case or the suspect's activities around the time of the incident. You memorialize his answers in a report and forget about it. What you have done is locked them into a statement that freezes them from showing up on the defendant's witness list to offer an invented exonerating alibi before a jury. The statement may mean nothing at the time it is given, but it could make a huge difference to the outcome of the case.

There is no magic to interviewing. Simply a conversation with a purpose, in this case learning about what happened; they generally don't become confrontational until you are zeroing in on a suspect because of all you have learned.

Eddie walked the hallways with a copy of the residents listing and knocked on doors of people who didn't have check marks next to their names.

He caught up with James Moccio, a resident who had used the function room for a birthday party on the previous Saturday night. Moccio told Eddie it was a small thirtieth birthday party for a friend with about ten people present. He said it was low-key with no drugs but some alcohol and that he had returned on Sunday to clean the room and left it in the same condition, as it was when he had entered on Saturday. He then stated that he had gotten the key on Friday and returned it to the office on Sunday. He also told Eddie that when he got home from work in the midafternoon on Monday he noticed the door to the function room was wide open. He said he popped his head in and saw the cleaning crew. He nodded to them briefly, and they nodded back.

To close the loop on the condition of the room before the fire, Eddie needed to talk with someone from the cleaning company. The building manager told him the cleaners only came to the building a few days a week and Wednesday wasn't one of them. Eddie knew there was plenty of time before the cadaver dog would arrive, so he contacted the company, got the location of the cleaning crew, and headed into Boston to speak with them.

What he didn't know in advance was that none of the crew spoke or understood English well enough to have a conversation. A quick call to the Boston Police solved the problem. They dispatched a Spanish-speaking officer to assist and he was on-scene within minutes. The conversations were brief. The crew all agreed that the room was spotless when they checked it on Monday afternoon, and they all remembered seeing someone who resembled Moccio standing at the doorway. That area covered, Eddie returned in time to meet with Trooper Barrett.

Gerard's earlier thought of getting together for lunch and updates were well meaning but unrealistic. We were all engaged in different phases of the case, and as important as food and eating was to the crew, we couldn't plan lunch around a set time. As it happened, we were all in the area around two o'clock when Johnny Rivers pulled into the parking lot. We came together for a quick review of new and updated information. Rivers was clearly agitated but insisted the others speak first. Duke and Eddie talked of their interviews. Duke mentioned the recovery of videotapes that might provide leads if we could identify any of the customers around the time of the fire, and Eddie spoke of his conversation with Moccio and how his simple task to speak with the cleaners became a little more complex. Johnny Rivers quickly got our undivided attention as he commented about what he had discovered when scratching the surface on Crouse background.

"Let me tell you," he started with his arms spread apart, "this guy is a hardcore scumbag. He has a rap sheet five pages long with stuff ranging from thefts and car chases to violent sexual assaults. He did five years in the can for an aggravated rape in Revere. He's still on parole for Christ sake. I did NCIC and Triple III checks on him too. They arrested him for a rape in Florida a few years ago, but they dropped the charges. If you look at the timeline on the charges, it looks like he screwed from Massachusetts when things heated up and then came running back home when he got in the shit down there. I don't think Florida jails are as kind to rapists as they are up here." He continued, "There is little doubt that Crouse is at the center of whatever the hell this is that we are looking at. I'm going to keep digging and see what else I can turn up. I have a call in to Revere detectives to learn what happened there, and I'll figure out how to get a contact in Florida as well to find out what happened there and why they dropped the charges."

Rivers information told me that we were right to focus our attention on Crouse's behavior and his movements. The initial alibis from him and his girlfriend were soft with sketchy details. Crouse's history opened yet another pathway for us to follow in our travels to find both the truth and a victim.

The sounds of yapping and whining coming from the back seat of Trooper Barrett's K-9 cruiser as she pulled into the parking lot interrupted our conversation. Kathy's assignment for more than a decade was the K-9 unit, and she had recently trained and received certification with her German Shepherd partner, Adam, in human remains recovery. Kathy was tireless and thorough, and her presence gave us a bit of hope that if a victim were concealed anywhere in the area, she and Adam would find them.

She wanted to start in the function room where Adam could pick up a scent from the bloody areas. Steve Ruelle unlocked the door to the room, and Adam strained on the leash and headed directly to the area of dried blood on the carpet. After a few moments of sniffing and barking, Kathy aimed him toward the door. He tugged and headed out to search the common areas, stairwells, and corridors of the building, with Duke and Eddie following close behind. After the interior search was complete, the entourage exited out the front door and walked at a pace just short of a gallop. Adam led them all around the perimeter of the building and the parking lot, tugging and snorting the whole way. He sniffed cars, bushes, and the area around the dumpster before lifting his leg and leaving his mark on a rusty sidewall of the dumpster. He headed off the property, walking up and down the bordering streets, occasionally sniffing at trees and barking at neighborhood dogs.

At the end of the search there was nothing new to report other than that whoever our victim was, they were no longer anywhere around the Malden Mills Condos. It was disappointing in one sense, but Adam's effort took away any thoughts that someone was careless enough to leave behind a body, which was not surprising since they took extraordinary steps when torching the building in hopes of eliminating evidence. If they were willing to potentially take the lives of dozens of others to cover their tracks, they were cunning enough to remove the body before setting the fire, which could very well explain why Crouse was pulling a kid's wagon in the parking lot while the other residents slept.

As the darkness set in, we suspended our work for the day. We met in the parking lot to go over what we had, what we needed to get, and how we would continue the exploration. We were only two days into it, but it was feeling like a lot longer, and a bit of frustration was obvious in everyone's voices. It was too early to be discouraged, and we parted believing our approach and methodology was correct and I remained confident that we were making progress.

Karol Setalsingh would be back on Thursday morning to work on the crime scene since it was now sufficiently dry. Ruelle and Rivers had court first thing, and Connolly and I had matters to attend to at the office. Duke and Eddie said they would be there to meet with him in the late morning.

We knew that a lot of the information we needed for source materials, like phone records and credit card checks, were going to require court orders or grand jury subpoenas, and that would take time to both request and, if granted, receive the results. Similarly, any search of Crouse's Chevy Blazer or condo would need a search warrant, and while we were hopeful, we were short on probable cause to request one.

The case could break wide open in a moment's notice with a comment from a witness or a clue from a piece of evidence, but it could also crawl along at a snail's pace. We prepared for any eventuality, but none of us thought it would be a quick ending, and all of us were mentally prepared for the long term. We also had to prioritize the writing of reports to memorialize what we learned before any information was lost or forgotten. We all knew Adrienne would be expecting them when she met with us on Monday morning, and we weren't going to disappoint.

CHAPTER 3

The Investigation Continues

Aside from some brief next day coverage in the local *Malden Evening News,* the reporting of the fire had been nonexistent until the third day. Buried midway through the *New England News Brief* column in the metro section of the *Boston Globe* was a one-paragraph note mentioning the fire, and that there was blood and hair found at the scene, and that K-9s searched the area with no results. It also mentioned the posting of flyers in the building offering a five-thousand-dollar reward from the Fire Marshall's office for information. The fact that a story was in the paper and it suggested intrigue meant that we could expect a flood of phone calls to both the Malden PD and the DAO. The media would want information, and their requests for interviews or a press conference was expected. The good news was that the responsibility of responding to those calls fell to the media relations people in the office. They were our blockers and shielded my team from any direct contact with reporters.

When Karol Setalsingh told us on Tuesday that he needed to return on Thursday to do a more thorough and complete search, I knew he wasn't just blowing us off due to the hot and humid working conditions. Karol was an extraordinarily talented forensic specialist who spent sixteen years in a handful of assignments before discovering his niche in the Crime Scene Services Section five years prior to this case. In a short period, he had earned the confidence of my homicide investigators, who knew that if there were something of evidentiary value remaining, Karol's attention to detail and painstaking methods of discovery would find it.

Once in the function room, Karol plunked his crime scene toolbox and camera bag onto the kitchenette counter and unpacked a few of his tools of the trade. He rummaged around and removed bottles of black and white fingerprint dust, brushes of varying thickness and size, a tape measure, a roll of tape, and a magnifying glass. He pulled on a pair of light blue neoprene gloves and covered his feet in paper booties before setting about searching the room and everything in it for areas of concern where he may uncover evidence and/or fingerprints for processing and development. His exploration was slow and scrupulous, and there were items he photographed and packed up for further evaluation, but nothing new or obvious grabbed his, Duke's, or Eddie's attention. As he was finishing up and getting ready to pack his gear, he took a moment to open all the sliding drawers and cubby spaces in the kitchen area.

"Just trying to be thorough, guys, I had a defense attorney question me one day on the witness stand about why I didn't search the drawers in a room away from the crime scene. It was a ridiculous question, but it got the jury's attention, and I was a little flustered and tongue-tied in trying to answer. Now I go through everything, so if they ask me I can quickly answer the question with an affirmative nod and a slight smile and shut down the line of questioning."

Duke helped, blindly running his hand over the upper shelves above the sink. He landed on what felt like a magazine. He pulled it down and found himself staring at the image of a beautiful blonde woman on the front cover of *Genesis,* a men's magazine featuring nude women. The date on the magazine was November of 1999, so it may have been sitting and hidden there for months and probably long forgotten by whoever left it there. Duke looked right at his partner and said, "Eddie, you gotta stop leaving your stuff where it can be found. You betta tell Karol how it got there before he finds your prints all over it."

Eddie's face flushed, and he just stared at Duke, trying to formulate a good comeback, but he couldn't. Duke got the best of him, and he couldn't keep the smirk off his face.

Karol said he would need to clear some light soot from the cover but he would make an effort to process it for prints. He photographed it before slipping it into a large plastic evidence bag and marking it with the date, time, and place of recovery.

When Karol left, he headed to the crime lab with a few potential pieces of evidence that had what appeared to be blood and hair on them that would require testing by the chemists. The magazine stayed in his possession, and he would do the latent fingerprint work at his workbench at the OCME.

Duke and Eddie wandered over to Malden Taxi to speak with the day dispatcher. She had spoken briefly with them when they interviewed Lester on the morning of the eighteenth. At the time, the morning rush of calls for service fully occupied her, and they told her they would come back later when things quieted down. Sue Ellen Hyde told them she worked for Lester Morovitz for the past four years on the five a.m. to four p.m. shift. Her work desk faced a large window and Eastern Avenue, and when not taking calls and dispatching taxis, she could gaze out and take note of life as it passed by in front of her.

Duke asked if she knew Lester's stepson, Tommy Crouse. She nodded, acknowledging she knew him and that he was a frequent visitor who came by a few times a week to speak with Lester. She added that he did not drive a taxi but did occasional jobs driving clients to special events in limos.

"I think he may also be working a construction job on the Big Dig in Boston," she said. "He lives in a condo across the street with his girlfriend and a couple of small kids. He drives a bluish-colored Chevy Blazer."

Duke asked if she saw Tommy on the morning of the fire. She thought before answering and said, "I'm not positive of the exact times, but I saw his Blazer pull out of the parking lot between five thirty and six a.m. and take a right hand turn onto Eastern Avenue, heading in the direction of the Mobil station." She added, "Then, a few minutes later, the truck returned and pulled into the condo parking lot. But shortly after that, the truck left again and this time took a left-hand turn." She also recalled, "The fire department pulled into the parking lot approximately twenty minutes later."

Eddie questioned if she knew it was Tommy behind the wheel or if anyone else was in the Blazer, and she told him, "The truck has tinted windows, so I couldn't be sure of who was inside, only that I saw it moving on three occasions that morning." She added, "Tommy came into the office the next day, and we talked briefly. I told him I saw him leaving on Tuesday morning and then coming back before heading out again, and he said that he had forgotten his wallet."

As they walked back across the street, Duke told Eddie he thought it was odd that the dispatcher knew Crouse but didn't refer to him as an employee of the taxi company even though she mentioned that he did special event chauffeuring.

"She did help with the timing of the events, and it sure looks like Crouse gassed up before heading up north, and neither he nor Esther mentioned a stop at the gas station next door before they left. I go back to what I said after we interviewed them. They both remember some things well but are really unclear, forgetful, or vague about the obvious and important stuff. I can't wait to get the Mobil gas station tapes to our media people so they can put them onto the right type of videorecorder for us to watch."

• • • •

Thursday was winding down, and I was sitting at my desk reviewing the reports of the first responders to the scene when I took a call from one of the three media specialists in the DAO.

"Bill, do you have a few moments to come over and meet with Martha and I about the Malden Mills fire? The press has been hounding us all afternoon for information, but other cases are tying her up right now. She wants to put something out, and we want to be thorough but careful in the wording of it."

I put the reports into a folder and walked across the hall to Martha's office.

This wasn't a homicide case yet, but it certainly had all the earmarks, and we were treating it as one—but without more, it wasn't. Without an agreement between her and the Malden PD chief about working together to manage the flow of information through press releases and public comments, this kind of case could get out of hand very easily.

"Billy," Martha started, "our media folks have been fielding a lot of calls from the media today about the blurb in the *Globe* about the Malden case. We need to come up with some answers for them. Right now, we are considering a brief press release, but if they persist, we may need to do a press conference. Is there anything new in the case that we can or can't share with them?"

"No, not really," was the best answer I could come up with. "Are you looking for something to go out with today, or can it wait until the morning when I can bring the group together so we can talk about it with Gerard and you? I would rather have direct input from those who spoke to the witnesses and with the crime scene people. I don't want to misspeak on their behalf. This is way too important, so we have to be somewhat guarded with what we can share because there is some info we just don't want out in the public domain," I continued, "but on the other hand, when we don't have a victim or even a reported missing person, we could use the public's help. I'm just always nervous about putting things out through the media that can come back and bite us in the ass at trial time. And while I know we are a long way from identifying a victim, making an arrest, or preparing for a trial, it's the early mistakes that become the larger issues once someone is charged. If we can hold them off until tomorrow, I think we can put out a much better statement for them."

After discussing the pros and cons of a press release, we agreed I would have a few of my investigators in her office at nine in the morning, when we would put our heads together and cobble together a unified statement.

Having our media office was a godsend because they were the buffer that kept the press at bay. Dealing directly with the media is a slippery slope for investigators because eventually they will burn you, and that should never happen twice.

An investigator who likes to speak and share pertinent information with the press either is new to the game or overly impressed with themselves. Their colleagues, particularly seasoned detectives, treat them with disdain and derision. It isn't that we don't trust the media, but our goals and objectives aren't usually the same. We are terrified of saying something or sharing information that might bring potential harm to the case because, for us, the successful prosecution of the case is all that matters. Their job is different from ours, and there are frequent areas of conflict, particularly when we are determined to preserve information for the integrity of the investigation, while they are just as determined to publish it when they learn of it. I understand their reasoning, but from our perspective, it is shortsighted.

On Friday morning, we convened around the conference table in Martha's office. Steve Ruelle said he had spoken with his chief and the department's public information officer, and they agreed there should be full coordination and cooperation between all involved agencies and that our office was the best vehicle for the dissemination of information.

We laid out all the information we had gathered up until that moment and talked about our next steps. Martha interjected with insightful and probing questions, while her media specialist scribbled notes onto his legal pad and began to create a document. By the end of the morning, a one-page press release was ready to share with the Malden chief and then disseminated by fax to the media.

• • • •

Adrienne Lynch was back in her office early Monday. We started our week together at the long-established nine o'clock leadership meeting, where we hunkered around a massive conference table in the office of the first ADA, John McEvoy. Martha, like her predecessors, brought team leaders, a few superior court trial attorneys, and representatives from all of the specialized prosecution and support units together to review the activities of the previous week and talk about the plans for the week and the weeks in front of us. The meetings rarely lasted less than an hour because there were always problematic, and often unique, situations that team members presented for discussion.

There were an awful lot of smart people in that room—true leaders and thinkers who freely shared their experiences and their knowledge for the guidance of others. I always walked away a lot smarter than when I had arrived. Adrienne spoke briefly about her time in South Carolina, and I spoke about the cases that came in during the past week, including a short burst on the Malden Mills fire. As soon as the meeting adjourned, Adrienne and I headed to the conference room, chatting as we walked to meet the rest of the team.

"You know, Billy, I was thinking on my drive back yesterday that it seems every time I go out of state for a couple of days the crap hits the fan and I come back to a complicated mess where I'm already miles behind everyone and rushing to catch up. One good thing about this trip, though, was that I was able to stop at home in Jersey and spend the weekend with my mom and dad. That is always a treat," she said with loving sarcasm.

Her father, always affectionately referred to as Big Ed, had been a prosecutor and clearly the number one mentor in her life.

"We sometimes sit and chat about the facts and complexities of a case, and he critiques things from another perspective. He offers advice and occasionally equates my case to ones he worked on in the past." Adrienne always spoke of him with reverence and with a laugh and a huge smile on her face.

Our backgrounds differed in many ways, but she and I shared a very basic connection: the respect and love we had for our fathers. My dad was a retired Boston police detective who commanded the Investigations Unit in the Suffolk DAO in the 1970s. Once I became a detective working on significant and complex cases, our general and casual conversations often took on a different tone. In the summer, we would sit in the screened-in porch of our house on Cape Cod, and in the winter, by the living room fireplace with a cold beer or a whiskey glass of Dewar's scotch nearby. We would discuss cases I was working, and he always offered sage advice and encouragement. The word "quit" was not in his vocabulary, and if I learned anything from him, he taught me that if I was going to succeed in this field, I needed to adopt the same philosophy in every case I worked. I am thankful that I not only share his name, but I acknowledge the privilege to be walking in his shadow with my feet eclipsing his footsteps.

• • • •

Connolly, Forster, and Donoghue were already waiting in the conference room since they had only needed to walk across the hall. Rivers and Ruelle arrived a few moments later. Finding a parking spot, whether legal or not, anywhere near the courthouse on a Monday morning was a total crapshoot, so punctuality, like parking, was a matter of luck.

Steve passed around copies of the initial Malden police and fire reports and talked about their search of missing person files and calls to hospital emergency rooms for any information on persons who may have presented with significant injuries. So far, their efforts were fruitless. The (OCME) said if they received any bodies with fatal injuries and no known cause, they would give us a call.

Adrienne sat, pulled out her partially full yellow pad, and opened the conversation. She said she had spoken with Gerard Butler several times over the past few days and thought she had a good understanding of the facts but wanted to hear about any recent information. We followed up with a more thorough and in-depth discussion and recollection of what happened from Thursday morning through to that morning.

She took notes as she listened before shifting the conversation from what we completed to what we still needed to do, including our immediate next steps. We had a person of interest to focus on but for what reason—an arson, certainly, but a serious assault or a murder. We had a lot of work to do before we could rule anything in or out, and without a victim; assault or murder charges would be extremely difficult, if not impossible.

I knew that even though we had accomplished a lot, we were still in the beginning stages, and it was highly likely that without a surprising turn of events we wouldn't be closing the case out anytime soon. There were still had a ton of questions that needed answers and bit by bit we continued to chip away.

Early in my career, I learned never to question anyone more than once because it gave the appearance you didn't trust their memory and any new information would taint their original statement. Over time, I learned that was ill-advised guidance coming from a lazy investigator because the truth is the opposite. Keeping an open dialogue builds trust it doesn't negate it. In the days following an incident, people talk about it amongst themselves and observe others behaviors and comments that they hear. When a detective stops knocking on doors that type of information is lost and gone forever.

A week after the fire, Eddie and Duke set aside the afternoon to go back to Malden Mills and knock on a few doors of people they hadn't yet met and a few that they had spoken with earlier. While on the first floor and in close proximity to Crouse's condo, they knocked on the door of Pete Grey and his girlfriend Nancy Cooper. There were brief introductions and small talk about the fire and the need to gather information by talking with all of the residents. "Did you check out the guy in Unit 115? His name is Tommy," Pete asked. "It was either the day after the fire, or two days later I ran into him in the hallway, he was plastered and "wired." He pulled me into his doorway and wanted to know what I knew and if I had heard anything. I took that to mean he was asking about the fire and I told him I hadn't heard anything." Pete went on to say he knew Crouse and they talked on occasion, but they were not friends. "About a month and a half ago we were talking, and he told me he had a key to the function room, and he brings broads there and does coke with them." Cooper spoke of Crouse in similar terms and related, "about a month ago I was alone and ran into him. He was looking for Pete, but he wasn't around. We made small talk and he kept saying he was a regular guy before showing me a white powder in a baggie a couple of times. I think it was cocaine and he was hitting on me."

The couple was clearly dealing with some life issues, but they were friendly, open, and cooperative. The little tidbits they offered were important because, among other things, they contradicted Crouse's earlier statement that he didn't have a key to the function room. That visit resulted in a short walk around the corner and a few doors down to Unit 115 for another conversation.

Crouse answered the door but didn't invite them in. He preferred to speak from the threshold and that was his prerogative. Eddie asked him a couple of general questions before probing a little deeper and inquiring about having a key to the function room. Once again, he insisted he did not have a key and the only two times he had been in the room were on the weekend he rented the room for his daughter's birthday party. He repeated that someone from the condo's management company opened and locked the room and he never had a key.

A few days later Eddie received a call from Karol Setalsingh with some incredible, unexpected news. He had processed the Genesis magazine and recovered a thumbprint impression on the lower portion of the front cover. "Well that's good news." Eddie said.

"Yes, it is, but it gets much better," replied Karol. "The print belongs to your boy Tommy Crouse! I matched it up with his print card from his Rape arrest in Revere."

The news of the discovery travelled like wildfire. Once again, just another step, but this one was a little bigger. Unless Crouse could offer a good explanation, it would shoot down his claims of only being in the room for a kid's birthday party. Generally, that was not an occasion to bring along a porno magazine for a little light reading while the kids swiped away at a piñata or dug into a dish of melting ice cream.

Eddie and Steve Ruelle visited with Crouse for a third time. They focused this encounter on the fingerprint. Eddie talked about finding the magazine hidden on a shelf in the function room and his fingerprint on the cover. Crouse was indignant and steadfast that he was never in the function room with a "dirty magazine" and intimated that someone had taken it from his apartment and put or left it there on the shelf. He dug his heels in and for the third time denied ever being in the room except for his daughter's birthday party.

Crouse was indeed a bad guy and evidently a liar with a nasty criminal past. In fact, a deeper dive by Rivers uncovered a lengthy record that included aggravated rape, assaults, and drug-related charges, with previous convictions and jail time served.

However, you can't convict someone of a crime you can't prove, and as the weeks turned to months and late fall approached, we still couldn't produce a victim. My guys checked teletype messages daily for missing persons or reports of similar crimes in other jurisdictions to no avail. They also made telephone calls regularly to police and social services agencies to ask if they had any unverified information about a violent, unsolved crime. I mentioned the case at monthly detective meetings, hoping to make a connection to crimes or unusual situations in other communities. We asked other detectives to keep their eyes and ears open for any information remotely connected to the fire or missing persons. Informants and arrestees are often willing to trade information for current and future considerations regarding arrests and incarcerations.

After the first couple of demanding but frustrating months on the case, our team meetings and daily attention began to wane a bit because we all had older and newer cases demanding our attention-ones with identified bodies and leads to pursue. In fact, Malden had a new, complicated murder, and Steve and Johnny were working on that with another

ADA and team of troopers. Our office was still fielding the usual dozens of calls each month for unattended deaths. They all required on-scene and follow-up investigation and Jimmy, Eddie, and Duke were part of the rotation that responded when they had the call. In addition, the ADAs prosecuting cases with indicted defendants needed to prep for court motions and trials and rightfully required the trooper's undivided attention at times.

We continued to track and follow whatever limited information came our way. We anxiously awaited the forensic results from the crime lab, the telephone records requested through Grand Jury subpoenas, and the hope that a private media lab with specialized equipment could clarify the video from the Mobil station and either confirm or refute that the first person to purchase gas on the morning of the fire was, in fact, Tommy Crouse. Any one of those findings or results could identify new opportunities and pathways for us to explore and quickly pull us back together. Although spread a little thin, we were still actively working the case.

One of our priorities from the first day was to try to cobble together enough information for a search warrant for Crouse's pickup truck. We wanted to do a thorough forensic search in hopes of recovering biological and or trace evidence that might be helpful in identifying a victim.

We had some helpful materials but not enough to reach the legal standard of probable cause. Duke was keeping a folder of relevant information and had already written the beginnings of an affidavit in hopes of eventually filling it in with enough factual items to cross over the threshold and pass judicial scrutiny.

As late summer turned to fall, updated information started to trickle in from several sources. The crime lab finished their testing on the blood samples. They confirmed the source of the blood was from a female and should contain DNA they could compare at a later point to DNA samples from other sources. The chemical samples taken from the fire for evidence confirmed the arsonist used petroleum products to start the fire, and that would help if the DA brought an arson charge. Grand jury subpoenas brought valuable information regarding Crouse's home phone, as well as the mobile phone he carried that his stepfather paid for through Malden Transportation. Similarly, the records from his Mobil credit card were very enlightening. The telephone and credit card statements poked sizeable holes in the original statements or alibis of Crouse, Fournier, and her parents.

It's fair to say that the enhancements of the video from the Mobil station exceeded all expectations. The folks at Avid Technologies, using new software that they developed, worked absolute magic. They were able to isolate and expand the four quadrant camera views that had appeared on one screen. They also cleaned up the haziness that came from poor lighting and overuse of the VCR tape, expanded and enlarged the visual content on each frame of the video, and then broke down the film into a huge collection of individual photos. The enhanced video clearly showed Crouse as the first customer at six o'clock in the morning. He bought five dollars' worth of gas and paid in cash. The video also showed him going outside, removing the nozzle from the gas pump, lifting the rear hatch of his Blazer, and pouring gasoline from the hose into some type of receptacle in the rear of the vehicle. Crouse had never let on in any of his interviews that he was at the gas station and bought gas that morning, let alone that he paid in cash. This was powerful and damning information and a major piece to the case he was helping us build against him.

During the last week of September, Duke spent a few days sitting with the old and the new materials spread out on the table as he arranged and rearranged them into a concise and understandable narrative with enough information for a strong showing of probable cause to search Crouse's truck. He enlisted the help of ADA Marguerite Grant and the search warrant team, and together they stitched together a document with enough connecting information to meet the threshold of probable cause.

On the first Wednesday of October, Duke met with a judge in the Middlesex Superior Court where, in the privacy of his chambers, they discussed the reason for the warrant request. The judge reviewed the paperwork, asked a few questions about the narrative, and was satisfied there was probable cause to look for evidence in the pickup truck. He signed the warrant authorizing a search.

At this point, Crouse and Fournier had relocated from Malden to the nearby city of Lynn, where they were living in another condo in the same building as his mother and stepfather. Jimmy and Duke arrived at Crouse's home around nine o'clock and presented him with a copy of the search warrant for the Chevy Blazer. When they asked for his keys to the truck, Crouse told them it was in a transmission shop for repairs and that he didn't have the keys. He gave them the name of the mechanic and a way they could reach him. The three had a short conversation in the hall outside of the doorway. As they parted company, both Jimmy and Duke noticed and commented to each other that Crouse's eyes had welled up with tears.

A half an hour later, Steve Ruelle and Eddie Forster found the truck in the parking lot of Malden Taxi and had it towed to the Malden PD garage. They cordoned it off with yellow tape and secured it until the techs searched it the following morning.

The intent was to process the vehicle in two stages. The chemists at the lab carried out the first phase on Thursday morning. Their search was specific for serology samples and trace evidence in both the seating and storage areas. The second phase would be done on Friday morning and focus on evidence of accelerants connected to the fire. Paul Horgan and Lucy would do that work.

The searches were important and necessary but also multifaceted. If they found residual evidence like blood, hair or fibers connecting Crouse to another person, it would strengthen the case against him. However, if they found nothing connecting him to the fire or a victim, that could work to his benefit by buttressing his claims that he wasn't involved in the arson and/or any bloody altercation inside of the function room.

The results of the testing from both searches were inconclusive and not particularly favorable to either side. The chemists found small traces of blood in the truck cab, but they belonged to either Crouse, Fournier, or were unidentifiable. Lucy hit on a grommet in the truck bed within seconds. Normally that would be an accelerant, but in this case, that sample, as well as a rug sample cut from the truck bed, turned out to be bleach. Both sides could try to use the results to their benefit if we were ever to criminally charge Crouse.

• • • •

Winter was sneaking up on us, and the holidays were approaching. Daylight savings time brought darkness at four thirty in the afternoon, and the weather was getting colder with each passing day. The snowfall and ice conditions that accompanied the winter months were only a few short weeks away. So, with little more to operate on, the Malden Mills case was quietly nudged over to a side burner. The case was never out of sight or mind and as it simmered, little bits of new information added spice to the pot.

Speaking with Adrienne one afternoon, Eddie opined that that they shouldn't lose hope or be discouraged about solving the case. "You know how this works 'A,'-it happens all of the time. A killer buries the body in a shallow grave when the ground is soft. They mean to bury the body six feet deep, but it's harder than they expected, so they stop digging after two feet. They stick the body in the open hole, cover it with dirt and crap, and run away. The ground freezes in the cold months, and when it gets mushy in the spring, hungry critters start digging for food and our phone starts ringing because someone's dog found a bone on a morning walk and they are freaking out. It happens every year somewhere around here." His comment may have seemed crude, but experienced investigators know it to be true.

• • • •

Mercifully, the Christmas holiday brought a few days of relative calm to the office and a chance for everyone to spend a bit of quality time at home with family and friends. The holiday fell on a Monday that year, and I was more than okay running with a skeleton crew for the week. Tuesday the twenty-sixth was bitterly cold with the thermometer registering below zero. There was just Duke and I in the office, and the phone had been thankfully quiet as we sat and talked about his first year with the Middlesex team. It had been a quick immersion for him; we had recorded sixteen murders so far that year, and Duke had responded to and worked on nine of them.

Shortly after eleven, Duke answered the first phone call of the day—and in an instant, it rocked our world. The call was from the dispatcher in the communications center at the Wakefield Police Department. He said all of their day shift officers were off at an office building for a call of shots fired. He had an address and could add little more but said the chief and the detectives were requesting us at the scene as fast as we could get there. He added that they also requested every available ambulance from the surrounding towns. Duke grabbed his coat, gloves, and a pack of notebooks and headed out for the fourteen-mile blue-light-and-siren trip.

Less than twenty minutes later, he was calling. "Boss, you need to be sitting for this."

"Okay," I answered as I sunk into my chair.

"There are at least seven shooting victims," he said.

"Sweet Jesus! Any of them dead?" I asked.

"Yes, all seven. The shooter is an employee who everyone seems to know. He's in custody and headed to the PD now. He hasn't spoken a word. There were dozens of people in the building at the time, and everyone who could run out the door did. A priest from a church across the street just unlocked the doors to offer them shelter. You need to get up here as fast as you can and call out the cavalry because we have a huge crime scene, a ton of people to interview, and a gathering crowd of police officers who are here to help, but I'm not sure what to tell them except wait. This is huge." He gave me the address and the name of the company again.

What followed in a rapid cascade was a callout through the office pager system to everyone, including those assigned to cases other than homicides. The order was to report ASAP for a multiple homicide at the offices of Edgewater Technology in Wakefield, and a similar callout requested that the Crime Scene Services Section send as much help as they could. I called John McEvoy and gave him the limited information, and he headed to the scene, calling for additional help from other homicide prosecutors and the search warrant team. Martha Coakley was at O'Hare Airport in Chicago, waiting for a flight back to Boston, when she saw live coverage on the CNN newsfeed on the overhead monitors. She was on the phone in seconds and asked for a pickup to go directly to the scene when her plane landed. Help poured in from other DAOs and local PDs, and soon we were putting together interview teams with folks we knew and trusted from previous cases.

Duke called while I was en route to seek my authorization to let a regional SWAT team breach the crime scene to do a protective sweep to search for additional victims or people who had sought shelter in hidden or safe spaces. It was a tough call in one sense because we needed to protect the crime scene, but out of an abundance of caution, I thought it was prudent for them to search—extremely carefully to avoid unnecessarily disrupting the crime scene.

Within the hour, we learned more about the shooter. Michael "Mucko" McDermott was an employee with significant, recent anger management issues aimed particularly at certain human resources personnel because of a financial debt he had disputed. The company was under federal government orders immediately to garnish his wages due to a failure to pay overdue taxes. The company had to remit the money to the IRS. McDermott was openly upset and vocal with his employer about what he saw as their intrusion into his personal life.

The victims, four women and three men, never stood a chance. All but one saw him approaching, but they were no match for his weapons. A few minutes after eleven, he pushed back from his desk, reached into his locker, and removed a high-powered rifle, shotgun, and semi-automatic pistol along with a gym bag full of ammo clips and loose ammunition, and he headed in the direction of the main entrance. He entered the lobby area where two women he knew acknowledged him with a warm holiday greeting. He responded by levelling his rifle, opening fire, and killing them where they stood. The sound of gunfire rang through the building, and everyone scrambled for his or her lives. Many exited through side doors to the street while others sought refuge under tables and desks. McDermott advanced straight ahead like a soldier on a mission, trudging his six-foot-three, three-hundred-and-fifty-pound frame down a long corridor before climbing up two stairs and entering an annex area full of offices, workstations, and people. With his rifle at the ready, he rapidly killed three more coworkers. Two men who had yelled his name and urged him to put down his weapon and a young mother who sat at a desk, turned away from him. He shot her several times in the back.

He left the office and calmly walked back down the corridor and took a seat in a visitor's chair in the foyer. As the sound of police sirens brought all the working members of the department to the scene, McDermott put the weapons at his feet and stared straight ahead. He offered no resistance when taken into custody.

We all took a few deep breaths as we processed the enormity and reality of the moment, but we didn't delay or put the scene on hold. This was where training and experience kicked in. We knew what we needed to accomplish and how to do it; we just had to sit for a moment and talk through it all. Yes, the scene was gruesome, terrifying, and chaotic, but it didn't matter if there was one victim or seven, the investigative template was the same, just magnified by seven. We had at least three search warrants to write, a massive crime scene to process and dozens and dozens of very scared and shaken people we had to locate and interview.

In addition, background work had to begin on McDermott's motive and the planning stages, including how he was able to procure the murder weapons. At the time, the most important task was identifying the victims and connecting with the seven families to make the death notifications. We could make our introductions, express our condolences, share what limited information we could, and begin to prepare them for what may lie ahead. We would later confirm this was the largest mass murder in Massachusetts history.

On Wednesday morning, McDermott, under heavy guard and wearing a bulletproof vest out of concern for his safety, exited the police van and headed into Malden District Court for his arraignment. In what one could only describe as a circus atmosphere, with media and spectators overflowing the courtroom, spilling into the courthouse lobby, and out the front door, ADA Tom Reilly made a short but thorough explanation for the charges against McDermott. His attorney spoke on his client's behalf. He hinted about mental health issues and the need for continued medical care. McDermott was held without bail and ordered to remain in custody at the Middlesex County Jail, located several floors above our office in the Middlesex Courthouse.

To the untrained eye, cases like this appear simple to prove. People are dead, a suspect in custody at the scene, and there are dozens of cooperating witnesses. However, it doesn't lessen the need to conduct a complete investigation because we still have to prove the case for first-degree murder beyond a reasonable doubt before a jury. What complicated the concerns of the prosecutors and investigators in this case was the best and only real defense for McDermott was insanity. These cases require a completely different approach. Insanity is a legal term, not a medical one, where the defendant pleads that due to an episodic or persistent psychiatric disease the Court cannot hold them responsible for their actions at the time of the murders. While the defense is rarely successful, it doesn't diminish the amount of work needed by the prosecution team to disprove the theory.

There was no doubt that for the following several months this case would consume a tremendous amount of time, effort, and energy by the investigators, victim witness advocates, ADAs, and support help assigned to it.

CHAPTER 4

Finding the Remains

Part 1

In my opinion, and to be fair, not one that everyone shares, the only good thing about New England winter is that it serves as a prelude to our New England springs. We suffer the cold, the snow, and the full darkness that consumes us before the workday ends so that we can truly appreciate the magnificent transformation that rolls in with the warming climate, extended daylight, and the re-greening of the lands. Winters are harsh and devoid of joy. Spring signifies a rebirth and it's a wonderful time to be alive and active. As the days get longer and temperatures rise, the snow melts, people take to the streets, and there is an unmistakable revival of enthusiasm and optimism everywhere. The bulky clothes and winter boots go to the back of the closet, and light-colored pants, pastel tops, and sandals are moved front and center. Restaurants rotate their menus from the comfort food and winter brews to lobster rolls and summer ales as they move their dining tables outside to rooftops and sidewalks.

North of Boston, in New Hampshire and Maine, people look to other signs that signify spring. Sadly, for them, the deep snow on the ski trails disappear, and the dozen or so resorts begin to retool for the transition to warm weather activities like golf, mountain trail biking, and climbing. The melt of the mountain snow floods the streams and rivers, and the sounds from the rush of the water can be deafening. As the winter white covering disappears and the trees begin to bud, the foot trails and jogging paths reappear to allow walkers and runners to resume their exercise routines.

The melt of the spring and the softening of the frozen ground is also a time for small woodland creatures to arise from their winter hiding spaces and scavenge the environment for nourishment. They spent the last few months hunkered down in hollowed out tree trunks or in the holes they created in the fall for winter warmth and safety from their predators. Their only food was what they had the foresight to tuck away before the harsh winter struck. By spring, they were out in force and ravenous. Their search could be for nuts and berries or for the carnivores, the opportunity to plunder the carcasses of the unfortunates that didn't survive the winter months.

Monday, April 23, 2001, a week after Patriot's Day, was a warm, sunny day in mid-New Hampshire. A local man sensed it was the beginning of an ideal morning. His old jogging route was clear and passable, and he was up and out early, happy to be back to his old routine. His run would take him through some differing terrains that ranged from narrow tree-covered shade to wide-open wasteland. As he entered a clearing and headed toward a paved road that circled a large and busy industrial park, he passed through a dormant sandpit littered with plastic bags of trash and discarded pieces of broken furniture and abandoned appliances. It was the least attractive part of his run, and he needed to keep an eye on the ground in front of him to avoid stepping into a small hole or onto a piece of trash that could cause him to trip and snap an ankle. A few hundred yards from the road, he stopped dead in his tracks. Sitting on the ground in front of him was a human skull with a few strands of hair attached. It was unmistakable. He could tell immediately that it wasn't a toy or sculpture tossed there or fallen from a trash bag. He circled around it, hoping someone else would come by to share the moment with him and confirm that what was lying in front of him was the real thing. It was a surreal and frightening moment, and he needed help ASAP. He grabbed for his cell phone, dialed 911, and told the dispatcher what he had found.

For Leslie McDaniel, his mundane overnight shift on the Hookset New Hampshire Police Department was ending and the bright morning sunlight was more painful than stimulating. As the shift commander, it was time to head into the station, exchange information with the day shift, fill out the end of watch paperwork, and head for home. At 7:05, a radio transmission from the dispatcher rerouted him to meet a man about a discovery in an area off Industrial Park Drive, between Peterbrook and Leroux Drives.

A few minutes later, McDaniel slowly drove his marked cruiser up the road with an eye out for the reporting party. He passed the General Electric Plant on his right and a couple of smaller business fronts before he came upon the jogger, who was waving him down from the edge of the roadway. The conversation between the two was quick and to the point. No time for an exchange of pleasantries, the frightened jogger was anxious to bring the police officer to the area where the skull was lying before another curious or famished animal carried it away. Together, they walked and talked toward the discovery, and the jogger explained why he was in the sandpit and how he had come across the skull. They were a few hundred yards in from the roadway when they found themselves on top of it. Even for a seasoned police veteran, the observation was ghastly and unnerving. McDaniel's mind was racing as he knelt and noted that there was still some dried skin attached to the cranium along with the hair fragments. His immediate thoughts were a coyote or larger animal dragged it there while foraging for food and left it behind. He could tell it wasn't an old artifact pilfered from a high school anatomy lab or bought in a joke shop and meant as a prank. No, this skull was human, and he thought there was a very good possibility that the rest of the body wasn't too far away.

Instinct and training overrode all other thoughts as McDaniel took a moment to consider what he was going to say over the police radio. He knew that the news stations monitored their police transmissions, and he didn't want them rushing to the scene, nor did he want to alarm town residents who also listened in on their police scanners as they readied for the day ahead. He took a deep breath, depressed the small red button that activated the microphone on his radio, and in a calm voice, called the PD's dispatch center. He simply asked for assistance at the scene from the investigations unit and requested they notify the chief to stand by for a telephone call. He then did what every police officer knows to do. He went back to his cruiser, got a huge roll of yellow crime scene tape, and with the assistance of the jogger, cordoned off a large area to keep everyone out except those who were necessary and trained to help. The first rule of any investigation is to protect the crime scene at all costs. Do not let it become contaminated, and do not poke around potentially disturbing unseen or unrecognized evidence. Bring in the specialists. McDaniel knew that there would only be one opportunity to process a crime scene, and he not only wanted to get it right, he never wanted anyone to second-guess about why he had trampled through the area.

The Hookset detectives were not yet on-duty, but they got the call and headed to the scene to start their day. McDaniel dialed up the chief and gave him a heads-up about the discovery. That resulted in a series of calls to the county DA, the New Hampshire Attorney General's Office, the New Hampshire State Police Major Crime Unit, and their OCME. In turn, everyone they contacted either went or sent at least one representative to the scene.

In most ways, the New Hampshire protocols for death investigations paralleled Massachusetts except the attorney general and not the county attorney have investigative and prosecutorial jurisdiction over death scenes. In turn, the New Hampshire State Police Major Crime Unit that took the investigative lead at the direction of the attorney general probed all sudden, unexpected, and violent deaths. There were a handful of cities in New Hampshire with experienced detective units large enough to handle frequent death investigations, but Hooksett was not one of them.

The discovery of skeletal remains is not very common, even in states with lots of rural, heavily wooded areas. If or when they identify the bodies, most often, they are those of missing hikers or hunters who never returned from their missions. In New Hampshire, this might happen only two or three times in a year. In many cases, the victims were unheard from for more than a year, and it is the next generation of hikers and hunters who discover their remains. With the small number of cases, the State had no need for a forensic anthropologist on the payroll. When necessary they consulted with Dr. Marcella Sorg, a world-renowned scientist and full-time professor at the University of Maine who also served as the on-call "bone doctor" for the OCME in Maine.

Finding a skull in the middle of a sandpit doesn't necessarily mean there is a homicide victim nearby. It could be that animals foraged through an old graveyard or excavation site and came out with the head of a person who died from natural causes decades ago. The final determination was for the medical examiner to decide, although not until the completion of the medicolegal investigation.

McDaniel set up a tactical position by the roadway to greet the arriving investigators and prosecutors while keeping an eye on the distant crime scene area. He would also be the scribe who took the initial notes about the scene, the weather, and lighting conditions, his meeting with the jogger, and anything else he deemed important. He kept a written crime scene log identifying all who entered, as well as the time they arrived. He introduced the jogger to the detectives, and they took over from there, but he remained on the scene until relieved of duty in the late morning.

• • • •

Trooper John Cody of the Major Crime Unit was on his way to the office in Concord, a few miles north of Hooksett, when he took a call from his supervisor telling him to redirect to the Industrial Park Drive location and meet with the Hookset detectives. Ultimately, he was the designated evidence technician with the responsibility of documenting, preserving, and collecting any evidence located at, and removed from, the scene.

Although crime scene processing was part of every major crime detective's job description and they all received training to the task, for most of the troopers in the unit, this kind of assignment was one to avoid, or at least not relish. Not everyone wants the lead in these kind of cases, particularly because of the intensity and responsibility of getting everything 100 percent correct and not missing or contaminating anything that had the potential of strengthening or weakening the case. Not to mention that when you come to work in a business suit and a polished pair of shoes you would prefer not to be on your knees, elbows deep in a fetid, anatomical, and biological tragedy.

Cody was different. He was the go-to guy at these scenes. As an eleven-year veteran with an extensive background in emergency medicine, he understood and appreciated the challenges that cases like this presented, and he welcomed the assignment.

At his own initiative, he had received specialized training by the New York State PD in the recovery of skeletal remains. With that as part of his backstory, Cody didn't shy away from this type of assignment; he thrived on it. Attention to the minutest detail was his specialty.

Cody joined the Hookset detectives who were already at the location, and together they walked to the area where the jogger had found the skull. After a quick look and discussion, they thought it better to call for the assistance of a body detection canine to search for any further remains rather than to tramp through the area and step on or walk past potential evidence. Cody also spoke with his immediate supervisor and asked for additional assistance from the office to assist with the search and, if need be, a recovery.

The canine and his partner arrived on-scene within the hour and set up for a ground search. After a few moments acclimating to the area, the canine put his nose to the ground and sniffed his way forward. He purposefully advanced to an area several yards away and closer to where the terrain dropped off to a running brook below. He alerted to an area of interest by simply sitting down, wagging his tail, and looking to his handler for a treat.

Leaves drifted from the surrounding trees from the previous fall covered the overgrown spot. There was a slight dimple in the ground, and the six-by-three-foot area seemed artificially disturbed. A walk around the perimeter and a lean-in look for closer inspection by Cody's trained eye revealed what appeared to be a long bone and some dirt-covered clothing protruding slightly from the pile of loose dirt. He detected a faint odor of decomposition as well. There was little doubt this was a burial site and not the final resting place of someone who had died of natural causes. Everything intensified with the realization they most likely had a homicide victim buried just a few inches below the ground surface.

A second, inner perimeter was marked off to keep gawking officials away and create working space for the people who would be involved in the reclamation process. Meanwhile, Cody hustled back to his office to pick up the crime scene van that held all the equipment needed for a proper forensic anthropological recovery. The canine team continued to search a wide area a few hundred yards in either direction in the event that additional human remains were nearby.

At this point, the investigators knew little, and since there is only one opportunity to process a pristine scene, they slowed the pace and prepared a game plan that would minimize site contamination and maximize recovery efforts.

The assistants for New Hampshire's chief medical examiner, Dr. Thomas Andrews, called him to the scene to oversee and supervise the recovery. Having the medical examiner report directly to a scene and not wait for the body's arrival to the morgue was a rare event, and the investigators took notice. Dr. Andrews would ultimately conduct an autopsy to determine the cause and manner of death, so he wanted an exhumation that was as complete and flawless as possible.

The process of recovering human remains is precise, painstakingly slow, and not for everyone. The tools of the trade are brushes, trowels, and plastic scoops along with measuring tapes, small wooden pegs, and twine to establish a perimeter grid and plastic buckets to collect the dirt. There is a sifting box or two for screening the dirt and debris to make sure they find every piece of potential evidence, no matter how small. No large or power tools are used that might damage or reposition the bones.

Photographs and diagrams are taken before the area is touched, and they are retaken every inch or so as the dirt and debris are slowly removed and more of the remains come into view. Every potential piece of evidence is marked, photographed, and bagged, as it is unearthed. Investigators are always thinking ahead to a potential arrest, trial, and testimony, and they are not going to allow the defense counsel to second-guess or berate them because of a flawed or incomplete process.

Members of the recovery team gear up before stepping to the gravesite. They pull full-body Tyvek coveralls over their work clothes and cover their footwear in paper booties and their faces in gauze masks. This protocol prevents them from unintentionally fouling the scene and protects them from any of the biological hazards that they might encounter.

This team started by clearing away the growth and brush from around the burial site; a sapling that was in their way required removal to give them unrestricted access. They cut away or removed branches and other debris inside the gravesite perimeter. They laid out tarps near the edge of the disturbed ground and dropped down onto their hands and knees. Slowly, they brushed and scraped away the dirt, scooping what they removed into five-gallon plastic buckets. They would later empty the buckets onto the top of a screen-covered box and, like goldminers of yore, shake them vigorously to separate out any teeth or small bones possibly dislodged, overlooked, or unseen to the naked eye. When they began, there was a very faint odor of decomposition, but as they cleared away the debris and mined down deeper, the smell intensified, and for some, natural gagging reflexes kicked in. It grew intense.

Several inches below the surface, the outline of a human started to come into view. The body presented in a facedown position and anatomically appeared mostly intact. The excavators noted that in the area where they would expect to find a skull there was a divot in the ground. As they cleared away more dirt from that area, they discovered a lower jawbone with a few connected teeth, which normally would be a part of the skull. Remarkably, in the same area they found a complete patch of thick auburn human hair held together midway with a dirtied yellow scrunchie. At first glance, the coloring of the hair seemed to match the few hairs still attached to the skull sitting a few yards away.

Cody made a freehand sketch of the discovery and recovery, and techs took photos multiple times, as more of the body was exposed. In the background, there was a more precise and to-scale method of recording in process. Trained specialists were employing a new category of surveying equipment that allowed them to create a map that contained both the geographic layout and the placement of all the evidence. The finished product would be accurate and specific to the inch. Surveyors, environmentalists, construction planners, and police accident and crime scene reconstructionists increasingly relied on this device, known as the "Total Station."

The technicians excavated the burial site until there was a total reveal of the entire body. While mostly skeletonized, there was still some "weight" left on the bones and inside of the clothing. They scooped out the dirt from below the body's midsection so a fresh new tarp could be slid underneath and pulled up along the sides and they could remove the body intact and all in one movement.

The investigators positioned themselves around the body at optimal leverage points and with slow, deliberate movements and strong, sturdy hands; they followed Dr. Andrews's commands. Pulling the tarp in unison, they gently lifted the body into a large evidence bag designed for the transport of human remains. The bag was zipped and the remains slowly carried to the crime scene van waiting to transport the remains to the OCME.

Cody took another evidence bag from the van and walked over to where the skull was still sitting. After ensuring they had taken all of the necessary photos and a Total Station plotting of the skull area was complete, he gently lifted it from the sandy ground, placed it inside the bag, took it to the van, and reunited it with the rest of the unknown victim.

A few feet from the burial site was an earth berm that was a foot or two high above the ground surface and dropped off on the other side approximately twenty feet down to the brook below. Sergeant Magee of the Major Crime Unit, while working with the Total Station crew, had earlier looked over the berm and saw what he thought were a couple of shovels lying down below. He pointed them out to Cody, and once they removed and secured the body, Cody walked several feet away, so as not to alter any evidence they might find between the upper surface and the brook. He cautiously proceeded down the steep embankment and retrieved both shovels as possible evidence. He photographed them in the position and place he found them. One had a black handle and a curved spade type blade, and the other was taller and had an orange handle with a flat blade. During his initial visual exam of the burial site, Cody observed distinctive tool markings along the perimeter. It appeared that whoever had dug this hole used both a spade and a flat blade. Cody was sure to note it in his report. He packaged the shovels as possible evidence and dropped them off at the crime lab for fingerprint processing and testing for biological fluids.

• • • •

Approximately twelve hours after first discovering the skull and nine hours from the beginning of the recovery effort, the investigators secured for the day as the sunlit day gave way to a purplish nighttime sky. Tomorrow would begin the next phase: the difficult process of identifying the remains and determining how the person met their death.

As the parade of cruisers headed out onto Industrial Park Drive and the drivers broke left and right onto Daniel Webster Highway toward their homes, Trooper Cody fired up the crime scene van and headed due north, directly to Concord Hospital.

Cody arrived minutes later and backed the van up to a side entrance where the two rooms dedicated to the New Hampshire Medical Examiner Office were located. He signed in at the security desk and asked one of the officers to unlock the evidence room for him. He grabbed a gurney and loaded the evidence bags from the back of the van onto it, wheeled it inside, and secured it all in the refrigerated evidence locker for the night. He took the time to catalogue everything he brought to establish a record that could be used later to show a trail of continuity of the evidence and erase any later claims that the evidence was left unattended and open to tampering or contamination. It may seem like an unnecessary step, but failure to do so gives a defense attorney an opportunity for attack by claiming that someone had access and could have altered evidence used against his client. The defense only needs to create reasonable doubt in the mind of one or more jurors. The prosecutions job is to prevent that from happening. They do so by scrupulously paying attention to every detail and creating documentation that supports their work.

On Tuesday, midmorning, Trooper Cody returned to the OCME and met with Dr. Andrews and Dr. Marcella Sorg, a frequent consultant to Dr. Andrews. The two had spoken the previous day during the recovery process when they were sure the remains were human and the death was probably not from natural causes. Dr. Sorg was able to free up her time to come down to Concord and assist Dr. Andrews with the postmortem examination. The nature of this kind of autopsy is difficult and complex because of the poor physical condition of a body. The fact that the identity of the person was yet unknown and a lack of a medical history for reference were other complicating factors. Having someone with the experience and expertise of Dr. Sorg was a huge advantage in the identification process of skeletal remains. Together, Andrews, Sorg, and Cody made a great team, each one bringing a slightly different background and proficiency to the autopsy table.

Dr. Tom Andrews, a board-certified forensic pathologist, had come to the state of New Hampshire as their newly appointed chief medical examiner in September of 1997. He arrived with a rich history from years of work in the city of New York's OCME. By his own estimation, Dr. Andrews had performed more than two thousand autopsies.

The simple difference between pathology and forensic pathology is that pathology is the study of disease or injury and its effects on the human body, whereas forensic pathology is taking those same principles and applying them to the investigation of sudden, unexpected, or violent deaths. In New Hampshire, as in Massachusetts, it is mandatory that the chief medical examiner be a board-certified forensic pathologist.

Dr. Marcella Sorg was a board-certified forensic anthropologist with a doctoral degree in physical anthropology. She was also a research professor at the University of Maine at the time and a highly regarded and well-published expert, particularly in the area of forensic taphonomy, the study of postmortem processes.

John Cody's two decades of experiences as an active paramedic, patrol officer, and detective brought a high level of experience and another set of skilled eyes to the panel.

There was no doubt that if Dr. Andrews were ever to determine the cause and manner of this death, he certainly brought the right people together to assist him. As the saying goes, this wasn't their first rodeo together.

• • • •

The OCME's autopsy suite was in the basement of New Hampshire's largest hospital. There was nothing Hollywood about it. It was a cramped, workable space with two stainless steel worktables with beveled sides set at a slight elevation from top to bottom and a drain hole, with an attached hose at the bottom to let the cleansing water and bodily fluids flush away. There was a hanging scale and drawers full of specimen bottles and syringes to extract fluids for lab testing and all the necessary tools and machinery required to get the work done. There was minimal room for anything else. "Unremarkable" would be the best word to describe the surroundings. The total space for the office was small in comparison to most other states, but it met their basic needs and requirements. The room was large enough to accommodate the three of them with enough extra space to spread out the evidence and do their work.

The medical tech brought the bags with the remains in from the evidence locker and placed them onto a seven-foot-long stainless steel table. Dr. Andrews undid the red evidence tape that sealed them, and with the help of the others, cautiously removed the evidence. He laid out the main trunk of the body onto the table and positioned the skull where it belonged anatomically.

Like the scene of the recovery, the external examination started with extensive photographing, measuring, and recording of the event. Then they carefully removed the clothing and placed the pieces onto coat hangers for inspection and further drying out under a climate-controlled hooded area. From the upper body, there was a sports-type bra covered by an undershirt and a flannel-type outer shirt, and on the lower body, a pair of flower-print underpants, and a pair of cut-off jean shorts.

They washed and thoroughly cleansed the body and removed the small sections of soft body tissue that would have no bearing on the medical inquiry. Next, they took samples of body fluids and preserved them for later testing at the crime lab.

Then, like putting together a puzzle of more than a hundred pieces, they reconstructed the body in anatomical position and laid it out with precision onto an adjacent table. While some bones remained attached to one another, most of the soft tissue—such as tendons and muscles that hold the skeleton together—had broken down during the decomposition phase, causing other bones to disconnect. Except for one rib and several small bones from the body's hands and feet, the body's skeleton was intact. The jawbones retained most, but not all, of the teeth.

Realistically, they were only one day into the investigation and couldn't expect that at the end of the day they would be able to determine with any certainty the cause or manner of death. The identity determination was doubtful as well. As information learned from the police investigation grew and was matched up to, or compared with, the physical evidence they recovered, Dr. Andrews thought he might be able to connect the pieces and make a definitive finding of the cause and manner of death. However, it wouldn't be right away.

The primary focus at the time was studying the external skeleton and searching for signs of trauma. There was a thorough visual study supported by several radiographs and microscopic exams. Dr. Sorg noted a few small marks on a couple of ribs, which was something to look at further but not the kind of trauma that might lead to someone's death. Ultimately, nothing remarkable about the skeleton presented as indicating force or life-ending trauma.

There was, though, a potentially positive development regarding the cause of death based on a close inspection of the hanging clothing. There was a significant amount of dried body fluids on the outer shirt, and Drs. Sorg and Andrews noticed not only a tattering consistent with animal bites and scavenging but also a "slit-like defect" that would correspond to the area just below the rib cage on the right side of the wearer. The doctors then looked at the tee shirt and saw a similar defect in the same positioning as the one on the outer shirt. This discovery could indicate a penetration with a sharp instrument consistent with a stabbing.

Dr. Sorg measured the length and thickness of the bones and made particular observations of the pelvic area, as well as the face and cranium. At the conclusion of her anthropological examination, she was able to give an initial educated opinion as to the sex, age, and stature of the body.

It was not necessarily her final determination, but it would certainly narrow the field of "possibles" and give the investigators a start while combing through their missing person files. The body, she said, was consistent with a female fourteen to seventeen years of age who stood approximately five foot eight inches tall.

As the process ended for the day, they delicately put the body back into the evidence bags and returned it to the refrigerated evidence room. John Cody would return two days later to take samples of vertebrae, skin, and hair from Dr. Andrews and bring them to the crime lab for testing that might assist in determining an identification.

Without more, Dr. Andrews could make no determination as far as cause and manner of the death and added the case to the Pending File for the time being. Their collaborative efforts weren't over; they were just beginning.

CHAPTER 5

Finding the Remains

Part 2

As I walked into the office on Wednesday morning, my hands gingerly balancing two trays of coffee and one Mountain Dew, Eddie Forster broke away from a conversation he was having at the back of the office and made a beeline toward me. He was clearly amped up.

"Hey, Boss, I know you have a lot of important stuff going on with that case in Lowell and everything else, but you ain't going to believe this. We may have an actual lead on the Malden Mills case. I mean, it isn't much, but it could be something, and it's the first possibility in months. I already talked to Adrienne, and she wanted me to talk to you about going up to New Hampshire to meet with the guys in their Major Crime Unit. They invited us up to look at stuff."

"Jesus, Eddie, slow down. I have no idea what the hell you are talking about, so take a deep breath, and start from the beginning."

"Okay, Dude, I got in around seven thirty this morning, and after I read *The Herald*, I took my coffee in the back room and started going through the teletype items from yesterday." He said on the restart, "There was one from the New Hampshire SP. They uncovered some human remains from a shallow grave in Hooksett. They appear to be of a teenage girl, and she was wearing the kind of clothes a girl would wear in the summer. Some guy out jogging found a skull, and then one of those cadaver dogs found the rest of the body kinda buried a few yards away. I checked a map, and she was found only a couple of miles from the Fournier's house in Candia."

He stopped for a moment, searching for my nonverbal reactions or for any sign or expression of interest before he continued. "So, I called up there about an hour ago and spoke with Sergeant Forey in the Major Crimes Unit. She filled me in with what they had and said they didn't have an identity yet and the person doesn't match up with anyone in their missing person files. She said we were welcome to come up and they would take us to the scene and fill us in on what they got. What do you think? Adrienne said she thought we should head up there but wanted you to approve it."

Eddie, like everyone else in the office, was a digger who never gave up on an unsolved case. He, Duke, Jimmy, and the rest of my unit always scanned through the yards and yards of daily and overnight teletype messages that came in from police departments around the country before feeding them into the office shredder. Although there was rarely anything of direct importance to any of our cases, the habit of never letting something go unread or not followed up on was ingrained in every one of us. That day could be one of those times that due diligence paid off.

The office was a little lean on available bodies because of a home invasion and homicide in Lowell that happened the previous Monday evening. One of the investigative teams had been up there with the Lowell detectives, working night and day. Eddie had already spoken with Johnny Rivers and Duke, and they could alter their plans for the day to make the trip.

"Okay, Eddie, you guys can start heading up. I'll speak with Adrienne once you leave and see if there is anything she wants, or doesn't want, you guys to do. Call once you get there, and let me know what the plan is going to be." As they headed to the door, with their coffees in one hand and notebooks in the other, I made one small request.

"Please, please do not go at warp speed or blue lights and siren. I'm okaying this without notifying GHQ that you're taking the cruiser out of state. I don't have the time or the desire to fill out the paperwork and listen to the bullshit questions that follow. So don't bring attention to your travels and we will be fine. If you get in an accident up there, you own it." They nodded in unison because we all understood how to play the game.

I walked over to Adrienne's office and slumped down into her guest chair. She was seated and gazing at her computer screen while typing up a response to a motion from a defense attorney in another homicide case she was preparing for trial. She seemed focused, and I wasn't even sure she saw me come in. She continued to pound at the keyboard but looked over, took a second to push her glasses back to the top of her nose, and simply asked, "What do you think, Billy?"

"Who knows?" I said. "I will say it is springtime and, like Eddie said last December, once the thaw sets in the nauseous odor from decomposing bodies grabs the attention of people and starving animals really quick. Same with people popping up in lakes and rivers once the ice melts. They're annual events, like the greening of the grass, baseball, and the return of the freaking Canadian snow geese. I do like the proximity of the remains to the Fournier home and the fact the remains are of a young woman wearing summer clothing." I continued, "Plenty of reason to follow-up but still a long way from being the solution to the investigation."

"Do you think you can pull everyone together for a meeting tomorrow morning?" she asked. "I don't have any court appearances and am pretty much free for the day. There have been some positive things going on with the arson part of the case, and I'm not sure everyone knows all of it. It would be nice to reconnect and find out what they learned but also to go over everything again as a group. I am narrowing in on Crouse for the arson and have been putting some evidence into the Grand Jury. By the way, Paul Horgan from the Fire Marshalls office is amazing—a true godsend. His knowledge and experience is unbelievable, and he seems to know everyone in the industry, particularly a few true experts who have been willing to help."

"I will do what I can to pull the troops together. Not sure everyone can make it, but we will do our best. If nothing else, we can put a new energy charge into everyone, especially if the guys come back with any promising info. We can try to do it in our conference room," I added, "but we may have to go to Malden if they can't make the trip."

"Sounds good," Adrienne replied, "now let me get this motion out of the way and upstairs to the court, and then I can turn my attention back to our case." She nodded her head toward a corner of the room where a few cardboard file boxes lay piled on top of each other. "I'll sift through those and be in touch later today."

• • • •

Our office had worked cooperatively with the New Hampshire troopers assigned to the Major Crimes Unit a couple of times over the past few years when there was a discovery of bodies of victims from Middlesex County homicides in their state. Walking in the door to their office at State Police Headquarters in Concord was more of a homecoming than a cold call. We had already established a good camaraderie as well as reliance and trust. Not everyone knew each other, but after a couple of introductions and handshakes, the atmosphere took on the air of a class reunion.

Duke called in the early afternoon with an update. "We're thinking there could be something here, Boss. The New Hampshire guys have been great to us. They have no identity or even any real leads on the body, and there are no reported missing persons in New Hampshire fitting her description. They are inundated with inquiries from across the nation, but so far, none of the descriptions of the missing persons or the circumstances around the disappearances seems to match.

"They showed us photos of the body and the clothing they recovered, and they have completed the autopsy, but because the body is almost completely skeletonized, the cause and manner aren't obvious. The medical examiner has more work to do, and he is pending the findings until the investigators learn more information. We are heading to the scene with a couple of the troopers now, and then we will head back to Cambridge. Depending on the traffic heading south, we probably won't get back until around five."

I told Duke that Adrienne wanted to meet with everyone in our office in the morning. "I'll walk over and let her know we talked, and we can't rule out that the remains may be tied to our investigation. By the way, how is Eddie doing?"

Duke laughed, "You know him, he is, well—let's just say enthusiastic. He's asking a million questions and has a big smile on his face. He is really bouncing. He keeps telling everyone how he told us back in December that we would find our victim during the spring thaw, and he may be right. I'll do my best to keep him grounded, but I can't make any promises."

• • • •

On Thursday morning around ten o'clock, the group started to gather in the state police office for what we all anticipated could be our most important meeting in months. The entire investigative team was on hand. Adrienne was the last to arrive, but we knew she was heading our way from the heavy-footed scuffling and cadence that we all recognized. Sometimes hearing those footsteps brought a smile to your face, but at other times, it produced an oh-shit-Adrienne's-coming-and-I-don't-have-what-she-asked-for moment from which there was no escape.

She walked in with an extra-large Dunkin Donuts cup in one hand and two huge three-ring binders cradled tightly to her chest supported by her free arm. She nodded with a smile toward the small windowless conference room behind Lana's chair, and we all filed in. We filled every seat at the table. The room was already a little warm as we hunkered down and prepared for a long meeting. After some light small talk, Adrienne turned to Eddie to open the discussion since he was the one who discovered the teletype message and got the ball rolling with the New Hampshire troopers. As usual, Eddie immediately deferred to Duke as the primary note taker.

Duke fully anticipated that would happen, and his notebook was already open to the previous day's notes. "It was an interesting and productive trip, and while it is too early to say we are on to something, there was nothing we learned yesterday that would rule us out." He continued with a *Reader's Digest*-style chronology, beginning with the discovery of the remains on Monday through the autopsy on Tuesday and their trip to meet with the New Hampshire troopers on Wednesday.

He provided some detailed information about the deceased. "For the autopsy, the medical examiner brought in a forensic anthropologist from Maine to assist him in trying to determine cause and manner of death but also to provide a profile of the person based on the bone structure. Cause and manner are still pending, but they were able to say the remains are those of a young woman between the ages of fourteen to seventeen and she was approximately five foot two to five foot eight inches tall. They also said the clothing on the body was consistent with that worn in warm weather, and because of the state of decomposition, they surmised she might have been dead since last summer. Another thing that was interesting was that her hair had dislodged from the skull and was lying in the grave where the head would have been. It was thick and long and held together in a ponytail with one of those scrunchie-type things. Her hair was a reddish auburn color."

Adrienne broke in with the first question. "Duke, did they say anything about whether or not they could extract any DNA for testing?"

"I asked them that, and the troopers said they would have to speak to the medical examiner and get back to us. The remains were in really bad shape," Duke answered.

"Adrienne," Eddie broke in, "you know that DNA testing takes forever to get lab results. I think the wait from the FBI is more than a year right now, and we don't even have a lab in Massachusetts that can do it. Anyway, after the O.J. trial, people are confused about how it works. The science stuff always baffles juries. And me, too, for that matter."

Some light laughter followed, but many at the table agreed with Eddie's comments.

"I understand the complexity of the testing process, Eddie. I'm just thinking out loud," said Adrienne. "Maybe if the New Hampshire Crime Lab can extract a DNA sample from a bone or flesh then we could send it down to BODE Labs in Virginia, and they can do a priority case for us. We have used them before, and they do excellent work. They aren't cheap, but they have a great reputation. They understand how to apply the science to the evidence, and they do a great job explaining the process to a jury. We have the blood evidence from the function room, and we can send a sample of that, as well, for the comparison. At least that way we'll know whether or not the remains are those of our victim." Everyone agreed, realizing that would be a huge step in determining whether the case was New Hampshire's or ours.

"I'm trying to be realistic and cut to the chase as quickly as possible," Adrienne added. "We all have a lot of casework on our plates right now, and we don't have the time to start chasing ghosts. This is the quickest and most direct way of moving forward. If testing is positive, we have a case; if it isn't, then we don't. It is as simple as that. I'm not downplaying what you learned, and like all of you, I am hoping we have the opening we've been praying for, but let's just slow the pace, and go about it the right way.

Adrienne continued, "Since everyone is here, let me share where we are with Crouse and the arson investigation. Then we can talk about our next steps. I have been working with Paul Horgan for the past few months to develop a solid case against Crouse for setting the fire in the function room. These cases are tough to prove because they are not only circum- stantial; they require forensic science evidence to support the charges. Sergeant Horgan had been nothing short of amazing in his ability to explain how they processed the scene, collected evidence for crime lab testing, and then presented their findings in a manner that a jury could understand. Everything they have done and all that they learned points to Crouse and no one else. If we had to go to trial today, Paul would be my key witness to get Crouse convicted.

"While I am hopeful we will eventually locate a victim and be able to tie her death to Crouse, we can't afford to let him roam the streets any longer. I couldn't live with myself if he victimized one more person." She continued, "What I am planning on doing is getting him indicted on the arson charge, having the judge set a high bail, and then move to revoke his parole for the rape conviction in Revere and get him back behind bars as soon as possible. If down the line we can hook him with a murder charge, so much the better."

Switching back to the New Hampshire situation, Adrienne asked a general question about the team's thoughts on a new approach and moving forward from there.

Johnny Rivers summed it up best. "We really haven't got together in a while or devoted any time to the case. Things went dormant once the winter arrived. I know Steve and I have been out straight with criminal activity, and likewise, the Edgewater Technology case and a few newer ones have had you guys totally consumed. I think we need to find a few hours to be together, away from all distractions, pull together everything we have gathered, and put it onto the table for discussion. Then we can decide our next steps forward.

"This is the first potential break in the case since we started," he continued, "and I think all of us have been reawakened and energized. Let's roll with the momentum and pick a day next week, and jump on it. We really need to do this regardless of what happens with the Hooksett find."

"Johnny's right," Adrienne responded. "If we are able to make a DNA match then the case probably comes back to us, and we still have no idea who she is. It would be a huge step forward, but we still need to identify her. It's time to tie up loose ends and come up with a new game plan, and it is better done now so if we do get DNA, we are ready to move on it and not have to start scrambling then. Let's get all of the reports, the interviews, the photos, Crouse's cell phone records, the video from the gas station, and everything else we have, put it all into boxes or three-ring binders, and bring it to Malden for a deep dive review.

"How does the end of next week look for everyone?" she asked. Everyone dug out their pocket calendars and, with some minor maneuvering of schedules, agreed to meet on the following Thursday morning at ten in the Malden Detective Unit. Their conference room and table was large, there were whiteboards to write on, and more importantly, there were a few good sandwich shops in the neighborhood for lunch.

The meeting adjourned, and I walked out the door with Adrienne, and we headed to Martha Coakley's office to brief her on what we knew, the direction we were taking, and most importantly, to get her advice and blessing on our path forward.

Adrienne's next step was to call the New Hampshire Attorney General's Office and speak with Kelly Ayotte, the head of their homicide investigation unit. Ayotte and Adrienne had spoken and shared information on cases in the past. It was not exactly a friendship but certainly a trusted and favorable working relationship. Ayotte, we learned, was the New Hampshire version of Adrienne Lynch: a down-to-earth, personable, and highly respected prosecutor with a phenomenal work ethic who embraced a team approach on all death investigations.

She had been in telephone contact with the major crimes investigators since the remains surfaced and knew that Middlesex detectives had been up the previous day to share information, so she expected Adrienne's call. She listened with interest to Adrienne's detailed explanation of our case, and she appreciated there was a real possibility that the human remains were those of our Malden victim. Adrienne explained why she thought DNA analysis was the quickest answer to all of our questions and concerns and asked if Ayotte would be willing to submit samples for testing.

Ayotte was understandably protective of her case and unwilling to turn over or invade any evidence without something more concrete than a hunch. Nevertheless, she was also committed to identifying the young woman, and if her death was ruled a homicide, bringing the murderer to justice regardless of who made the arrest and prosecuted the crime. Adrienne's argument was persuasive, and she convinced Ayotte there was good reason for the testing. Ayotte also realized that if it were not our victim, she would already have a DNA workup for her files that would allow them to compare the unknown victim's profile to names submitted from other jurisdictions in their unresolved cases.

Adrienne told her about our conversation with Martha Coakley and said that our office was willing to pick up all of the expenses related to the testing. She emphasized that by using a private lab we could expedite the process and have an answer back within a week to ten days, versus months or a year from the FBI. After more thought and discussion, Ayotte agreed to request their crime lab technicians work with the medical examiner to put together samples of tissue and bone and forward them to BODE Labs. Adrienne would make a similar request of the Massachusetts Crime lab to forward bloodstain samples for comparison testing. She added that her next call was to BODE Labs to explain what we hoped to accomplish by submitting the two sets of samples and that we were willing to pay them to expedite the testing. Adrienne would be the point of contact for the information flow as well as the billing.

Adrienne hung up the telephone, took a deep breath, and smiled; pleased with the huge forward steps we had taken. After months of shade covering the Malden investigation, she could see there was a sign of light emerging on the horizon.

· · · ·

The task for the New Hampshire and Maine crime techs was complicated because they were working with badly decomposed and moldy soft tissue, and they knew there was only a small chance that there was testable DNA present. Nevertheless, they did their best and extracted four samples from different patches of skin. They were a bit more optimistic about a small piece of bone they removed from a vertebra because they knew it was more likely DNA would survive inside a bone. They did their best and were hopeful about the samples but far from certain. They packaged the items separately to prevent any concerns about contamination and shipped them to BODE Labs via FedEx.

The Massachusetts crime lab had an easier assignment since they had been able to recover and preserve blood samples at the crime scene within hours of the event. Their blood evidence was relatively undamaged in comparison to the remains discovered in NH, so would make for a better testing sample. Out of concern that the sample may get lost or damaged in transit, Trooper Peter Sennott hand delivered it.

BODE Labs received both deliveries by the first week of May, and their testing started on Monday the 7th. We would later learn that they eliminated the skin samples from the remains because of exposure to severe weather changes postmortem had resulted in a growth of mold that eroded the DNA. The bone, while also showing some signs of mold, did produce a small sample that they could work with.

• • • •

As we like to say on the state police, it was now time to hurry up and wait—time to pay attention to our other cases, to catch up and clear out space in the event that suddenly there was a reason to turn our full attention back to the Malden Mills case. We met at the Malden PD on the following Thursday and put together a general game plan for reviewing the volumes of cell phone records that were produced by the telephone companies in Massachusetts and New Hampshire. They had arrived piecemeal and several months after the requests. We made quick reads when they came in, but it was time for a deeper dive into the contents. It was slow and tedious work. There were hundreds and hundreds of rows of mind-numbing numerical data. We had to crosscheck everything page by page with a clear head, a pad of paper, and a fistful of pencils with erasers. When completed, though, it would not only establish a timeline for the calls to and from Tommy Crouse, but it would also possibly match in a more general way to the geographic location when his phone was in use. Although a monotonous and wearisome task, we had to be thorough and correct. Similarly, scrutiny of Crouse's Mobil credit card would help understand his spending habits and travel patterns on the day of the fire and the days that followed. There was plenty of work to keep all of us busy.

Adrienne and Jimmy needed to focus their attention on another homicide trial scheduled for the first week in September. With summer and vacation time quickly approaching, the follow-up and preparatory work had to begin. It was a case of domestic homicide where a husband bludgeoned his wife to death midmorning in their apartment. It was a gruesome scene and, like Malden, presented with a lot of circumstantial physical evidence, including fingerprints and DNA, along with a few witnesses with substance abuse and veracity issues. For the first time in Adrienne's trial practice, she would be presenting documentary evidence recovered from a public computer at the town library and computer center. Interesting and,¬ with new legal issues to pursue, there were still a few months to go before the trial, but with everything else going on, Adrienne's usually efficient juggling act was becoming a little heavier and more difficult to manage. The balls in the mix were growing in number and were beginning to feel more like bowling balls than beach balls.

CHAPTER 6

Connecting the Dots

As the days turned to weeks, the wait added to the frustration and anxiety all of us were feeling but not admitting to each other. By nature of our work, none of us had the gift of patience. We expected rapid answers, and as each day passed, and our enthusiasm waned and uncertainty grew, our spirits started to sink.

Every time the office phone rang, I hoped it was Adrienne calling with the answer. Whenever I heard her voice or the cadence of her walk coming from the corridor outside our office, I expected her to be coming in to announce the results. It was the feeling you got as a kid hanging with your buddies on a sweltering summer day thinking the distant sound that was getting closer was the music from the ice cream truck, but as the anticipation grew, the song grew fainter as the truck made a turn and headed away in another direction.

It was Wednesday, and Memorial Day Weekend was almost on top of us. I'd resigned myself to the fact that there would be no word on the DNA testing until the beginning of June. We had family plans to head to our getaway townhouse just out outside of Waterville Valley in New Hampshire. It would be a great chance to mentally check out for a few days and turn my attention to some spring cleaning, yard maintenance, and maybe take a hike or two in the wilderness. If all went well, a couple of ice cubes and a few fingers of Power's Irish whiskey would be a perfect ending to each day!

Then, like the New England weather, everything changed in the blink of an eye. Around noontime, the call came from Adrienne. She was short, direct, and calm.

"Billy, Charity from BODE Labs just called with their test results." There was a split second of silence on both ends. All I could hear was my heartbeat pounding in my ears.

"AND?" I pleaded.

"We got what we were hoping for! I think we might be back in business. I'm over with Martha now, and she wants to gather everyone quickly so we can get a game plan together before the news hits the press."

What a jolt of energy! I couldn't get off the phone fast enough to get the news to the team. While I was making my calls, Martha and Adrienne were on the phone with Kelly Ayotte in New Hampshire. There was a consensus that the investigation and any potential prosecution belonged in Middlesex County and not in Hookset, NH. They would ultimately transfer the case and the evidence to Middlesex County, but it couldn't happen overnight. Ayotte agreed to forward some photographs from the New Hampshire State Police Crime Scene Unit for display at a press conference the next day. Our hope was that pictures, more than words, could stimulate people's memories and create a discussion and a chance to bring an identity to our human remains.

The message of the DNA results spread like wildfire, and marshaling the troops didn't take long. We had all of the team in her office within two hours. It is hard to describe everyone's reaction. Renewed excitement and a shot of adrenaline, for sure, but there were no high fives and whooping calls. More like tightened fists, elevated heartbeats, and muted enthusiasm. To survive in this business and to stay focused you really have to stay away from the real highs and lows so you can live in the moment and stay productive.

The news was certainly encouraging, but having no idea about the identity of our victim continued to hinder any opportunity to advance the case. All we knew about her was she was a teenage girl and the clothing she had on was appropriate at the time of the fire in July, but there was no one in the missing person files that fit her profile, and no one had come forward with as much as a hint at her identity.

Martha brought her media relations specialists to the meeting, as well as a couple of experienced ADAs. It was standing room only, and the energy level was intense and elevated. Martha had a measured eagerness in her voice as well, as she talked about our next steps. She wanted to hold a press conference on the next afternoon at the Malden Police Station, where with the Malden chief, Adrienne, and the rest of us surrounding her as a backdrop, she would provide some historical background about the Malden Mills case as a refresher for the press. Then, she would segue neatly into the revelation that the Malden Mills victim linked through DNA testing to the recovery of partially buried human remains in Hooksett in late April. To add intensity and emphasis to her words, she wanted that visual display featuring poster-sized photographs of pieces of evidence from the gravesite propped up onto easels and set at eye and camera lens height. Her sense was that cleaned up pictures of the clothing and thick clumps of auburn hair held together with a scrunchie might help jog someone's memory and start a conversation or prompt a phone call. If she delivered the message fittingly and the public received it correctly, it would be a dramatic feature for that night's newscast and the next day newspapers.

The media specialist circulated a rough draft of a press statement that everyone at the news conference would receive. Recognizing that not every paper or news station could attend, he would fax the statement and images simultaneously to every news outlet on the office's media mailing list.

Martha asked Steve and Johnny to share the news and the press release with their chief and media relations officer. The relationship between the DAO and the Malden PD had been harmonious throughout the case, and she wanted to ensure we not only continued to speak in a unified voice but that we all agreed on the direction we were headed. We could never lose sight of the fact that the chief was an appointee and answered to the mayor, the city council, and the residents of Malden. We didn't want him ever to feel that he or the people who worked for him did not have equal input into every step of the process. We also didn't want the city officials to be blindsided by the information when they watched the news Thursday night.

Our media relations people spoke later in the afternoon with the Malden chief on the wording of the release, and they planned on meeting in his office the following day an hour before the press conference to go over the plan.

• • • •

I don't know why I thought finding a parking place near the Malden PD on Thursday at noontime would be easy because it wasn't. At least it was that way for a good reason. A collection of media vans at both the front and rear entrances to the downtown station, as well as several cars with placards on the dashboards indicating their owners were members of the working press, filled every available spot. I found a spot a block away and headed to meet the rest of the team in the detective's office.

After identifying myself with a "flash of the tin" at the front desk, the desk officer buzzed me in, and I walked the dozen or so steps to the detective's office. When I turned the corner, I could see the guys huddled at one end of the table in the conference room. It looked like they were reviewing a handful of papers in beige file folders. Eddie looked up, saw me, and waved at me to come join them. As I drew closer, he stepped toward me and spoke in a whisper because there were so many people standing around that we didn't know, and said, "Dude, you ain't gonna believe this, but Johnny Rivers may have the identity of the girl. The story is unbelievable, but I'll let him tell you."

Johnny usually begins every conversation with a joke or a wisecrack, but not this time.

"I think we got her," he said. "We have a lot of work to do to confirm it, but it looks like she is a local kid. A juvenile runaway who took off from DSS (Department of Social Services) custody last July, and as of today, still hasn't been located. DSS never reported her as a missing person, but there is a warrant in the computer for her as a Child in Need of Services (CHINS). Steve and I don't know her, but we know the family. Her father is a tough guy with a good-sized rap sheet. He has had a few run-ins with a couple of our officers, and he doesn't like us very much."

My mind was racing. "How did you find all of this out now? We haven't even made the news public yet. Has someone been holding back this information and not sharing it? This is great news, but you have to admit the timing on this is really fucked up."

"Oh, more than you can imagine. Wait until you hear the whole story," Johnny responded. "So, this morning we were getting all of the stuff ready for the press conference and had some of the photo posters lying out on the table. One of the midnight guys was looking at them, and when he saw the one with the big hank of hair, he picked it up, studied it for a moment, and said, 'I haven't seen hair like that since Kelly Hancock was around.'

"I asked him who Kelly was, and he said, 'You know her. She's that kid who is always running away from DSS. She's a troubled kid but has a lot of street sense. We locked her up a few times on CHINS warrants. We would find her wandering the streets at, like, three or four in the morning. The Court kept putting her into foster care, and she would always run away and come back to her old neighborhood. Her family's from Malden.'"

"Then I asked him when they last saw her," Johnny continued. "He thought it was sometime last summer. They grabbed her early in the morning, and she went to court later that day, but the last they heard she had run away from her caseworker.

"So, Steve and I pulled her file, and sure enough, we do have a CHINs warrant, and it was entered into the computer, but that won't show up when you are running a missing person check. It looks like she ran away from her caseworker on July 17, the day before the fire at Malden Mills, and she hasn't been arrested or heard from since."

The news hit us all like one swift, unpredictable leg sweep. One minute, you are standing still, having a conversation, and the next you are on your backside, bewildered and wondering what the hell just happened. You never saw it coming even though it was all right in front of you. Incredible!

Our next step was to capture Martha and the chief after their meeting and before they met with the media. We brought them into the conference room, shut the door, sat them down, and broke the news. They were as astonished with the development as we were. They asked the same questions that all of us had and a few more. Johnny Rivers restated the information as thoroughly as he had earlier and said they were still sifting through reports and files to be sure they had all of the information correct. There was much more to do before we would be prepared to share the information or issue any kind of a statement.

It wasn't as though we didn't know what our next steps would be, but we were so taken off guard we found the suddenness of the information flow a little bewildering. More than nine months of investigation with little real progress, and in less than a day we had tied our crime scene to the recovery of a body in another state and might have identified our victim by pure happenstance. Our good fortune was an awful lot for us to digest in a short time.

The press conference went on as scheduled with no mention of the new information. If somehow any of it had leaked out to members of the press and there were questions about the identity, Martha was prepared to comment that there was no positive identification to this point but that investigators would certainly be pursuing any lead or information regarding the case. We didn't want anyone with knowledge of the case to think we had wrapped up the investigation and his or her information wouldn't be important to the investigative team. We still needed all the help we could get to prove a case to a jury.

The coverage by the press was all we could have hoped it would be. It was one of the lead stories on all the major television and radio newscasts in Boston that night. On Friday morning, there were stories in all of the newspapers, most either showing the photos or describing the clothing and hair in depth. Interestingly, at least for the moment, there was still no public response, and Kelly Hancock's name was obviously not one about which people were thinking.

We reconvened after the media moment and worked on a plan and an approach, particularly how and who would meet with the Hancock family. A quick review of Mark's criminal record and his prior negative issues with the Malden PD made it evident that neither Ruelle nor Rivers should be standing there when we knocked on the Hancock's door. Our initial contact had to be delicate but direct. If our instincts were correct, we were essentially making a death notification to a young teenager's father, and our collective history told us this could get very bad, very quick. Unless you have been at the receiving end of one of these visits it is impossible to know how you might react, but a violent response is common.

From the very beginning of this case, we had done everything together. It was a rare moment there wasn't a combination of state and Malden detectives at each other's side. In this instance though, the pairing might not be the best fit. We decided because of the history between the Hancocks and the Malden PD that Jimmy, Eddie, and I would approach the family and Steve and Johnny would work internally, review the police logs and reports, and interview their officers that had prior contacts with Kelly. They would also be available to assist us if we got information that required immediate confirmation or follow-up.

The fact that her name hadn't come up in the nine months since the Malden Mills fire was a baffling to all of us. There had been lots of publicity, particularly locally, and talk of a very violent act and a plea for assistance in locating a victim. It was one thing for no one on the PD to mention her name but equally alarming was that no family, friends, DSS workers, etc. came forward with Kelly's name as a "possible." Having her name wouldn't have taken us to her body any quicker, uncovered a murder weapon, or given us probable cause to make an arrest, but it may have helped with things like interviews of her friends and family. In the end, it wasn't overly relevant, but it was certainly a head-scratcher.

From a review of the Malden PD reports regarding Kelly, we learned that Mark was Kelly's birth father and his current wife, Jackie Shepard, was Kelly's stepmother.

On Friday morning, Jimmy, Eddie, and I met at the office. With two coffees and a Mountain Dew in hand, we piled into one cruiser and headed to the address we had for the Hancocks. As it turned out, their family home on Newhall Street was only a few streets away from Malden Mills. There was no one home, and we learned from neighbors the family was in the process of relocating. We learned that Jackie worked at a hardware store one town away, so we headed there to visit with her.

She was cordial but a little concerned the police were looking for Mark again. Jimmy spoke for us, and after a very basic introduction, he told her we needed to speak with Mark but didn't share the reason for our visit. She said he was at an address in Walpole, a town twenty miles south of Boston where he was rehabbing an old family home for their family. After assurances that he wasn't in any trouble and we were not there to arrest him, she reluctantly gave us the address, and we headed out to Route 93 and south through Boston and eventually onto Route 95 and into Walpole.

We purposely had a loose game plan for our discussion with Mark, partially because we had no idea how he would react with the police showing up at his doorstep, particularly if his wife had called to let him know we were coming. Jimmy Connolly would once again make the introductions, talk about Kelly as a missing person, and ask Mark if he knew of her whereabouts. If he did, we could move on, but if he didn't, our questions would become statements and we would move in the direction that we had recovered human remains and that we were exploring the possibility they might be those of his daughter.

Beyond a few anecdotal comments from cops, all we knew about Kelly and Mark Hancock came from a pair of computer printouts. The larger one revealed Mark's criminal record, and the smaller was of Kelly's juvenile record as a chronic runaway. That little bit of knowledge is never the best way to understand or evaluate a person, or as in this case, a family dynamic. All we really knew was she mustn't have been happy with her home life, and he had a volatile temper. That was it.

It wasn't unreasonable to think that Mark would be upset seeing us, regardless of the reason. In fact, we expected it. As we approached the doorway to the home, he came outside and met us. We never had a chance to introduce ourselves before he blurted out, "What can I do for you guys. What's this all about?" He wasn't being friendly, but he wasn't confrontational either. It was evident that he wanted to be assertive and control the conversation, and we couldn't let that happen.

We stuck to the plan and let Jimmy ask the opening questions. In a calm manner, he said, "Mark, we are investigators with the state police, and we have a couple of questions to ask and hope you can help us out." Mark nodded, and Jimmy continued, "Are you Kelly Hancock's father?"

What happened next was pure agony for all of us. Mark's head jerked up, and his eyes widened as he went into a rage and peppered Jimmy with questions.

"Why? Where is she? Is she okay? Why are you asking me about her? Is she dead?" With each question, the level of his voice rose, and he was clearly in great distress. His body was convulsing, and his eyes filled with tears. "What can you tell me?" he demanded to know.

We were used to playing supportive roles when delivering death notifications and often resorted to eye contact instead of words to communicate. Jimmy looked over at Eddie and me with a look that told us, "Hold on, boys, this is going to be a difficult few minutes." We returned the look with small nods and buckled in for what was about to happen.

"Mark," Jimmy said in a soft, measured voice, "we have been investigating a fire that happened last July at the Malden Mills Condos on Eastern Avenue. We have reason to believe that the fire was used to cover up a homicide."

"What does that have to do with Kelly?" Mark asked, his body still shaking.

Jimmy continued, "Last month the body of a young girl was discovered in New Hampshire, and we have tied the two scenes together through DNA. When we were looking at evidence yesterday Kelly's name came up as someone from Malden who hadn't been seen in several months, and we are just running out any leads or tips we get."

"So, you *are* telling me my daughter was murdered!" he countered.

Jimmy took a deep breath before answering. "No, but we are asking for your help. When was the last time you saw or heard from her?"

Mark exploded in pain and torment. "Back last July. She was in DSS custody, and she ran from them. They took my baby from me, and they wouldn't give her back. They had no right to do it. They killed my daughter! They killed my daughter! We were working things out so she could return home. She was a good kid; she just kept running away. She never did anything else wrong."

The three of us stood silent for what seemed an eternity as we watched an anguished father pace the ground like a cornered animal looking for an escape route or a chance to attack. Knowing the exact words to offer comfort was impossible. We all have had different experiences on death notification calls: people have punched, tackled, spit on, and sworn at me. I have been yelled at and told I was a liar or mistaken and to leave. One mother put her hand to my face to prevent me from delivering the news that she knew was coming, and others refused to open the door because they sensed why I was there. Others have simply sat and stared vacantly ahead in silent reflection. Everyone processes and grieves in their own manner, and it is always completely unpredictable.

It is the absolutely worst news any police officer has to deliver. It has to be a straightforward approach, but it is never simple.

Eventually, Jimmy was able to restart the conversation. He told Mark we needed his help in making a final determination whether or not the remains in New Hampshire were those of Kelly. He talked to him about trying to collect any of Kelly's belongings like a tooth or hairbrush or even an article of clothing that she wore a lot. It may be possible to have a lab technician locate and extract a sample of DNA from any of those items. I asked if the family had a dentist whom Kelly might have visited. He said there was a dental clinic the family went to but he couldn't think of the name right then.

Mark excused himself to go into the house to call his wife and break the news to her about our visit. The two spoke for several minutes, and we stayed outside and out of view and earshot to give them privacy. When he came out, he told us the news devastated her and he needed to be with her as quickly as possible. They needed to be together, and they had to figure out the best way to break the news to Kelly's siblings. He told us she was the oldest of his five kids, and she was particularly close to Lisa, her twelve-year-old sister. Jackie, he said, was his second wife and Kelly's stepmother.

Mark hadn't calmed down, but he was certainly more in control of his emotions after venting at us and then speaking with Jackie. Still very angry, though, he continued sporadically lashing out at the Court and the state agency that had taken Kelly from her family.

Jackie had given him the name of the dentist and the location of the clinic. I wrote down the information and he told me that someone would be calling the dentist office within a few moments.

We awkwardly asked Mark if he wanted to ride back to Malden with us because he was so shaken up. He declined, saying that he really just wanted to be alone to think things through and he felt he was composed enough to drive himself. We were hesitant to leave him alone but couldn't force the issue; we took him at his word. We left and headed north back to Cambridge.

It was coming up on noon when we pulled away. I called Dr. Kate Crowley, the forensic odontologist at the OCME, as soon as we hit the highway. I had primed her with the facts of the case a few days before and prepped her earlier that morning that we would be visiting with the father of the possible victim and that if we got the name of a dentist I would call her and let her know.

She answered on the first ring. I updated her and gave her the name of the clinic and the dentist. She said she would call him right away and see if Kelly was his patient. If she were, then she would ask him to produce any records, particularly x-rays, as quickly as possible. Her requests for dental records often met with pushback because of privacy concerns, but she was quick to familiarize them with the Massachusetts law that requires medical personnel to cooperate with the OCME on death investigation cases and provide any and all medical records, and that included dental information.

Dr. Kate, the name she prefers, was always persistent and relentless in her approach and that day would prove no different. The office informed her that the dentist was not at work and unavailable. Undeterred, she found a way to get his personal phone number. It ultimately took a raised voice and some not-so-subtle coaxing to get him to return to his office, search the files, and come up with recent x-rays and records and leave copies of them for Steve Ruelle and Johnny Rivers to pick up later in the afternoon. Then she called the New Hampshire OCME's office and asked if we could send someone up to get copies of their dental photos and x-rays to match them to a possible victim. They told her they would be ready for pickup when the officers arrived.

As I was talking to Dr. Kate, Eddie was on the phone with Johnny Rivers explaining the importance of getting both sets of dental records to the OCME that afternoon. We didn't want to have to wait out the Memorial Day Weekend for answers when we were this close.

Ruelle and Rivers dropped what they were doing and flew up to Concord, NH, where they met with John Cody, the trooper who had led the recovery effort for the Major Crime Unit. He turned over a sheet of six radiographs taken at autopsy. They headed back south to the dental clinic to pick up Kelly's dental records before heading to the OCME, arriving shortly after five o'clock. Dr. Kate and I met them in the lobby.

She brought us in to her office, rifled open the envelopes, and went right to work. Months and months of investigative work came down to this moment. What looked like a complex puzzle to us came together very quickly for someone with her experience. She averaged more than three hundred identifications a year and knew exactly what she was looking for in making comparisons of the teeth and bone structure.

It took all of three minutes for her to reach a conclusion. She looked up at us with a set of images in each hand, smiled, and said, "Your victim has finally been identified. It is definitely Kelly Hancock." She went on to show and explain the reasons for the surety of her decision. We were half-listening as we reached for our phones to share the news.

While certain of her identification, Dr. Kate still wanted to consult with the forensic odontologist for the state of New Hampshire before memorializing her finding in a final report. She made the phone call and explained the situation, and he said he could be available in his private dental office in Concord on Saturday morning. She told him she would be there at ten thirty. After getting the address, she ended the conversation. As she was putting down the phone, she looked over at me and asked if she could get a ride to New Hampshire the next morning.

"I'll meet you here at nine," I said, "and I'll bring the coffee." Not exactly the family trip to New Hampshire I was anticipating, but if all went well I could make a second trip later in the afternoon.

The Memorial Day traffic heading north into New Hampshire was heavy but moving along at a good clip. We arrived at the office in little more than an hour. His office was in a big, beautiful sprawling residence in an old, well-preserved section of the city. He greeted us with muffins and more coffee, and after a few moments of acquainting ourselves, the two went into a side room, pulled out the evidence, and went to work. She pointed out every place where she saw a match and told him the amalgam used in the filling in one of her teeth matched the type used in the clinic and recorded in Kelly's record. The two compared, discussed, and ultimately agreed on all points of the review and came to the joint conclusion that the human remains recovered in Hooksett, NH, were those of Kelly Hancock, the victim of a horrific homicide in Malden, MA.

I called Adrienne with the definitive news right away, and she, in turn, notified Martha, and the rest of the legal team. They would wait to release the news to the press until there was sufficient time to notify the Hancocks and for them to contact their other family members. I called Jimmy Connolly, and he shared the news with the other investigators.

Sharing the information with the Hancocks was not the type of news you delivered by phone. Eddie Forster, who above all was a gentle soul, agreed to visit their home in person to break the news. Dressed in suitcoat and tie to show the respect and solemnity of the moment, he walked up the stairs and rang the doorbell. While his visit and the news he carried was probably expected, his words to them were conclusive and ended any thoughts they might have harbored that Kelly would walk through their front door again. While not as traumatic perhaps as the initial shock of Friday's news, it was, nevertheless, devastating. Before leaving, Eddie talked to them about the legal process of returning her body to Massachusetts for a proper burial and that we would be in constant touch with them as our investigation continued. He left them alone to bring the kids together and have the conversation that no parent ever wants to have with their children. Mark and Jackie would later tell us it was impossible to describe or put into words how devastating the news was to the family or how each of them reacted to it.

• • • •

What a whirlwind roller coaster ride we had all been on for those previous three days: we had gone from a completely stalled out investigation to a DNA match of the two crime scenes to a photo of a hank of hair to a dental examination that led us to our victim and her family. The dots were all connected. It was excruciatingly sad but, at the same time, exhilarating to know we finally had an opportunity to vindicate the death of a young girl and solve her murder. We felt as if someone had pulled back a curtain that opened us to a new landscape, one with family and friends to interview, as well as people in the criminal justice system who had contact with Kelly. It would also help us focus in on Crouse and positively determine if there was a connection between the two.

There was a weekend to reflect on our good fortune and to be proud of the effort put into the case by the whole team, but there was also the awareness that we were not finished, just entering a completely new phase of the investigation. With no actual direct evidence or eyewitnesses, we needed to build a very strong circumstantial case. These cases are always more difficult and challenging to prove. However, they were also the most rewarding.

On Tuesday, we would reconvene with a jolt of energy and a new perspective on the case. To the person, we were confident that with Adrienne at the helm we could pull everything together quickly for a presentation of our information to the Middlesex County Grand Jury. That would be our total focus. We were not going to put any horse before the cart and think about a trial. Just one step at a time would serve us well.

CHAPTER 7

Moving Forward

It was a few minutes past nine on Tuesday morning, and I was running late for the weekly supervisor's meeting. I ran up the two flights of stairs and into the main office before pausing to catch my breath and listening for a break in the DA's opening comments before entering. There was only one way in, and Martha sat just inside the doorway at the head of the conference table. I tried to tiptoe behind her, but it was one of those rare moments when being a six-foot-three-two-hundred-and-thirty-pounds man put me at a distinct disadvantage. Uncomfortable would be an understatement. I survived the intrusion, but only after Martha stopped talking in mid-sentence and shot a glare in my direction that served as a quick, humbling, and deserved punishment—not the first and probably not the last time I would earn "the look."

When it was Adrienne's turn to talk, she delivered a short, clean synopsis of the past week and the developments that had allowed us to identify Kelly as our homicide victim. The group barraged her with questions and comments, and she responded to all of them. I sat quietly on the low baseboard heater in the far corner of the room, itching for the meeting to end.

By ten fifteen, we were out and on the move. She was upbeat, and there was no doubt she had been thinking about the case all weekend and was enthusiastic about pushing forward. Her energy and enthusiasm was apparent and infectious. Once in the room, she pulled yet another yellow legal pad from her valise and threw it down onto the table. The dog-eared look of it made it obvious that she already filled the pages with comments, questions, and directives. Her notepads were her playbook: one we would all study and follow.

"Good morning, everyone," she said with a smile, "I just need to say at the start that identifying Kelly Hancock as our victim was surprising, but it wasn't a bolt out of the blue. It happened because you never abandoned what looked like a hopeless case. It was because of your persistence and attentiveness that we now know who this girl is; no longer is she just an unidentified victim. She has a name and a family, and shortly, we can return Kelly to her family and they can give have a proper funeral and burial. Even though we can't reverse history, we can damn sure stand as her surrogates and fight like hell to put her killer behind bars for the rest of his natural life. We all need to recognize the great work we've done to this point and use it as our catalyst moving ahead."

No one rallies a team better than Adrienne does. A sincere pep talk with a light pat on the ass to get back into the arena was the only motivation we needed.

"I am so glad we treated this case like it was a homicide from the moment the smoke and water cleared from that function room. By no means are we done, but because of our preparation, we are certainly a lot closer to an indictment, arrest, and trial than we would have been. Now we have to further develop and firm up the investigation. We have a sturdy foundation, but it still isn't going to be an easy case to prove. All of our evidence is circumstantial. We have many good statements, an alibi or two shot full of holes, and bags of physical and trace evidence that need to be tightly tied together to make our case as strong as possible. It is fair to say that everything we've collected so far points in the direction of Tommy Crouse, but us believing that is a whole lot different than proving it to a jury beyond a reasonable doubt. So let's get started.

"Knowing our end goal means we first have to set and meet several short-term objectives in order to get there. We have to be meticulous in our collection and review of information and evidence, and as best we can, verify and then document everything we learn. I will need reports completed as soon as possible. Once we get an indictment, you can bet that Crouse's lawyer is going to file an avalanche of discovery motions, and they will begin at the arraignment.

"I've expanded our core team to include Anne Foley as our victim witness advocate in helping us work with the Hancock family. That will be no small feat, but we need to have the Hancocks united with us and not against us. Right or wrong, they are pissed off that their daughter was in state custody when she died and have already made their feelings known to the media and us. We need to convince them that we were not part of their past and our sole goal is to vindicate their little girl's death."

She continued, "I have also brought in Nat Yeager and Marguerite Grant to help me work through all of the legal issues that are going to arise as we move forward through the grand jury and on to trial. I know we have all worked together on other cases at one time or another and I think it is safe to say we will all work together flawlessly again this time."

Jimmy, Eddie, Duke, and I, as well as Johnny and Steve, smiled and agreed. We all recognized that Adrienne had significantly strengthened our team.

"Now that the media spotlight is back on our case and people are learning that our victim was a fourteen-year-old girl, we need to capitalize on the sudden illumination from the bright lights. We have to start with a complete re-canvas at Malden Mills, and we need to reinterview others who saw Crouse that morning and on the days that followed. We all know how and why that works. Many people know more than they let on but withhold information, hoping either we just go away or we won't call them to testify to what they witnessed. Or they know something that they thought was unimportant or insignificant so they didn't share the information, but later, they or we realize that what they held back might turn out to be critical to the case. We need to create a little more face time with a few of those folks and jog their memories a bit. Maybe they will be a little less guarded and a little more forthcoming now that they know the person brutally murdered in their function room was a young teenager.

We need to learn everything we can about Kelly. Pardon the term, but we need to humanize her." The emotion in Adrienne's voice was noticeable.

"She was just a runaway kid, not a criminal. It's clear from her parents' reaction to her death that she meant a lot to them. They did not see her as a cast-off child but as their oldest daughter. We need to go way below the surface and speak with her family, friends, neighbors, school authorities, and social services providers. We need to discover the real Kelly. She was not a skull in the road or a pile of buried remains. She was a fourteen-year-old kid with a chip on her shoulder and a boatload of unresolved issues who had been heading in the wrong direction in life, but most of all, she had been a troubled child in need of help.

"I'm open to all ideas and thoughts on how to divide up the responsibilities. We just need to get on it now. Beyond the interviews, we need to start looking for clues and information from things, like the telephone records. We can spend some time reviewing the enhanced videotape from the Mobil station and see if that may produce another lead or two. We can always ask the Grand Jury for more subpoenas for the contact telephone numbers that appear in Crouse's records around the time of the fire in July. Find out whom he called on July 17 and 18. What did he say? Did he show any emotions? You know what I'm saying. I'm not trying to tell any of you how to talk to people, but these are the things we need to find out."

As our quarterback, Adrienne always saw the whole playing field and had a plan and a purpose behind every movement. For months, the fact that we didn't yet have the evidence to charge Tommy Crouse with a violent assault or a homicide did not mean that we couldn't hold him accountable for the fire that he started to cover up the crime.

Through the winter months, while the rest of us caught up investigating other cases, the fire at Malden Mills remained very active with Adrienne. She, too, was working on other cases, but she was determined to bring the arson evidence to the Grand Jury with a minimum expectation of getting Tommy Crouse indicted on an arson charge. She was working with the troopers from the Fire Marshal's office and a couple of subject matter experts and had already made presentments to the Middlesex Grand Jury. She surmised that if she could get him indicted, she might be able to get his probation revoked on the violent rape he committed in Suffolk County and have him returned to jail to finish out that sentence. One way or another, she was going to hold him accountable for what he did and hoped to return him to the custody of the Commonwealth.

While we were friends and colleagues with the troopers in the Fire Marshall's office, we travelled in separate lanes. They were prepared to go forward to seek an indictment, and we were striving to catch up.

The meeting went on for the better part of an hour, and when it ended, we headed to the cafeteria. We had them wrap our sandwiches to go and headed for the back room of our office to eat and discuss our approach to the recanvassing and to decide who would be best suited to work with the Hancock family.

Steve and Johnny thought it best that we remain as the primary contact with the Hancock family. Over the years, the relationship between the family and the Malden PD had been rocky at best, and with our recent progress, we didn't want to stumble or lose momentum because of differing personalities. We would still work together on evidence review and recanvassing the building and the neighborhood.

Jimmy, Eddie, and Duke would work with the Hancocks to not only learn about their family and Kelly but also to locate friends, schoolmates, social service personnel, and anyone else who may have insight or knowledge about her and the events that led up to her attack and death.

The addition of Anne Foley to our team was a true blessing. Victim-witness advocates are a godsend in all cases. They are crisis intervention specialists and natural caregivers trained to support crime victims, the families of victims, and prosecution witnesses. By definition, their primary responsibility is to ensure victims of crimes and their families receive the services and protections that the laws of the Commonwealth guarantee. In reality, their role is so much more involved than that. At the most difficult, unfathomable time in a person's life, they are the advocate who stands waiting at their front door to offer comfort, guidance, and assistance. They are compassionate and empathetic to a fault under the most trying of times. They are there to bring stability when there is nothing but chaos and uncertainty. They are also there to tend to the emotional and physical needs of victims and witnesses, and to address any safety concerns. In homicide cases, the "vic-wits," as they are known in our office, become the central point of contact for both the families and the investigators when questions or concerns arise.

So, with Anne leading the way, we were able to find the needed common ground with the Hancock family to move forward, uncover, and discover the person we only knew as Kelly.

• • • •

Aside from Constitutional boundaries, there isn't a guide or handbook of hard-and-fast rules for homicide investigators to follow. There are some obvious dos and don'ts and a few things you only learn after you have miss stepped a time or two. For me, and those investigators and ADAs I have worked with through the years, a fundamental, unwritten rule is to not prejudge or pigeonhole anyone. It is easy, based on years of experience, to slip into a simple, stereotypical way of assessing and judging people and situations, but it doesn't take long before you realize you have made a huge mistake and retreat back to clear, objective thinking.

Kelly was a prime example of why we needed to remain open-minded. From a distance, she was like many fourteen-year-old girls from a blue-collar neighborhood in a small urban city. She walked the streets day and night with her friends, looking and acting the part of a tough, street savvy kid who was mature beyond her years. Although Kelly projected this image, it wasn't an honest reflection of who she had been.

She'd had a mischievous smile, a gregarious personality, and a fierce independence. She had been a jeans and halter-top girl. She hadn't owned stylish clothes or expensive signature sneakers. No one had ever made her an appointment to have her nails done or her hair styled. Her one striking physical attribute that people remembered and women envied was her rich, thick, reddish auburn hair that she had pulled back and held together with a scrunchie.

Kelly had led people to believe that everything in her life was just fine. However, it hadn't been. Beneath the veneer was a troubled, mixed-up child who masked her pain and problems with street bravado. The truth was that for her, home life was difficult.

The more we spoke with the Hancocks the more we learned about them, their family, and their difficulties with Kelly. They were a blended family. Mark and his first wife, Barbara, were the parents of Kelly and Lisa. They had divorced but had shared joint custody, and the girl's primary residence was with their mom. After their breakup, Mark met and eventually married Jackie. She had a son, Thomas, from a prior relationship. He was a few months older than Kelly. Ultimately, Jackie and Mark grew their family with the additions of Taylor, Sammy, and Mathew.

When Kelly was seven and Lisa five years old, Barbara suffered a catastrophic medical episode one afternoon while at home with her daughters. The girls had witnessed her seizure and sat alone with her limp, unresponsive body for hours until someone arrived to help, but it was too late; she had already passed. That evening, the girls went to Mark and Jackie's home, where they would remain from that moment forward. Kelly and Lisa remained a big part of Barbara's family though and they visited with their grandparents and extended family often. They had spent time together during the holiday season, and they had travelled with them on family vacations to New Hampshire in the summer. On occasion, they had visited their mother's gravesite in a cemetery within walking distance from their home.

While we knew of Mark's criminal past and a few adversarial run-ins with the police, we were just starting to learn about him as a father and husband. Neither he nor Jackie were under any obligation to meet or talk with us, nor was he a person of interest in the investigation, but there did seem to be a genuine desire to get to know each other better, to build trust and reliance with each other. I'm not sure whether it was the fact we shared in his grief over the loss of Kelly or that we presented in a non-confrontational way that allowed them to be open and candid in our talks.

Mark characterized himself and Jackie as strict but fair parents. All of the children had chores each day, and on school days, their homework had to be completed and reviewed before they could go out to be with their friends. Whenever possible, the whole family sat together for meals and conversations. The Catholic Church and Sunday school provided them with a spiritual anchor that played an important role in their lives. In fact, Kelly, Lisa, and Tommy were altar servers at their local parish church.

Mark was candid about the troubles and problems he faced, but said that for him "work was work and home was home," and for the most part, he left his work outside the door of his home. "Just because I was a thug on the streets and collected debts from people didn't mean I was a bad parent. They were two different things." He said, "We were strict parents, not bad parents." He and Jackie found work when and where they could, and that money kept a roof over their heads and food on the table. When Jackie wasn't at work, she was home checking homework, cooking, cleaning, and spending time with the kids. When Mark was at home he spent a lot of his time playing with the kids in their yard or they would walk to the basketball courts at the Malden YMCA, where they would spend hours shooting baskets and playing games.

"I was the oldest of seven when my father, who was extremely abusive to my mother, abandoned us. He never spent time with us, and he left us with nothing," Mark told us. "I had to watch over all of my brothers and sisters so they would grow up right. I did the best I could without anyone to guide me. I dropped out of school after the sixth grade. I was strict with them and made them toe the line, but I also had to do what I had to do to make sure we had food. I was good at shoplifting, and more than once, I broke into our neighborhood market and stole half a cow to bring home for my mother to cook," he said with a broad grin.

"After watching the way my father treated my mother, I swore I would never raise my hand against a woman, and I never have." At a point years ago, Mark did have a restraining order brought against him by his ex-wife, Barbara. When I asked him about it, he grinned, "Oh that. I never touched her, and she wasn't afraid I was going to hit her. I was around her house a lot visiting my kids, and she said I was scaring away her boyfriends, and she was mad at me and told the police I was threatening them. I may have been scaring them away, but I don't think I was threatening them."

Kelly's running away wouldn't be a major issue at trial, but it would be part of the prosecution's presentation, so we needed to know more about Kelly, why she often had run away and gotten into mischief. Mark and Jackie spoke of her independent spirit and her absolute fearlessness of everything and everyone. Beyond that, Mark seemed legitimately baffled by her behavior. "It wasn't a lack of communication," he said, "because we talked all of the time, even when she was on the run we spoke almost every day. She would call from pay phones and friend's houses. She'd tell me not to worry and that she was fine. She'd also tell me, 'Dad, I don't know why I do these things.' I tried to stay calm with her, but at times, my temper got the best of me. I felt like the devil was talking to her and making her do these things."

He added that when Kelly ran, she rarely went far from home. "I think she liked the safety of the house but she loved the freedom of being alone." He noted that when she went to live with a foster family or a group home she would run from there as well because she didn't want to follow their rules.

"She'd be on the run with a warrant out for her arrest, and she would be walking around the neighborhood. She would climb a few fences and be in our backyard playing with the kids. In fact, when she ran the last time, a day or two before she was murdered, one of my kids came into the house and told me she was in the backyard. I looked out the window, and there she was. I yelled out through the screen and told her I was coming to get her, and she took off jumping over fences to get away."

He added they later learned Kelly would speak with Lisa and they would meet away from the house. Sometimes, when the weather was bad, Lisa would unlock the back door and Kelly would slide in late at night and sleep in the stairway, leaving before they woke in the morning. Lisa would also find a way to get Kelly food and money to keep her going. They had been through a lot together, and they were best friends. Lisa was not nearly as adventurous and always worried about Kelly. They were just kids. Kelly was fourteen and Lisa only twelve when they saw each other for the last time.

Jackie recalled that Kelly started running in the sixth grade, and the episodes continued through the seventh and into the eighth grade.

Delving a little deeper into the family history, because we knew it would be an issue at trial, we spoke with them one afternoon about how and why DSS had entered their lives. We knew the family involvement with DSS and the juvenile court system was acrimonious at best. It was the first thing Mark said to us on the day we first approached him in Walpole after Kelly's remains were identified; Mark later spoke with the media and vented his anger at "the system," squarely blaming them for her death.

I asked Mark how DSS had come to be involved in their lives, and I clearly nicked a nerve. "I was called down to the Malden Police Station and was only told it was about Kelly. I went down there, and there were a bunch of detectives and school cops there. They brought me into a room and accused me of sexually assaulting Kelly. They came at me hard, and I was furious that anyone would accuse me of touching one of my children. I was like a bull. They let me speak to Kelly, who was in another room, and she told me she never said that I had touched her in any way and that they were making stuff up. They never charged me with anything, and she left with me that day, but DSS showed up at my house a few days later. They made us do family counseling and other stuff. It was their decision to remove her from my home, not ours."

He said what angered him most was that DSS questioned and interfered with their style of parenting and when she went to other places she was allowed to smoke, as well as wear makeup and tight clothes: three things that were absolutely forbidden in his house. In his words, "It drove me crazy." He also believed that Kelly learned to play the system by pitting one segment against the other so she could retain her freedom and lack of responsibilities. He said, "She ran from us, but she also ran from every placement home." He repeated that she did things in DSS care that she never would have done if she were home.

When you are fourteen, unsure of where you fit in your own family and resisting help in finding that place, home is not a place you want or choose to be most of the time. You are happiest when hunkered down at a friend's house on a cold and snowy night, and when it's warm, you want to be wandering the streets of your city without rules or restrictions. You've picked out your safe places where you can hide and disappear like a field mouse in the high grass. You worry more about the police catching you than falling into the grip of a sexual predator. In your immature mind, you consider yourself clever, sensible, and confident. You can survive under any circumstances.

Such was the life and beliefs of the rebellious and self-determined fourteen-year-old Kelly Hancock in July of 2000. She survived but barely. The days and nights of dodging, bobbing, and weaving to avoid the authorities became more difficult and stressful. Therefore, it was that on a muggy, uncomfortable summer night as she walked the streets alone, she met up with thirty-something Tommy Crouse. He offered her comfort and a place to spend the night. As it turned out, climbing into his car that night was the final bad personal decision she would ever make.

As we learned more about Kelly, her family life, and her interactions with the Court and the DSS, what emerged was a picture of a fourteen-year-old girl that was different from the one any of us expected. She was not a nasty street urchin but a big sister with a mothering instinct who loved and protected her younger siblings, in particular Mathew, who was two when Kelly died.

For me, the most poignant, heartbreaking image of all came when Mark related how when Kelly was away from home but nearby, she often wandered into the cemetery where her birth mother was buried and curled up beside her gravestone, where they would spend the night together in peace.

• • • •

Maybe the second unwritten rule or truth that investigators learn is that you never put your hands on a suspect unless you are placing them under arrest. Similarly, nothing good ever comes from losing your cool and yelling, screaming at, or smacking a suspect. There is nothing to gain except personal satisfaction and potentially everything to lose if the judge excludes statements and evidence from the trial because of your ham-handed bullying tactics.

In addition, that was why as much as every one of us wanted to grab Tommy Crouse by the throat, pummel the piss out of him, and scream into his face, "She was fourteen years old, and you took her life, and you could give a fuck less. We will make sure you rot in jail!" we didn't.

None of us would jeopardize our investigation because we couldn't keep our emotions in check. We wanted Crouse in jail because of what he had done, not in the hospital because of something we did.

CHAPTER 8

Grand Jury Indictment and the Arrest

The grand jurors got their first whiff of this case on August 3, 2000, two weeks after the fire. Gerard Butler spoke with them about what happened and what we had learned so far and suggested to them that subpoenas for telephone records for a couple of telephones might help us advance our investigation. They obliged, and from those subpoenas, we learned more about the timelines and connections between Crouse and others. The records helped us challenge Crouse's alibi for the night of July 17 and the day of July 18.

After that initial appearance, Adrienne replaced Gerard in the room. She presented them with further updates, had witnesses testify under oath about the arson investigation, fielded juror's questions, and made suggestions and requests for subpoenas for additional records.

This Grand Jury had been recalled a couple of times after their mandated three-month term because there was additional work to be done before we could ask for them to vote to indict Crouse on any charges. Each time they voluntarily returned, Adrienne presented them with updated information and asked for more subpoenas to further the investigation, and each time, they granted her request. Adrienne wasn't purposefully dragging the case out, but before she made the request on one count of arson against Tommy Crouse, she was holding out hope we would locate a victim and request additional charges based on new facts.

Then, with the identification of Kelly Hancock, she had what she needed and formally requested that the jurors reconvene one more time. She chose Paul Horgan and Eddie Forster to appear as her final witnesses.

The jurors heard from them in earlier testimony, so there was already a familiarity, and they both knew the facts of the case inside and out.

On the second day of the last week in June, Adrienne brought them the news that they'd located the remains of a young girl in Hookset, NH: and how we had connected her to the Malden Mills fire scene through DNA analysis. She recapped all they had heard and seen over the past several months and asked that they consider indictments against Crouse for murder in the first degree and arson.

Later in the day, the jurors completed their discussions and deliberations about the case. They voted to return true bills per Adrienne's request. Almost eleven months after the Grand Jury opened an exploratory investigation into the fire at Malden Mills, their work was complete. In quick order, the paperwork arrived at the clerk of courts office, and at the request of the DAO, warrants were issued for Crouse's arrest. Jimmy Connolly took possession of the paperwork, and afterward, we met to develop a simple plan to affect Crouse's arrest without fanfare or danger.

During the course of the investigation, we kept a distant eye on Crouse. We learned that he was working for a large construction company on a major road project in Boston at the time. A couple of days earlier, surveillance had confirmed where he reported for work most mornings. The plan was to set up on his vehicle and arrest him as he was leaving the worksite. Although not always possible, this is a preferred way of making a planned arrest. It takes the drama and trauma away from a person's home and family and isolates it solely on the arrestee.

A team of four arrived at Crouse's workplace at six thirty on the morning of Wednesday, June 27. They spotted the white Lincoln Navigator he was driving and set up surveillance with the officers split into two cars.

Late in the morning, Crouse walked briskly to his car, and before they could approach, he was in and gone at a quick rate of speed. They fell in behind him as he drove in and out of highway traffic, cutting people off and speeding through yellow lights in congested urban areas. The cruisers were close behind. They weren't sure if he knew they were pursuing him or that was how he drove all of the time. They decided not to call it in as a police chase but did request the services of the state police Air Wing to give them helpful eyes from the sky. The helicopter pilot easily located them and locked onto the pursuit. After almost a half hour, Crouse drove onto a residential street in the town of Swampscott before pulling over and coming to a stop. The helicopter lowered to several feet and hovered over the SUV as Crouse stepped out. He saw the officers running toward him and heard the commands to kneel on the ground with his hands over his head. With a bewildered look, he followed their orders and offered no resistance. The detectives quickly cuffed his arms behind his back, bundled him into the backseat of a cruiser, and escorted him to the Malden Police Station for booking.

Adrienne was elated when Connolly called her with the news. She asked that they bring him to superior court that afternoon so she could arraign him on the charges and request that he be detained without bail and held upstairs in the jail until trial.

They hustled through the booking process and allowed Crouse a phone call to his family before whisking him off to the Cambridge Courthouse. In the meantime, Martha and her staff were polishing off a press release for distribution to the media. Anne Foley was reaching out to the Hancock family to forward the good news and to let them know media outlets might be calling and looking for them to comment as well.

The arraignment went smoothly with Adrienne reading a synopsis of the facts and asking the Court to hold Crouse without bail. Attorney Jack Baccari, a criminal lawyer Crouse's stepfather had previously retained to defend him, argued for a modest monetary bail so his client could rejoin his family. Lastly, a probation officer weighed in with information regarding Crouse's past criminal record. In Massachusetts, it is extremely rare for a monetary bail to be set at arraignment on a first-degree murder charge. This time was no different, and the judge remanded Crouse to the county jail to await his next court appearance.

CHAPTER 9

Custody

The Middlesex County Courthouse is by far the largest building in the city of Cambridge. Rising twenty-two stories above street level with more than 458,000 square feet of space, it encompasses a small city block. Located smack in the middle of a mixed-use section of the city, it casts long shadows over the district and probate courts, single-family homes, and rehabbed brick factories packed with lawyers, architects, and start-up hi-tech companies.

From the outside, it is an unremarkable looking building. The windows are recessed and shielded from direct sunlight. The only color that offsets the drab neutral façade is a red stripe that encircles the building below the seventeenth floor. Most have no idea of the stripe's relevance, but those who do, recognize it as a subtle signature statement separating good, from evil. Above the line is the home of the Middlesex County Jail where the residents await trial on their criminal charges.

The northbound ride on the prisoner's back elevator from the eighth-floor courtroom to the seventeenth-floor lockup is not the same as a trip on Led Zeppelin's mythical "Stairway to Heaven." No soft music or soothing voiceovers, just nine quick dings, and in less than thirty seconds the door opens and the defendant is home in the Middlesex County Jail. It is the prisoner's pathway from the courtrooms to the Receiving and Booking Office of the Middlesex County Jail and the only travel route inmates will know until either acquitted, convicted, or sent to live in another jail or state prison.

Tommy Crouse made the trip following his arraignment on the murder and arson charges. Shackled and flanked by two unsympathetic court officers, he presented at the booking desk with a plastic bag full of his personal belongings and the paperwork from the Court ordering him to remain in the sheriff's custody without the opportunity for bail.

The jail's intake process is simple, straightforward, and the same for everyone. The only hiccup is the wait for your turn at the counter, which can take a few hours depending on when you arrive and how many are already up in front of you. The court officers brought Crouse into the holding area, where a booking officer reviewed his paperwork before exchanging both custody and the handcuffs from Crouse's wrists. The jailer's cuffs were similar, but there were a few extra links because one cuff latched onto his wrist while the other went through an eyebolt and stapled him to a metal bench where he sat and waited for his turn, just as everyone else did. There is no booking desk hierarchy based on the crimes of which you were charged or if you were a friend or cousin of someone in the front office. There is no express or courtesy lane for the frequent flyers either. Crouse just had to sit until the jailor unsnapped him and brought him to the desk.

Crouse answered all the booking questions about his personal identity, health issues, concerns, prescriptions, and finally his next of kin in case there was a need for notification. After being fingerprinted and photographed, they brought him into another room for a more in-depth strip search and a brief look-see for hidden contraband. Finally, they issued him the standard prisoner's uniform: a loose-fitting grey jumpsuit previously worn by someone else and reeking of institutional laundry detergent and bleach.

Regardless of the severity of the pending criminal charges, in Massachusetts, the county jail is where you wait prior to trial. It is common for men with a history of violence and lengthy arrest records to sleep soundly a few feet from rosy-cheeked, scared shitless kids from the suburbs busted for comparably minor, nonviolent crimes. The newbies lie awake at night, listening to their rapid heartbeats pounding loudly in their ears, terrified to close their eyes. Often, two dozen or more inmates awaited trial on first-degree murder charges were intermingled with a much larger group held for nonviolent crimes.

Unless predestined for either maximum security or protective custody cell areas, new arrivals are assigned the next available bunk space. No one is special or receives anything better than the guy in front or behind. You aren't there because you are a good guy. There are no reservations, king-sized beds, or opportunities to purchase an upgraded accommodation.

For the foreseeable future, it would be Tommy Crouse's mailing address. His movements and his time, like those of his peers, were limited and controlled. Privacy was at a minimum. The administration regulated all visits and visiting hours and could shut them off without warning, and they recorded all of his phone calls except the ones from his attorney. He lost control of his life, he was in an environment with guys who were a lot tougher and smarter than he was, and he knew it. It was a change in lifestyle but not one that was foreign to him. He had been in this position before when he served time for the violent rape he committed in Revere.

There is no fixed pecking order among inmates, but there is a certain deference given to those charged with crimes that are more serious and violent. It is more about fear than respect, but either way, it exists. If you are awaiting trial for stealing a car or breaking into a widow's home you are at the bottom of the ladder, but if you killed someone in a robbery or took a shot at a cop, you are at the top. Everyone knows the unwritten rules, or they learn them quickly and usually the hard way.

Whether the perception is true or not, inmates generally consider men awaiting trial for murder as the toughest guys in the joint. They've already taken another person's life. What if they lose their shit again and decide to take someone else out? Many of them have serious mental health or personality disorders, and it doesn't take long to realize, "That guy ain't right in the head." You don't want the "what if" to be you, so you stay away the best you can. Speak when spoken to, and in some instances, do what that person asks of you.

On paper, Tommy Crouse looked like he might be a tough guy. Murder and arson were serious charges, but when you peeked into his file and saw his charge was brutally murdering a fourteen-year-old girl and then setting the building on fire to destroy evidence while dozens slept, it was clear he was not. He wasn't a lion they needed to fear, he was a trash-talking weasel. It wasn't information he could hide because it was all over the news. Nothing tough about what he did. He wasn't Michael Corleone in the Godfather; he was Fredo. He wasn't someone to look up to; he was made of the stuff you scrape off the bottom of your shoe. He wrote and owned his history. He only attacked women, never men, and when he got in legal trouble, he ran to his mother and stepfather for protection and financial support.

Not surprisingly, Tommy wanted nothing to do with the general population; he sought the protective custody route, a safer haven with a diminished fear factor. No request was automatic, but it helps when your stepfather, a prominent member of the Malden business community and a good friend of the sheriff, advocates for your request.

G Tier was on the nineteenth floor and officially titled the "Special Management Unit." (SMU). On one side of the corridor were fourteen cells with automatic locks to keep the inmates safe at night. On the other side of the aisle was a corresponding line of bunk beds for the overflow of inmates seeking refuge.

No safety walls or locked doors separated the fourteen bunkbeds in overflow from each other or from the cells. The bunks were spaced three feet apart, and the inmates jammed their belongings into grey footlockers stored under the bottom of the beds. The double stacked beds blocked some of the sunlight, and without any insulation, that side of the room got very cold in the winter and miserably hot in the summer. Cell Number 2 was unassigned, and the toilet and sink were for those in the overflow. There was no air conditioning in the jail, and in an extended summer heat spell, the temperatures in the jail were brutal, and the inmates didn't always suffer it well. The inmates on this tier had their own shower area and had their meals delivered so they never had to mix with the general population. During meals, the jail was in lockdown while the guards moved the inmates to and from the dining area in shifts. It was impossible to lockdown the people in overflow, so they stayed in the common area where they gathered around a couple of steel picnic-type tables bolted to the floor. There they could eat, watch one of the two televisions, use the pay phones, and depending on the circumstances, use the shower area.

The SMU is unique because, with limited exceptions, everyone requested the housing and the protection that comes with it. They didn't want to be in general population where they feared an attack or challenge. There were public servants, pedophiles, clergy, and gangbangers who worried about reprisals from rival gang members. There were also people who were known police informants or planned to testify against another inmate, and there were guys like Crouse who allegedly murdered a child, or Mucko McDermott, our shooter who had murdered seven of his coworkers the day after Christmas.

They lived in a safer environment, and from the sheriff's perspective, there was less chance of confrontation or violence than if they placed the protected prisoners with the other inmates. Hard to call it a win-win, but that's the way it played out. There were limited behavioral issues in the unit because no one wanted to test their survival skills if sent into "population."

Crouse's prison history made his reentry smoother than most. He knew the rules and the daily regimen for eating meals, taking showers, and being in the common area during lockdown. He also knew what and whose buttons he could push versus the ones that would earn him a disciplinary report and a loss of privileges, like visitors and canteen purchases.

The tier had its share of characters. There were no Kumbaya moments of unity or solidarity. There were certainly friendships that developed, but everyone took the other's measure at arm's length before sharing personal data or case information with one another. Generally, people either decreed their innocence or admitted they did it but professed a rationale that their acts were defensible and winnable in court.

Crouse blended well. He got along with the corrections officers and most of his peers and rarely challenged anyone. He didn't earn "D reports," so he had visitors, and thanks to his benefactor and stepfather, Lester Morovitz, he had plenty of money in his canteen fund for the necessities of life and a few goodies he could either consume or share with others. The inmate term for canteen funds was "their kick."

In any prison, where the comforts of life are practically nonexistent, the canteen is king. It houses the simple everyday needs, like toothpaste, batteries, and shaving cream, as well as writing paper and pens, envelopes, and stamps. You can also buy nonperishables like canned soups, boxes of cereal, and cookies. Some jails even sell radios and small televisions with headphones for private use.

Beyond the everyday items, you can purchase other things, such as friendships, or avoid beatings, settle debts, or cure other issues that might arise. The "price" for those items fluctuates based on demand and supply.

An inmate can either buy things out of their kick and give them away or ask a friend or family member to add money to another inmate's account so they can shop on their own. There are no rules against that. All someone needs to do is present at the main desk, fill out a form indicating to whom you are donating, and then slide a few dollars through the slot and you are an instant hero to someone. Crouse saw this as an opportunity to ingratiate himself to a favored few, and Lester was more than willing to make things smooth for his stepson, oftentimes donating to the canteen funds of others.

Undoubtedly, most give the financial help out of benevolence, but there may be payback required, and the favor can quickly turn to something sinister and unexpected. For example, the giver may demand favors of the recipient to procure or deliver drugs or deliver messages to someone on the outside. Oftentimes, they want someone threatened or hurt whom they think may be setting up to testify against them. On occasion, it can be a demand for sexual favors.

On the other hand, the introduction of money into someone else's canteen may not be out of friendship but because of a threat of harm if they don't. The guards do their best to stay on top of this, but they can't prevent or question the reasons for donations from people who don't know the person receiving their gift.

We were all curious about how Tommy would adapt to jail life and asked our colleagues who worked in the jail about him from time to time. If he had any rough patches, they weren't obvious. They said he kept his head down, followed orders, and did his best to blend in with the others. He didn't get in fights, pick up D reports, or complain about the living conditions. For the most part, his time in the unit fit into the category of unremarkable. Somewhere along the way, he figured out that it is never good to act tough when you are around real tough guys.

There are few opportunities for paid work positions, but Crouse had grabbed one of them. The official title was tier cleaner, but the inside term was "runner." The responsibilities were simple: keep the floor swept and the tables clean, empty the wastebaskets, deliver messages. It paid fifty cents an hour, but it was more about the freedom to roam the tier, engage with the officers, and on occasion, enter other cells without challenge: Not much, but in jail anything is still something, and something beats the hell out of nothing.

Crouse liked to hear his own voice but in a sociable way. He could be a wise guy but not disruptive or challenging. He had a swagger because he had a murder charge hanging over his head, but it was different from that of a true tough guy. When Cell G-14 opened up a few days after Christmas, Crouse moved from an overflow bunk into the privacy of a cell. It was located at the end of the row and furthest from the main corridor.

• • • •

Louie Barone came to the tier on February 11. He was a veteran of the system and had done time before for a variety of crimes, mostly nonviolent but a few violent. He was a quiet kind of tough guy. He wasn't a braggart and didn't talk freely about his life or his criminal past, but everyone sensed he was not someone you wanted to mess with. He was of the "you-did-the-crime-now-do-your-time" philosophy and never complained; he just bided his time.

He had been living "across the river" in the Suffolk County Jail awaiting trial when he was approached by an inmate who wanted him to "take care of some business" by killing a few people. One was the victim of a gang rape who was planning to testify against him. Barone notified the jailers who reached out to the Boston Police and, when interviewed, said he was willing to cooperate but he needed to relocate and move into a protective custody unit. Barone didn't talk to his tier mates about why he had chosen to be in protective custody. Most don't, and everyone understands that.

The entire jail was overcrowded, including G Tier. Barone's bunk assignment was a lower bed in the overflow area, second from the end and almost directly across from Crouse. The two acknowledged one and other on the first day, and in the days that followed, they spoke and sat together frequently.

In their early conversations, they compared notes about where they were from, and as it turned out, there were people they knew in common. Barone mentioned that he had met Crouse's father-in-law, Lester, several years earlier when he was hanging around in Malden.

Crouse asked Barone if he knew about the murder charge against him, and he seemed surprised when Barone said he didn't. Crouse told him it was in all the papers and on the news and Barone said he just watched out for himself and never paid attention to the news. Crouse seemed equally surprised when Barone told him he didn't know, or seem to care, who Mucko McDermott was and that he had killed seven people. He was just another guy on the tier awaiting trial as far as Barone was concerned.

He let Crouse know he was perfectly content doing his time in peace. He wasn't there to make friends, nor was he star struck by the celebrity of a mass murderer.

Although Barone was hesitant to interface with Crouse at first, as the days turned to weeks, the two men spent a lot of time hanging out and talking. With permission, Crouse eventually moved his belongings out of his cell and into a footlocker under the bed next to Barone. He continued to talk almost nonstop about his case and he shared copies of some of the discovery materials his attorney brought to him. He frequently asked Barone for his thoughts and input on his case.

On a Tuesday morning in the middle of April, Barone was up early for a court date. He packed up his belongings and said his goodbyes, and the guard escorted him out of the tier and the jail and into a waiting van for a trip to Woburn District Court, where he had a court appearance relative to some check forgery-related charges. He was relatively sure he wasn't returning that afternoon because the judge on his case had already indicated he would be revoking his probation on a previous conviction.

Barone appeared before the Court, and as expected, the judge ordered him to the Billerica House of Correction to finish the eighteen months left on his previous sentence. The judge continued the current charges for a later trial date.

• • • •

Late that afternoon, Duke received a call from a trooper assigned to the Danvers Barracks. "Duke, listen, brother, I'm down at Woburn Court on a case, and there is a prisoner in the holding tank waiting for transport to Billerica. He told one of the court officers that he wanted to speak with a trooper about the murder of Kelly Hancock. They grabbed me because I was here, but this is way out of my league. I figured this is your case because it happened in Malden. Do you guys want to come up and talk with him?"

Duke thanked him for the call and told him he would be en route shortly. Duke turned to Connolly, who was sitting five feet away and halfway through a burrito and a Mountain Dew.

"Jimmy, are you free?" Duke asked.

Connolly answered hesitantly, "Maybe, why?"

"I just got a call that there is a prisoner at Woburn Court who wants to talk with us about Kelly Hancock."

"What are we waiting for?" Jimmy shot back, "Let me finish up, and we can head out before he changes his mind and we lose an opportunity." He wolfed down the rest of his lunch, grabbed his coat, and together they headed out the door.

"I'll call Adrienne on the way and let her know where we are headed."

Duke drove while Jimmy connected with Adrienne. It was a short twelve-mile trip to the Woburn Courthouse, but they had enough time to talk over a quick game plan.

"Did you ever do one of these kind of interviews, Duke?" Jimmy asked.

"No. Is there something different about them?" Duke asked.

"Oh yeah, a whole lot different and with a few distinct unwritten rules to follow," said Jimmy. "Sometimes in these situations inmates are truthful and for whatever their reason, want to cooperate with you, but those kind are rare. Most of them are treacherous, conniving bullshit artists trying to scam their way into a deal. You know the kind: they tell you they will testify but only if you can cut them a deal. You have to be very careful when you are talking with them. They overhear a few casual conversations on the tier, think they can use the information as a get-out-of-jail-free card, and then try to pick your brain for more facts that they can weave into their story. I'm telling you, these can work out well—or they can be the worst nightmare you'll ever encounter.

"So, our best approach is to listen and take notes. We encourage him to talk but give him no information about the case. We don't tell him if he is on track or anything like that, even if he asks. We don't question the truth of his comments or his motives until after we get a chance to fact-check everything he tells us. Let him talk as long as he wants and don't call him a liar, just write down everything he has to say. If he brings the truth, we will know it because we know the case. If he has gaps in his story or appears to be dancing around the important stuff, then he is probably full of shit. Nothing ventured, nothing gained, and at the end of the day, it is Martha's decision on any kind of deal making.

"The most important thing we tell him," he continued, "is to lay out from the very beginning that we can't make deals, only the DA can do that. The only promise we can make to him is that we will relay what he tells us to the DA, and she will make any decisions regarding requests for leniency, etc."

They badged their way through the security checkpoint because they were armed and headed right to the holding cell area. It was late in the afternoon, and it wouldn't be long before the transportation van would be taking all of the folks in custody off to Billerica in time for check-in and dinner. The trooper had left, but the court officer watching the holding area knew the story and identified the person as Louie Barone.

"He's being held on a probation surrender. His legal counsel is here, and he knows his client wants to speak with you."

Jimmy and Duke spoke to Barone's attorney first and asked if he wanted to sit in on the interview. He declined and told them he had no problem with them speaking to his client as long as it wasn't about the pending forgery and larceny charges.

The court officer directed them to a room where Barone sat isolated from the rest. There was a quick exchange of introductions before Jimmy took the lead and started the conversation. He reminded Barone that he and Duke were there because he had asked to speak with them, and while they wanted to listen to what he had to say, they couldn't promise him anything in exchange for his information.

"Louie," he said, "The only promise we can make is that we will go back to the ADA that's prosecuting Crouse and let her know what you tell us. I just want you to understand that from the beginning."

Barone said he was familiar with the rules of the game and that he had testified for the Commonwealth previously. With that understanding out of the way, Barone got right to the point. He said he had several conversations with Thomas Crouse in the Cambridge Jail, and Crouse had admitted to him that he had murdered a fourteen-year-old girl named Kelly Hancock. He said Crouse and he had been together in the Protective Custody Unit up until this morning and Crouse had talked almost non-stop about his case. With very little prompting from Jimmy, he delivered a short synopsis of what he knew.

They barely started talking when the meeting abruptly ended. The pick-up van had arrived, and understandably, the sheriff's only concern was getting everyone on board with the right paperwork and heading out of there as soon as possible.

Jimmy told Barone he knew their time was going to be short that day, but at least they had met and gotten the dialogue started. He asked Barone about meeting for a more in-depth interview at Billerica on the following day. Barone said he wanted to continue the conversation and would leave the arrangements up to them and the people at the house of correction. His only concern was for his safety and that they did not call him out in front of everyone for a visit with the police.

"Not a worry," Jimmy told him, "we have a great relationship with the staff of investigators there, and believe me, your safety will be the first thing on all of our minds."

On the way back to the office Jimmy called Adrienne, told her what happened, and said he would arrange everything in the morning to go back for a lengthier interview. Jimmy told her that preliminarily it sounded promising but far from certain. She was glad for the news but was quick to mention how wary she was of using inmates and people with criminal records as a witness in a homicide case. She also wanted to make sure they made no promises on behalf of the office. She made her point, but it didn't stop Jimmy from rolling his eyes and saying back, "I got it, Adrienne. We covered it, and we'll repeat ourselves every time we talk with him."

Midmorning of the following day, Jimmy and Duke met in the parking lot of the Billerica House of Correction. Jimmy had called and cleared their visit through one of the investigators at the jail, and he got a return call assuring him that Barone was expecting them. Arrangements were already in place to bring Barone to a private room in the Investigative Unit. He would have to sign the standard Visit by Law Enforcement Form acknowledging his willingness to speak with the police, and then they would bring the detectives in to speak with him. Because Barone had arrived less than twenty-four hours earlier, there was limited concern that his going with the guards out of the population would be a cause for concern or questioning by other inmates.

The meeting was informative, and the conversation flowed well. Jimmy started with the no-promises spiel, and Barone again said he understood. He said he was serving an eighteen-month incarceration on a probation surrender, and he had a few pending charges in Woburn Court for passing bad checks. He said he wanted to make it clear he was meeting with them because the victim in this case was a fourteen-year-old girl and the guy who did it was bragging about it without any remorse. He added if the DA could help him with his charges because of his cooperation that would be nice but that was not why he was willing to share the information. Barone clearly did not like Crouse and described him as a fat, bald loudmouth. He added that he took the first opportunity he had to share the information with the investigators.

Jimmy asked Barone if he could lay things out for them in chronological order, and he said he couldn't because he got the information in dribs and drabs over a couple of month's period. He added that when you are doing time, days and times all blend into one large heap.

"In jail," he said, "you don't keep a calendar or watch a clock. They tell you when it's time to eat, go to the gym, and turn the lights out at the end of the day. The only surprises may be a visit from someone or your lawyer. You don't write things down or keep notes. But there are things you hear that you can't forget."

They talked for more than an hour, and Barone shared what he knew. He said he met Crouse the night he went into the Cambridge Jail Protective Custody Unit. His first thoughts were that Crouse was a gangster. Crouse told him he was a leg breaker for some bookies, and he had taken a baseball bat to a guy's head in Newton before bundling him into the trunk of a car. He told him the FBI got involved and they were looking for him. Barone said he soon realized that Crouse was a storyteller and a blowhard who thought if he talked like a tough guy it made him a tough guy. He said he thought Crouse might be a skinner (an inmate term for a pedophile), but Crouse vehemently denied it without anyone asking him directly.

Barone said Crouse was somewhat surprised that he hadn't heard of his murder charge, and after a few days, most of his conversations revolved around his case. He shared all of the details of what he did, and how he got rid of her body, and how he was going to win his case because the police had nothing that pointed directly to him. Barone turned his attention to Duke and said Crouse "is really shaken by you. You have found a way under his skin." Duke just flashed one of his often-seen impish grins.

Barone continued talking and covered a wide variety of topics about their conversations. He said Crouse talked about using escort services to get girls and bring them to the community room where he lived. He said he'd had a key to the room. He talked of distrusting people who lived in the condo complex whom he had spoken to, and of his girlfriend, Esther, and how he wanted to marry her so she couldn't testify against him. Crouse also told him about how he distributed the gas around the room, that he bought it with cash, and that he bought 2.83 gallons of gas with his five dollars. He seemed shocked that it didn't cause a huge fire. Barone believed that Crouse talked about the case because "he got off on it."

Barone mentioned Crouse talked about a shovel found at the burial site and said there was "no fucking way the police would find his fingerprints on it" because he had been wearing gloves. Barone added that at some point Crouse received information that the police had found a blue fiber and he went ape shit over the news. Barone recalled that Crouse was so upset he stayed in bed for the next four days.

During their conversations, Barone said Crouse mentioned he had done time for a previous rape. He said it was his ex-girlfriend and that while he was serving his five-year term she had hung herself. He said she left a note saying he didn't do it.

What seemed to bother Barone more than anything was that Crouse knew a few things about Kelly and his description of her was that she was a "problem kid who wouldn't be missed." He talked of her as though she was just some piece of trash that he could dispose of without anyone being concerned. Crouse had simply said, "It was something that had to be done."

It was good to hear that Barone had a conscience and Crouse's arrogance truly bothered him. As the meeting ended, Jimmy told him that he and Duke would share his information with Adrienne Lynch and would be back to let him know her thoughts.

As they headed across the parking lot to their cruisers, Jimmy said he thought it was a positive meeting. "The information he talked about came without any prompting, and while a lot of it was about things we already knew, it's really important because it has never been in the public domain or the media reports.

"That," he told Duke, "is crucial in establishing Barone's veracity and legitimacy to a jury. Where you run into problems is when the guys give you stuff that anyone could have read about in the newspapers or seen on the news. Defense attorneys feast on those guys when they are on the stand because it looks like they are making stuff up to get a deal to get out of jail. It can really damage the prosecutions trial plan and take away from the momentum when you have to waste time on redirect trying to rehabilitate and correct their statements. But when inmates are testifying to things that only the defendant would know and they prove to be true, the defense runs into a brick wall.

"I told Adrienne we would head in to meet with her once we were done. I'm going to grab a sandwich on the way back in. Do you want anything?"

"I'm all set," Duke replied, and they both headed southbound back to the office.

· · · ·

"How did it go?" Adrienne asked to no one in particular as we walked into her office.

Jimmy shrugged his shoulders, "I'd say mostly good. He's a legit hard scrabble guy, but he knows what he's talking about, and he didn't learn it from us."

"You know he's testified for us before?" she asked.

"What? When?" I asked.

"Tell him," she said, looking over at Jimmy.

"I honestly don't know what you're talking about, Adrienne. Can you refresh my memory?" he answered as if he was on the witness stand and had forgotten an important point.

"Jimmy, it was your case! He was the guy who testified in the Jones case out of Ayer. The one where the defendant strangled his sixteen-year-old girlfriend with a freakin' bicycle chain and then wrapped her up in plastic bags, and he and his buddy dumped her in the woods in the middle of the winter. Don't you remember? They needed portable heaters to loosen up the earth before they could remove her, and then it took two days to thaw her out before they could do an autopsy."

"That's the guy?" Jimmy asked with a look of shock on his face. "Are you kidding me? I never met him. Steve Belanger got the call on that, and he handled the interview. I was never involved in that part of the investigation. Because they sequestered us during the trial, I never saw him testify. If I ever knew his name, I certainly forgot it. We'll talk to Steve about him. It was Johnny McEvoy's trial, so he can shed some light on him too."

"I'm new to this kind of process or decision-making about using inmates as witnesses," Duke said, "I can see the pros and the cons, pardon the pun. On the one hand, Barone brings a lot to the table. He comes across as believable, and we can document everything he says, including the time he spent upstairs lying in bed across from Crouse every night. But he has a good-sized record, and there is some violent crime on his BOP (board of probation record), so he's no saint. Correct me if I'm wrong, but we aren't going to find saints hiding out in purgatory. But I am interested in hearing how things worked out in that other case."

"Things worked out well," Jimmy recalled. "The jury convicted Jones, and Johnny McEvoy thought the testimony from the inmate was a critical factor. Jesus, I can't believe I didn't know it was Barone. He never mentioned anything about it today either."

"We have a lot to do to verify everything," Jimmy said to Adrienne, "I'll write our conversation up in a report for you, but I think his info is really important. Think about it. Right now, he is the only guy we got who can testify about Crouse admitting what he did to Kelly and how he disposed of her body. We spoke to Crouse several times, but he never told any of us that he did it. In a case built completely on circumstantial evidence, I think his statements are wicked important."

"It is definitely an important and positive development," Adrienne said, "and it's good he isn't trying to barter or hold us hostage for his testimony, which helps. Let's just see how things develop over the coming weeks. We don't have to make a decision now. I'll look into his pending cases and talk with Johnny. You write it up, and we'll just have to go from there."

• • • •

On the Wednesday following Memorial Day Weekend, Jimmy Connolly took a call from an investigator at the Billerica House of Correction who said he had spoken with Louie Barone earlier that morning about concerns regarding threats Barone received from another inmate about testifying against Crouse. Jimmy thought it best if he and Duke met with Barone in person later that afternoon, and the investigator agreed.

On the way to Billerica, Jimmy talked to Duke about why they had to go to Billerica in the first place.

"You remember how I said these kinds of situations sooner or later turn to crap? Well, this is exactly what I meant. Adrienne isn't sure she is going to have Barone testify, but we can't talk about that with him, and we have to uphold our end of the bargain by keeping him safe and out of harm's way. Meanwhile, he is getting threats to scare him into not testifying, and he is probably nervous as hell. We have to deal with that because it is a legit concern. I think we need him on board, but I also understand Adrienne's apprehension about using inmates as witnesses. Unfortunately, whether he testifies or doesn't, Adrienne had to turn our report and the information over to the defense, so Crouse already knows that Barone ratted him out."

When they got to the house of correction, the investigator met them at the door. They went through the usual process of signing in, showing their identification, and surrendering their weapons to the desk officer for security purposes. Once through "the trap" and inside, they walked through the maze of corridors and checkpoints before arriving at the Investigations Unit. Simultaneously, another corrections officer separated Barone from his unit and brought him to the interview room.

This meeting had a very different tone from the last time the three were together. Barone was clearly unnerved as he related a series of events that began the previous Friday and were still ongoing. He said more than one inmate was threatening him because Crouse had put the word out that he was going to testify against him in his murder trial. Barone was concerned for his physical safety, but he also didn't want to wind up in trouble for defending himself against the others if it came to that.

When asked who made the threats, he said that they all served time together in Cambridge and knew each other. Barone related that a guy named Jaime came to him on Friday and asked, "What's going on, Louie? We got this message from Tommy." Jaime told him Crouse said Barone was going to testify against him.

"Jesus Christ, that's a fucked up thing to do," Jaime said. He then told Barone he was "going to take care of things for Tommy" and he was "going to fuck him up" because he had to "take care of business."

Barone denied speaking to police and told the threatening inmate, "You have nothing with my name on it, but as far as I'm concerned Crouse is a murderer and a rapist and if the state police talk to me I probably will do something." He said Jaime continued with threatening comments for the rest of the night and said he was "going to get paperwork to prove it."

Barone said that after his conversation with Jaime, he told another inmate about the threats. That inmate, who he only knew as Mike G, had also been in Cambridge with them. He was not a sympathetic ear. He told Barone that one recent afternoon Crouse had been in a three-hour meeting with his attorney, and when he came back, 'he was mad as hell.' Mike G. said, 'Tommy just found out you were planning to testify against him. He knew I was heading to Billerica after my next court appearance and he asked me to speak to Jamie for him. Crouse thinks Jamie is his 'enforcer' and he wanted me to tell him to hammer you." According to Barone, Mike G. told him he was instructed to tell Jamie to 'take care of business in whatever way he wanted.' Mike G. also said that, Crouse told him to pass the word on to others and that the proof was in the paperwork and that would be forthcoming soon. Barone said Mike G. felt that hurting him was something they needed to do for Tommy.

Situations like this one present a host of issues and there is never a one-size-fits-all answer. Barone wanted Jimmy and Duke to know what was going on, but he wasn't overly concerned that he couldn't handle his own business. That is what real tough guys always say. The Billerica investigator assured him they would do all they could to protect him and if he wanted to be moved to another area, they would accommodate him. However, Barone knew that moving would not fix anything and in some ways would only secure in their minds that he was a rat and that the story would follow him wherever he went.

While there was no doubt in anyone's mind that the conversations took place, the question was whether Tommy's enforcer might follow up with the promised violence or was it just trash talk meant to intimidate him. Most viewed Crouse as a loudmouth knucklehead, and although they might like him, he wasn't someone another inmate would be willing to go to bat for and pick up additional criminal charges. The general idea was to get out of jail sooner than later and not do more time for getting into a fight defending someone else's business. Everyone agreed that for the time being Barone would stay where he was, but they all understood there might be a change in plans without notice.

When Jimmy and Duke returned to Cambridge, we all sat down with Adrienne. She listened with her usual calm, head-nodding manner before speaking.

"Look," she began, "we all knew this kind of thing could happen, but I think we, and I mean Barone too, will be alright. Here is what happened. I had to provide the information to his attorney that we had a witness from the jail. I filed for a protective order to prevent him from making copies of the report and sending them to Crouse in jail. We met with the judge last week and argued our positions. Baccari said that under the rules of discovery, his client had the right to have a copy of the report. I argued that he didn't because it was a security and safety issue and my motion request was an exception to the rule. Surprisingly, the judge took it one step further and told Baccari that while Crouse had a right to the information, he did not have a right to the written report. He told Baccari that he could read the report in the clerk's office and takes notes if he wanted, but he could not physically possess a copy."

Her words clarified how the information had gotten to Crouse. While not comforting, they explained the flow of information. We discussed how Barone should deal with the issue and decided it would probably be best for him to continue to deny that he would be a witness. First, Adrienne still wasn't convinced she would have him testify, and second, Crouse's claim that he would produce the paperwork wasn't going to happen. So any further discussion would be a he-said-he-said battle of words and Barone could argue, "Then show me the paperwork to back up what you are hearing," because he knew that would never happen.

The next morning, Duke arranged to speak by phone with Barone. Duke told Barone about what we had learned and discussed in our meeting with Adrienne. Barone said that at least for the moment things had calmed down he would stay put and, if needed, would use the show-me-the-paperwork argument.

CHAPTER 10

Trial Preparation

The difference between case preparation and trial preparation is relatively simple to understand. Case prep is the sum of the entire body of work from the investigative team. Trial prep is the domain of the prosecution team. Their mission is to sift through the voluminous collection of data to harvest the information and evidence they believe will best prove the charges against the defendant. Then they shape it all into a cohesive, refined, and persuasive production to present to a judge and jury.

Think of case preparation as the creation of the artist's palette and trial preparation as the work the artist creates from the palette. If you give the same set of facts and variables to ten attorneys and ask them to prepare a case for presentation to a jury, there would be multiple similarities in their finished products, but no two would be identical. Each would create a portrait in their own style based on their individual perceptions, experiences, trial-preparation styles, and beliefs. Each artist would also consider their final product a unique masterpiece. Beyond proving all of the elements of the crime, there is no one right way to proceed, but there is a long and regretful history of wrong ways on both sides of a trial.

• • • •

Mucko McDermott went to trial in April—several days of grueling, gruesome testimony about the homicides of his seven coworkers, were followed by days of medical expert testimony regarding his mental health leading up to and during the killing spree. The jury deliberated for sixteen hours over three days before convicting him of seven counts of first-degree murder. He was sentenced to serve seven consecutive life terms in a Massachusetts correctional facility. With that investigation and trial successfully behind us, and the summer months in front of us, there was an opportunity to take a few deep breaths before refocusing on the case of *Commonwealth vs Crouse*. Adrienne was well into her early prep and building her foundation for the trial.

She excelled at trial preparation. Her history and experience in homicide trials allowed her to foresee what the rest of us might not. She spotted the little issues or points that if unexplored or unanswered by us could explode in her face with a few pointed questions of a witness by a defense attorney.

Like the director of a Broadway play, her preparation and planning began with an immersion into a lengthy and convoluted script already created and written by others. She didn't stop reading and studying until she knew every scene and every line by heart. She couldn't change the facts, but she could arrange the presentation of the play in a way that she thought would be logical, understandable, and have the biggest impact on a jury.

After creating the scene structure, she designed and staged the background setting for each presentation. The actors who presented the dramatic information were our witnesses. They had already memorized their lines, because they had lived them. It was the best way for a jury to become engrossed in the story. Then she determined the best way to introduce and spotlight the main actors, allowing them to share their first-hand knowledge or expert opinions in a manner that brought out critical information. This, in turn, allowed the audience to absorb the depth and importance of their words and to understand the level of complicity the defendant played in the life and death of the victim. As she created her strategy, she built in a pace and a rhythm that captured the undivided attention of the jury, ending each act with the audience anxious for the next.

• • • •

As was often the case after a battle through Boston's Monday morning traffic, I arrived at the office on the wrong side of nine o'clock. There was no scheduled Monday morning staff meeting, so my tardiness did not concern me. It was the beginning of August, a few weeks away from opening statements in the Crouse trial. The case was clearly the number one item on the office agenda, but it wasn't the only one. There were a couple of other homicide cases in trial preparation phase, and the daily calls for sudden, unattended deaths and homicides didn't slow down to accommodate our schedule. In fact, in the heat of the summer, they were more likely to tick up just a bit. There is nothing like a few 90-degree days in a hot apartment to accelerate the decomposition process to alert a neighbor's discerning sense of smell that death was nearby and they needed the cops to come find the source and remove it.

Lana looked up as I walked in, and with a wry smile said, "Adrienne came over looking for you and wants you to give her a call as soon as you get in."

"Was she pissed that I wasn't here?" I asked.

"More like annoyed," she replied.

"What did she want?" I probed.

"Sorry, it isn't my day to ask the questions. Why don't you just give her a call? She had a couple of three-ring binders in her hand, so I'm guessing it's about the trial," she answered with a friendly smirk that I was more than used to by then.

With the trial date nearing and the framework for her presentation nearly complete, Adrienne was beginning to concentrate on the finer points and possible areas of contention from the defense. She was deep into the minutiae of each segment of the case. Her preparation was thorough but, at times, maddening to the investigators because it usually meant more interviews with folks they had already spoken to multiple times. While the questions often seemed meaningless, we knew she wanted or needed the answers to plug gaps or to open up other areas for questioning. We were all thoroughly committed to the case even though at times, when she scrutinized our earlier work to the nth degree, it was annoying. A little tension arose at times, but it quickly dissipated, and we did what she asked. To be honest, I was usually the first to redden and stiffen up because, selfishly, I don't like to feel that I am being second-guessed, nor do I enjoy being the middleman, delivering someone else's orders to the investigators.

I knew that after a weekend spent in the office alone, working without distraction, Adrienne would have a laundry list of questions and tasks that needed our attention. So, instead of picking up the phone, I headed to the cafeteria, picked up two large coffees, and made my way across the second-floor foyer and through the back entrance to the DAO and into her office.

When she is in pretrial mode, Adrienne's already cramped ten-by-sixteen-foot office resembles a hoarder's den. There were more than twenty cardboard boxes containing case files piled four high sitting a few feet behind her chair. A dozen or so three-inch black trial notebooks, crammed with information she would need to produce at trial, were already put together and lined up in an orderly and systematic way on a shelf within her arm's reach. She had used this method of preparation for years. Once seated at the prosecution table, information and evidence like police reports, witness statements, lab findings, and everything else she deemed important for that section of the trial needed to be at her fingertips. The trial wasn't the time to be fumbling through paper-work looking for critical information while the jurors daydreamed about their lives away from the courtroom. She needed to capture their undivided attention and keep it. Adding to her quagmire of paperwork were several small piles of appellate decisions and prewritten briefs, sorted and stacked on the floor like discrete land mines. She kept these nearby because they may come into play when arguing points of law and procedure, and she wanted to be able to immediately produce the ones that supported her position if or when they became an issue at trial.

There was a shelf above her desk crowded with thick treatises about the fire sciences, DNA, and forensic anthropology. These would be her bibles when dealing with the expert witnesses in our case. Adrienne was an attorney by trade, but in complex cases such as these, she needed more than a basic knowledge of the sciences to support her theories at trial. She needed not only to understand the science but the hypotheses behind it so she could ask smart, relevant questions of her experts to help inform and educate the jury. She also needed to prepare cross-examination questions to probe and discredit the opinions and testimony of the expert witnesses called by the defense.

The only part of her desk that she kept clear of paper was the area near the telephone that she always answered on the first ring, and the framed photos of her family members, which were there to keep her grounded.

"What, Adrienne?" I asked with a cautious smile as I put a cup of coffee onto a small landing strip in front of her. I sat gingerly, not wanting to cause an avalanche of paper.

"Good morning, Billy," she said in her usual soft-spoken tone. "I've been trying to put this case into some semblance of order, and while I'm making a lot of progress, I still have a ways to go before I'm comfortable with it. I'm getting just a little nervous because we are only a few weeks away from picking a jury. The guys have been good about writing follow-up and supplemental reports from the steps in the investigation they took a year ago. I need them done so we could argue motions and satisfy the discovery orders from the Court. I still need to prep a few witnesses for their trial testimony, and I know that is going to cause us to speak to more people and write additional reports. I realize the guys are busy with other things, but we are approaching crunch time, and I think that as much as we can, we need to make this case their top priority.

"Ann Foley is doing great work staying in touch with the Hancock family, while also dealing with many of our other witnesses. I have scheduled some of them to come in for reinterviews over the next week or so. A couple may need transportation, and a few sound a bit reticent to testify.

We need to sit them down and not only go over their testimony but get them to understand the importance of their assistance in the prosecution of Crouse. They gave the information to us willingly to help us build the case against him, now we need them to testify for the same reasons they were willing to be cooperative in the first place. We also still need to locate some of Kelly's friends, many of whom were no longer in the Malden area. This guy needs to go to jail for the rest of his life. I don't have to tell you that this isn't the time for this case to start to develop holes in the fabric. There is just too much at stake.

"I am waiting to hear back from the judge on some of the trial motions that were filed. Until I see those findings, it is hard to be precise about how I am going to present the case and line up my witnesses, but I have put together a general game plan. I'm confident that Marguerite and Nat's well researched and written briefs will result in rulings in our favor. I think you know I filed my statement of the case with the Court back on June 27. I have a copy here for you. That pretty much lays out the facts I have to present and prove to the jury."

"Don't worry, Adrienne, I will set a fire under everyone and get us into trial mode," I answered. "Where are you seeing weaknesses or potential holes in the case? It will make it easier for me to explain to the guys why you are looking into certain areas and where and why you may have concerns."

"Look," she said, "I certainly don't want anyone thinking we have a weak case or that they haven't done incredible work to bring us to this point. Everyone has been great, and the team is the best I have ever worked with. It's just that we are so close to the start of the trial I don't want to let up or get complacent and miss something or not pay attention to what the defense is doing in preparing their case. I'm concerned that the defense team's investigator could find a new witness or twists the words or thoughts of one of our witnesses and compromise their testimony. I don't want them to give even one juror the opportunity to find reasonable doubt in this case."

I reassured Adrienne we were all of the same mindset and that she could count on us to do whatever she needed for the case, and I stood to leave.

"Billy, this is probably the one case that we will all be talking about long after we retire. The way it all came together is remarkable. In fact, it is so unbelievable that it is almost impossible to believe that it is true. As we always say, 'You just can't make this stuff up.' Seriously, these facts could be the story line for a great book. I believe we have a strong case, but we built it on lots and lots of circumstantial evidence, and we have to be able to show the jury all of the pieces of the puzzle. And we have to connect those pieces so that when I make my closing argument the jurors see a masterpiece and not a confusing puzzle with a couple of pieces missing. I mean we don't have any eyewitnesses, or a confession, or a weapon, and Kelly's remains are just a skeleton, so the pictures we will be showing them don't even resemble a human being. It's going to be a tough road for us, but I'm confident we will meet our burden of proof—as long as we don't drop the ball."

As I stepped from Adrienne's office and headed back to mine, the significance of her words and the passion in her voice made it very clear to me that it was time for all of us to elevate our game. We needed to concentrate with laser precision on the case that we had all worked harder to solve than any other case in our careers. I also knew that when I told my people about my meeting with Adrienne, selling this to the rest of the team wouldn't be a problem.

CHAPTER 11

Adrienne's Game Plan

Late on a beautiful, sunny afternoon during the last week of August, I was packing up to head out of the office for the day. My plan for the evening was to stop for nine holes of golf and when I got home, sit on the back deck with a Sam Adams or two and toss a couple of cheeseburgers on the grille. Adrienne had other thoughts, and in the blink of an eye, so did I.

I can usually hear the echo of her shoes scuffling along the cement floor as she crosses from her side of the hallway to ours, but my thoughts had already shifted away to the first tee box and whether to hit driver or three iron. I never heard her come through the front door. "Hi Billy," she said as she poked her head into my space, "Do you have a minute?" My head shot up from what I was doing, "Not really," I thought to myself as I smiled and said, "For you Adrienne, I have all the time in the world."

"Are the other guys around?" she asked, obviously referring to the Hancock team.

"No, Jimmy worked an overnight construction detail on the Pike, and I think he has another one tonight, so he took a few hours vacation and went home early to sleep. Eddie and Duke are together with Johnny Rivers and they are running around trying to serve the rest of the subpoenas to our witnesses. We are almost there, but there is still a handful left. No one has outright balked or seemed surprised they have to testify, but that doesn't mean they are happy about it. More about nerves and the fear of the unknown than an unwillingness though. What can I do for you?" I asked with some hesitancy.

"Have you got time to go over our working game plan for the trial?" she asked, "Nat and I have been weaving together a schedule of witnesses and evidence presentation that we hope will keep the jurors absorbed and engaged throughout the trial. We think we are almost there, but I want to share our thoughts and reasoning with you guys, and get your input as well. By last count, we have almost sixty witnesses and depending on how long it takes to get a jury, the trial could last up to three weeks, and maybe a few days longer depending on the defense strategy.

"We are going to need a lot of help from you guys and Anne Foley to keep the herd together and get people in and out of the courthouse and on time each day. Judge Grabau is not a fan of us running out of witnesses. He demands full days of testimony unless there is a pre-agreed upon plan for a shortened day.

"Even with a structure in place, we need to stay flexible with our timing and our line-up, particularly with our experts. I've already heard from a couple of them about limited availability and scheduling is going to be a problem because of their other professional commitments. At least one is already slated to testify in another trial out-of-state. I'm confident I can get everyone's testimony and all of the evidence in, but I really worry about breaking or disrupting the continuity and flow because witnesses won't be appearing in the exact order I'd like. It is entirely possible the doctors from Maine and New Hampshire will be explaining the cause and manner of death to the jury before they know that we found Kelly's remains. I'll just have to deal with it."

My thoughts of golf on this night quickly evaporated. "Sit down Adrienne, and let's talk about your working blueprint." We slid in to the worn-out cloth chairs on opposite sides of my desk and she continued.

"I've met with all of our experts and I am really pleased with what they have to add and how their testimony is going to strengthen our case. I'll tell ya, the fire science expert that Paul Horgan sent me blew me away. He's a local guy with a national reputation. He is not only brilliant, but knows how to relate to a jury. He breaks his work product down so anyone can understand the points he is making and more importantly, the steps he took to reach a conclusion and render an expert opinion. When Paul was talking to him about the case, he told him this is a criminal matter about the murder of a fourteen-year-old girl and not a civil case about a fire where both sides are arguing over a bundle of insurance money. He was appalled and intrigued, and offered to help in any way he could. Seriously, he is all but doing the case gratis, which helps because we don't have the money in our budget for an expert of his caliber."

"By the way," she continued, "I hope no one got bent out of shape thinking I was excluding them from those interviews. It's just that when experts start talking about their training and experience and why they are qualified to render an expert opinion and then launch into what they did and how they reached their professional opinions, it can get highly technical and blurry. I think it's best if I do those one on one and not have other people asking questions because that interrupts my learning process and makes it more confusing for me. I need to have them educate me to their science so I can understand where they are coming from and explore the areas that I need to read up on to be better prepared. They often get lost in the scientific weeds and I need to pull them out and untangle their information so it is understandable to me so in turn I can present it in a way the jury can understand. You've been there a dozen times, so I know you understand. I just hope all of the other guys do as well."

She was doing fine, and I wasn't about to interrupt.

"In a circumstantial case like this one, I can't leave anything hanging or unexplored for the defense counsel to exploit. I need to get all of their information into the record or I look unprepared, and if the jurors see gaps in my presentation that can open the door for reasonable doubt. I've learned through the years that the best way to avoid that is to have the experts work with me to develop a list of questions they want me to ask to keep them on point. If I go off script and ask them about something they aren't prepared to hear, they can get tongue-twisted and confused and their credibility takes a hit. They have all testified many times and know their stuff, but if I don't ask the right questions, they can't just blurt out unsolicited answers. They need me to crack open the door for them so they can expand and explain themselves."

"Honestly," I remarked with a smile, "No one is ever concerned when you are preparing for trial and don't include us in your visits to the lab or the OCME. We know what you are trying to accomplish and we don't need to know what you need to know. We are happiest when you leave us out of those conversations. It gives us the time to do the other things like chase down possible new witnesses and re-interview others, as we get ready for trial. Like you, we want to build as close to an ironclad case as we can. We don't want any surprises coming from the witness stand.

"Adrienne," I asked, "when you were growing up were you like the school Brainiac that won the Science Fair and was the Captain of the Debating Team?"

"Huh?" she answered with a squint in her eyes, "Where the hell did that question come from? I'd expect that one from Eddie Forster, but not you. The simple answer is no, but I guess I did well enough to get into Boston College. I always wanted to be a lawyer like my Dad. I never thought of being a scientist or a CPA when I grew up, so I did what I needed to do to meet my goals, and not a whole lot more. But, you know how competitive I am, so I never really let myself suck at anything when it came to my schoolwork. I will say that over the past few years I have become fascinated with the forensic sciences. Partly because I have to know the stuff, but also, I really enjoy learning the science, so I do read a lot of books and articles about things like DNA and Forensic Anthropology. Why did you ask me that?"

"Because," I answered, "I sucked then and will continue to suck in science and technology for the rest of my life. I went to law school to study and learn about the law and not the sciences. Today, we have the constantly evolving forensic science advances in areas like DNA, blood spatter, and fingerprint enhancements and if a criminal trial lawyer doesn't understand them and stay up to the minute with court decisions, they will get buried at trial. You can add cellphones and computers and the technology behind them to the list of areas ripe for new forensic exploration. The internet and social media can be of great help to us, but only if we know what we are looking for and where to find it. Trials are getting increasingly more technical and complex and jurors now have heightened expectations of us because of fictional television shows like CSI. Traditional lawyering has become a thing of the past.

"In our case, the forensic anthropologist and the Medical Examiner are going to be crucial to explaining the cause and manner of Kelly's death based on her skeletal remains. It's going to be your job to get the jury to buy into what they are saying and without any reasonable doubt. Seriously, I'll bet if you were to poll the jurors on the first day of trial and ask them what forensic anthropologists or pathologists do, maybe one or two of them would get it right. I admire the hell out of you, but I don't envy you." She just smiled and shrugged her shoulders again.

"All right," she began, "let me lay out our working plan. I can come back later and explain it to everyone else or you can take care of that. Just let me know and I'll make myself available."

"Let me use an analogy by comparing a courtroom trial to a Broadway play. As the Director, I will compartmentalize the facts and present them in stages like the acts in a play. Our witnesses are the actors who will narrate the story for us and present the information to the audience or jury. I will follow the timeline as close as possible to reduce any confusion for the jurors. The drama and anticipation will build naturally, day by day. Pacing is important too, because I don't want to put all the drama up front or at the end. I'll start with some eye-opening information that gets their attention and hooks them from the beginning. Towards the end of the trial, I'll come in with the heavier scientific stuff and then wind it down with some emotional witnesses who talk about their relationship with Kelly. As best I can, I will intersperse the experts where they'll have the most impact.

"Once we have a jury, we'll begin with the usual road trip to visit the crime scenes in Malden and New Hampshire before we make our opening arguments, The Malden firefighters who were first on the fire scene will be the first to testify. They'll explain why they thought it was an Arson, and, in a not-so-subtle way, let the jurors know that at the time of the fire the building was full of sleeping residents forced to hurriedly evacuate while still in their nightclothes. I'm going to have them describe what they saw, heard, smelt, felt and found after they arrived and entered the room. Their recollections should have the jurors sitting up straight and focused."

"Then I'll backtrack to a few minutes before the fire was discovered and bring on the guy from the gas station to acknowledge Crouse as a customer and authenticate the store's videotapes. The woman from the taxi company will testify that she knows Crouse and saw his truck leave the parking lot minutes before the fire engines showed up. The people who live in the condo complex and saw Crouse coming and going before the fire that morning will round out that block of testimony. I'm not sure who I will use yet, but I need someone to describe the function room and the good condition it was in prior to the fire and following the birthday party that happened there on the Saturday night before the fire."

She continued, "Once that scene is set, I will call Lester Morovitz to discuss his phone calls with Crouse that morning and how he provided the information that led you to the Fournier's house in New Hampshire. I'm bringing in the Fournier's to testify about their conversations with our guys that night, but I'm not sure if I'm going to use them both or not.

"With that part done, I'll get a bit technical when I put the mobile phone folks from Massachusetts and New Hampshire on the stand to explain how cell towers work and how the phone companies record all of the hits to the towers from cell users. Then I'll have them explain how they pinpointed Crouse's phone and produced a record of all of the telephone calls for the day before, the day of and the day after Kelly was murdered. I'm going to follow them with the two women from NESPIN to explain how they utilized a software program to pinpoint and tie together everyone that Crouse spoke to, as well as when and where he was when he spoke with them. They have some fantastic demonstrative graphs and charts to show the jury. One shows the ridiculous amount of calls Crouse made and received during those days and the other ties his phone to those of other people that will testify to their meetings or conversations they had with Crouse. The visual effect should really hit home with the jurors. Talk about a picture being worth a thousand words."

Adrienne took a deep breath and continued, "This might be where my game plan goes a little sideways. I am trying to plot out each day and the next group of witnesses I want to bring in are the folks Crouse was friendly with at Malden Mills and the Eagles Club. Looking at the daily schedule though, that might conflict with the timing of putting Doctors Andrews and Sorg on the stand. They will be traveling together and their available time is limited. I may have to start a day off with them and then put on the condo people.

"I have to improvise and make sure the judge and defense counsel understand and allow me to take them out of order. It happens all the time and shouldn't be a problem; it just screws up my flow. The same is going to be true with the two dentists. I will have to start a day with them so they can get in and out and return to their practices. I don't like that it puts the horse before the cart because I'm having the body identified and the cause and manner of death determined before the New Hampshire Troopers will testify about finding Kelly's remains in Hooksset. I don't really have a choice. I gotta deal with the hand I'm dealt.

"I'm almost done," she said, "hang with me for a few more moments. The next package of witnesses will be lab people from both Massachusetts, New Hampshire and Maine to testify about what they recovered at both scenes and how they extracted and packaged the DNA evidence and sent it to BODE Labs for testing, comparisons and results. Then Kenny Martin can talk about and explain the blood spattering on the floor and walls of the Function Room and offer his expert opinion on how he used that information to recreate the scene of the fight and the stabbing."

"All of the New Hampshire Troopers want to come down together, so I'll start off a day with them and run right through all of the information about the discovery and unearthing of the remains. I'm not sure what day that is going to be, but I want it towards the end for the most impact. Not that I think any of the jurors will ever forget what they are going to hear and see, but the closer to my wrapping up the case, the better.

"I'm struggling a bit with the right places to get in both the social worker that Kelly ran from the day she was killed, and Crouse's probation officer who tells about his erratic behavior and some of his comments to her around the time of the murder. But, it's a little complicated because of privacy issues and their government positions, so I need the court's permission to put them on the stand. I filed the motion and don't have a response yet, but judges generally allow it if I show a need for their testimony.

"I need to get Tracy Heffernan in as well because she was the last person we know that saw Kelly alive and I could also bring in how well she knew her because her son had dated Kelly. As far as character witnesses to talk about Kelly, the court usually limits me to use a friend and a family member. Judges understand why we want character witnesses, but they draw the line at one of each testifying. For the family witness I haven't decided yet between Mark and his wife. Mark is the logical choice, but I need to see how he reacts to the evidence during the trial before I make a final decision. His criminal past doesn't help him, but he is honest and straightforward about his relationship with his daughter and I think it is important for the jury to hear and recognize that he may be imperfect, but his love for his child is unquestionable.

I'm still trying to figure out if I'm going to put Crouse's jailhouse buddy, Barone, on the stand or not. His information is important and damaging, but he carries a boatload of baggage including a few Restraining Orders. I realize you don't find swans in the sewer, but I really need to figure out if the beating his credibility can take from defense counsel outweighs the value of his information.

"Overall I think we have a great case to put before a jury." Then she laughed, "I mean with the exception of no murder weapon, no eyewitnesses and no confession we have it all. I do like circumstantial cases though because they make you work harder and you have to be incredibly thorough or you will let reasonable doubt quietly sneak in and put cracks in the foundation and everything could come crumbling down."

Sam Hancock and 3 others.

Kelly and her siblings Tom, Lisa, Samantha, and Taylor
Christmas 1995

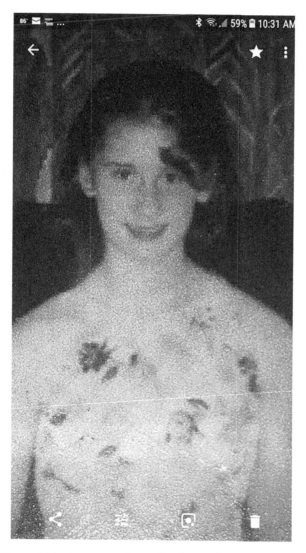

Kelly at 12 in her new dress for her 6th grade dance

Kelly and her little sister Lisa before Kelly went to her 6th grade dance. Kelly is holding flowers from her father.

Collage of photos made by Kelly's family to display for the unveiling ceremony of Kelly's Rock in the Peace Garden

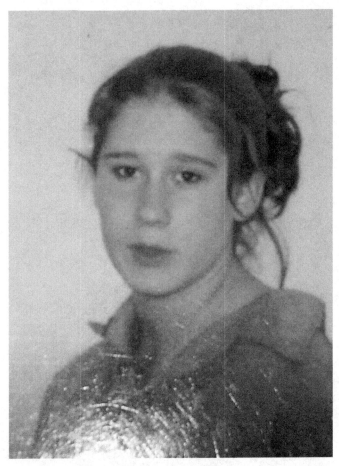

Kelly at age 14, taken shortly before her death

Kelly's Rock at the Peace Garden in Boston

Kelly's Gravesite with roses from her family, Walpole, MA

Kelly's sister, Lisa Hancock, with her parents
at her engagement party.

Thank you, Lisa, for generously sharing your photos.

CHAPTER 12

The Trial: Days One and Two Impaneling the Jury

Long before sunrise on the second Monday of September, a deputy sheriff made his early morning rounds and clanged on the steel bars of Tommy Crouse's jail cell, ordering him to wake up and get ready for the important day ahead. The jailer's call always comes early on a day when an inmate has a scheduled court appearance.

It was their responsibility to get him up and ready for travel to the courtroom on time. It was Crouse's responsibility to get up, shower, shave, eat breakfast, and get dressed and ready for his day in court. Today wasn't just any court appearance, it was the first day of his murder trial, and he needed to be alert and on his game. No drab gray prison attire or unshaven face, he would be all scrubbed up and decked out in his Sunday best, with shirt and tie and the shiny shoes that his mother had delivered to the jail for him. Jury selection would be the first order of business, and Tommy had to appear engaged and on his best behavior. He knew there was never a second chance to make a good first impression. He also knew that some of the evidence, testimony, and allegations against him would be brutal and he could hardly hope for sympathy, but if his positive courtroom demeanor could convince a couple of jurors to consider a conviction on a lesser charge with a sentence short of life in prison then he could deem that a small victory. He had been down this road before in his trial for aggravated rape, and he knew—and his attorney reinforced—this was not the time for him to act or appear to be aggressive or disagreeable.

Shortly after eight o'clock, a deputy sheriff came for him. He patted Tommy down for weapons and contraband and escorted him to the holding area where court officers were waiting. They shackled his hands and fect, signed him out, and loaded him onto the elevator for the quick seven-story drop from the jail to the holding cell, outside of Courtroom 10B. During the trial, the guards would remove the hand and foot cuffs while he was in the courtroom and in the jurors' and the public eye. The conventional wisdom of trial judges is that removing the cuffs eliminates claims of prejudgment of the defendant because he was already in custody and, therefore, must be guilty. Although the favored method, it is not etched in stone. The judge always has discretion to make changes based on the situation and environment. Any outburst or signs of behavioral concern exhibited by a defendant can quickly result in a loss of that privilege and a swift return to the restraints.

• • • •

The potential jurors began arriving at the courthouse by eight thirty and, after passing through the security checkpoint, shuffled toward the elevators where signage directed them to the floor and room number for jury service. Once inside the restricted juror's area, a team of court officers would guide them throughout the day. After presenting their identification and signing in, each received a file card with two numbers written on it. The first number designated their panel and the second their placement on the panel. There were ten panels each with ten people. The numbers were their temporary identification card. From that point on, court personnel would refer to them by their numbers and not by their names.

The one hundred adults in the pool of jurors, known in legal terms as the venire, were a blend of ages, ethnicities, religious leanings, social strata, political persuasions, and sexual orientations. A computer had randomly selected their names from files that contained lists of eligible jurors submitted annually by each of the fifty-four communities that make up Middlesex County. For each day the courts were in session, the computer compiled a new list. The rules governing jury selection is often referred to as "one and done," meaning that unless you are selected for a trial that day your service is complete. If selected, you remained locked in until the conclusion of the trial.

Prior to their arrival that morning, each had filled out and mailed back a questionnaire providing information about their personal and professional lives. The survey inquired about any involvement by them or family members in prior legal proceedings, a few questions regarding their spouse's education and employment, and their education, employment, marital, and parental status. The last segment of the survey included questions to help in determining whether anything in their overall history might affect their ability to serve as a fair and impartial juror. Both legal teams already had copies of their summarized answers, so they could look for openings or answers that would guide them in both the initial questioning phase and the selection of those that were determined by the judge to be "indifferent."

The hundred members of the jury pool filed into Courtroom 10B and took the seats on the back rows of solid wooden benches normally reserved for trial spectators. Moments later, a court officer bellowed, "All rise!" and they stood in unison as the door from the judge's chamber to the courtroom opened and Judge Grabau strode in, took the step up to his desk, and told everyone to be seated.

He had been a superior court judge for sixteen previous years and had presided over dozens of homicide trials. His reputation was of neither a prosecution- nor defense-leaning judge. He was even-tempered, fair to a fault, qualified, and competent with a keen knowledge of statute and case law, the rules of evidence, and the Massachusetts rules of the court. He was an excellent choice to preside over the trial.

Dressed in his usual conservative business suit and tie and enveloped in the customary black judicial robe, he stood to the side of his desk and chair, which was perched on an elevated platform located dead center and against the front wall of the courtroom. The positioning not only gave him the best observation point, but it also left no doubt to anyone in the courtroom that he was at the helm and directing the proceedings. The court clerk's work area was in front of and below the judge's desk. The prosecution team sat at an eight-foot-long table approximately ten feet in front of the judge and to his immediate right. The defense team and Tommy Crouse sat at a similar table a few feet away from the prosecution and to the judge's left side. During the trial and the voir dire process those offering testimony would sit to the immediate left of the judge. Once the final jury selection was complete, those selected would sit in two rows against the left wall and facing inward, giving them an unobstructed view of the witnesses, the lawyers, and the judge.

The clerk of court opened the day's events with the words, "Your Honor, the next matter is Commonwealth versus Thomas Crouse, Docket Number 2001–733. The defendant is present in the courtroom."

The judge introduced himself and slipped into his standard introductory remarks, explaining the jury selection process to everyone. Then he asked the attorneys representing both sides to face the pool of jurors and introduce themselves. Moving forward, he read from an abbreviated version of the "statement of the case" and followed with a recital of the names of the more than ninety prospective witnesses. He ended the segment by asking the eleven questions that the attorneys agreed were necessary to assist them in the selection and shaping of the final jury.

Once his remarks concluded, the guards escorted them back to the juror's room where they waited until called back for their personal interviews.

Individual voir dires are conducted in identical fashion with the same probing questions asked of each potential juror. The inquiries focused on their personal backgrounds and if they believed that they could be fair, and impartial in deciding the case. Additionally, the attorneys asked those who raised their hands earlier in response to one or more of the eleven questions to define or refine the reasons for their answers. The judge allowed deeper inquiries when there was a need to clarify an answer or two.

Some answered that they were biased, or unprepared, or unfit to serve for a multitude of reasons. Others referenced prior negative dealings with the court system, or that they had children the same age as the decedent or that they worked with at-risk students like the decedent and would most likely favor the prosecution. Several either recognized a name or two on the witness list or said they had family members or friends who were police officers or firefighters and that would affect their impartiality. The judge removed them all "for cause."

A segment of the questioning focused on the credibility of witness testimony, primarily if they would tend to give greater weight to the testimony of a police officer versus that of a civilian witness. Eleven answered they would believe the police officer over a civilian. The judge dismissed them as well.

Because the prosecution would present testimony regarding the possible sexual assault of the victim prior to her death, Judge Grabau incorporated an area of questioning as the fourth topic for discussion. In search of any possible unfairness, he asked, "Have you, or any members of your family, or a close friend, been accused of, a witness to, or the victim of a crime of a sexual nature and, in particular, child abuse?" A handful stated they could have a bias based on prior situations that involved family members. He excused those people from the jury pool.

Another area for consideration related to whether or not viewing of photographs of the skeletal remains of Kelly Hancock, might cause the juror trouble making a fair decision in the case based on seeing the photos. Judge Grabau stated, "In this case, it is expected there will be testimony and photographs depicting the remains recovered in Hookset, NH, allegedly identified to be the remains of a fourteen-year-old named Kelly Hancock. Some of the photographs and testimony may be of a graphic, disturbing nature concerning the conditions of the remains. Recognizing that this might be unpleasant and unsettling, would you still be able to listen to the testimony and look at the evidence to render a fair decision in this case?"

Three responded they believed the photographs would create a bias against the defendant, so they were released. Before the judge made a final decision to keep or remove the juror from the candidate pool, he asked each person if he or she had any personal reasons or hardships that would prevent them from serving. A small avalanche of responses came forth ranging from college, medical, and law school students who had just begun their classes for the year, to self-employed tradesmen who would be unable to work or earn a wage while serving on a jury. There were single parents with childcare issues, as well as those who were the sole or necessary caregivers for children and elderly family members. A few had advanced medical conditions with doctor's notes indicating that they required constant treatment. With limited exception, the judge excused them all for cause.

Once the inquiry was complete, Judge Grabau determined if the person was indifferent. If yes, they remained in the pool, if no, he removed them for cause and dismissed them.

The first day of the hearing ended at four o'clock. The thirteen people remaining in the pool received instructions to return on the following morning at nine.

On Tuesday, a new group of one hundred jurors supplemented the Monday venire and was available for questioning. Once the returning thirteen from the first pool finished questioning Judge Grabau began the process all over again with opening remarks, a statement of the case, and the reading of the witness list. After almost two full days of the voir dire process, only forty-seven of the two-hundred potential jurors questioned were determined to be indifferent.

The final and quickest phase of the selection process was for the prosecution and defense to use their peremptory challenges to eliminate prospective jurors without having to provide a supporting rationale. Armed with the personal questionnaires and their notes regarding comments made during the questioning phase, both sides used the opportunity to add or remove those they thought might or might not be favorable to their presentations. The overall procedure was similar to a chess match or a Major League draft. It was an inexact science and process to be sure, with both sides relying on their collective trial and jury experience to pick jurors they believed were knowledgeable, fair-minded, and in the end, who would be favorable to the presentation of their case. In less than half an hour, the final number of jurors reduced in number from forty-seven to sixteen. It had been a thorough, tedious, and exhausting vetting procedure, but at the end of the second day, sixteen fair and impartial jurors had been selected and seated.

Judge Grabau addressed the new jurors as a group and briefly told them to return on Wednesday morning at nine o'clock, when he would swear them in and then board a bus to view the crime scenes and other pertinent areas in Massachusetts and New Hampshire.

CHAPTER 13

The Trial: Day Three
The View

As I left the house that Wednesday morning, my thoughts were simple and focused on the beginning of the trial. Most of the events scheduled for the day were routine and repeated several times a month as jury trials came and went. The tasks were completely out of the control and responsibility of my office, but I still prayed that nothing new or disruptive had happened overnight. Even a small hiccup could throw the whole day off and create a cascading effect on the rest of the trial schedule. I just wanted to know that by nine o'clock Tommy Crouse would be sitting in the holding cell, the sixteen jurors would be standing by in the jury room, and the judge and legal counsel would be present and ready. Most of all, I wanted to know that the bus for the view would be idling outside the rear entrance of the courthouse stacked with box lunches and drinks for the jury and the court personnel. The only firm assignment for my staff was to provide security and lead the bus for the trip. Two cruisers: one to guide the bus and blue-light it through heavy traffic to the crime scene in Malden and the burial spot in Hooksett, NH, and the other as a "follow car" at the rear of the bus as an added layer of security. We knew to stay out of sight and refrain from talking to any of the jurors.

As I headed through Boston on the expressway, the eight o'clock news was just beginning on WBZ Radio when, out of the corner of my eye, I spotted a 747 aircraft rising slowly and majestically from Logan Airport. I lost sight of it for a moment as it passed behind some of Boston's largest buildings before reappearing and banking ever so deliberately to the left as it headed south toward New York City and beyond.

It was the same as every morning. Flights departed from Logan hundreds of times each day, and while we noticed, like so many other things we see on a daily basis, we generally ignored them. However, as much as I wanted it to be like every other day, it couldn't be. It was September 11, 2002, the first anniversary of the terrorist attacks on New York City, the Pentagon, and an open field in Shanksville, PA. The two flights that struck the World Trade Center had left Boston's Logan Airport less than an hour earlier, and right around this time.

The sight of the plane was like a lance, ripping into the then-dormant memories I had wrapped up and packed away months before. The Department of State Police, including all of the officers from my unit, played significant roles in the early stages of the investigation and in the weeks that followed. Before the towers had collapsed that morning, we were already at the airport paired up and working together with special agents from the FBI's Boston office. Together we conducted more than a hundred interviews, followed at least as many leads, and by days end had identified all of the terrorists who had left on the flights from Boston. We recovered a treasure trove of evidence and information, including the vehicle they arrived in, the luggage they left behind, and the messy hotel rooms in nearby Newton and Portland, ME, where they had finalized their plans before leaving on their death march earlier that morning.

We valued the importance of our work, and the feeling of accomplishment was certainly a moment of pride for all of us, but the devastation and loss of almost three thousand lives, including hundreds of Massachusetts residents, overshadowed, and suppressed any sense of achievement or triumph.

As I parked and walked from my cruiser to the courthouse, I crammed all those awful life-altering memories back into their crate and again buried them in the far back of my memory closet. There was work that needed doing, and it was in real time. Those memories and the emotions they evoke will never go away, but I just wasn't in a position to deal with them that day.

The good news to start the court day was all systems were still green-lighted, and everyone and everything was where they were supposed to be. The weather report wasn't great but 80 degrees and overcast with a slight breeze was fine; there was no need for rain gear or sunscreen but maybe a few cans of bug spray for the wooded area in New Hampshire.

The newly formed crew of jurors arrived on schedule and reported to the tenth-floor jury room where the court officers who would be their guides and security throughout the trial greeted them. Fifteen entered the room and tried to get comfortable and establish some personal space.

The sixteenth juror didn't enter the room but approached one of the court officers and told him she needed to speak to the judge because of a concern that she needed to address before he swore in the jury and began the trial.

Aside from asking her name for the check-in roster, the officer asked no questions and immediately took her to Judge Grabau's chambers, where the two met privately and she explained her predicament. She told him that she had been doing some serious soul-searching since her selection on Tuesday afternoon, and her conscience brought her to the realization and conclusion that she could not be an indifferent or unbiased juror. She was visibly upset, and the judge probed a bit to learn what had evoked such a strong visceral reaction. She explained that a year ago a schoolmate of hers had been raped, strangled, and murdered. She went on to say that overnight, thoughts and memories of those events had come flooding back, and she knew it would be impossible for her to set them aside and view the evidence and deliberate on the guilt or innocence of the defendant in a clear and fair-minded manner. The judge told her he appreciated her coming forward and for her honesty and was inclined to excuse her from the jury, but before he could do that, she would have to repeat what she had told him on the record and in open court.

A few minutes later, they were in Courtroom 10B with the trial lawyers, Crouse, the clerk, and court reporter present but without the other jurors. The bailiff swore her in, and she repeated her concerns and the reasons for them. The attorneys had no comments or questions and Judge Grabau, with limited comment, dismissed her from the jury. The trial would proceed with fifteen jurors seated in the box. Her assigned seat would remain empty.

If there was ever any question or doubt as to why a murder trial begins with sixteen jurors as opposed to twelve, the answer was evident before the presentation of any evidence. The swearing in was minutes away and already there was one less. There is always the possibility of personal or family illness or death, or other hardships and intrigue that might require the removal of a juror. If there were no alternates and the number of available jurors slipped below twelve there would be just cause for a mistrial and the trial process would have to begin all over again.

Moments after she exited the courtroom, the guards led the remaining panel members into the court and to their seats. Judge Grabau entered seconds later. He asked them to remain standing while the Court observed a minute of silence in memory of all those who lost their lives in the terrorist attacks on 9/11. All heads bowed out of respect.

The next voice they heard was that of the clerk of the court, who asked them to remain standing and to raise their right hands and repeat the juror's oath after him. He told the defendant to stand as well. He read aloud from the sheet of criminal charges against Crouse for arson and murder in the first degree. He ended by turning to the jurors and saying, "To these indictments, members of the jury, the defendant has pleaded that he is not guilty, and for trial therefore has placed himself upon the country, which country you are." He continued, "You are now sworn to try the issue. If he is guilty, you will say so; if he is not guilty, you will say so and no more."

The trial was technically and officially open. Judge Grabau took several moments to speak with the jury. He made quick work of explaining that he found it necessary to excuse one of their number due to an emergency. He talked about the solemn oath they had just taken to be fair and impartial and that he expected they would follow their oath. He spoke about their roles and responsibilities as jurors.

"Your function in this case," he said, "is to listen carefully to all of the evidence, observe the witnesses—observe their demeanor while they testify. You are the finders of fact in this case. You are the judges of the facts. You decide credibility. You can believe everything a witness says, or you can disregard, or disbelieve everything a witness has testified to, or in the alternative, you may find that parts of the testimony are more credible than other parts of that individual's testimony. So, you are the fact finders, and you'll also be determining credibility in this case."

He went on to explain his role as both facilitator and referee on points of criminal law, criminal procedure, and the rules of evidence. He talked about the necessity of sidebar conferences, described what they were, and explained why the jurors would not be privy to the discussions. He moved on to the roles of the prosecution and the defense during the trial and a little about evidence. He told them how it is ultimately his decision whether or not to allow information to be included as testimony but what, if any, weight or relevance it deserved was completely up to them to decide.

Unlike most cases, this one would have several witnesses providing expert testimony. He went on to explain why it is necessary for the Court to allow the experts to testify. "Expert witnesses are individuals who by reason of their training, study, or profession in a particular field are permitted to express an opinion." He followed by saying, "Expert witnesses are called because you and I don't have sufficient knowledge in a particular area to understand certain types of matters whatever the subject matter; we aren't trained in those fields. These individuals are called to testify, but ultimately, it's for you to decide what weight or value you put onto their testimony."

He told the jurors how important their personal observations would be of the witness's frankness, the basis of their opinions, and whether or not they felt that the expert witness seemed to have enough training or knowledge to make their statements, and finally, did they appear biased or impartial toward one side or the other.

He also spoke of "limiting instructions," which allow certain information to be brought into evidence but only for a specific, limiting purpose. Although he couldn't mention it at this point, this instruction would make more sense later in the case when he would admit evidence of an alleged sexual assault even though a sexual assault offense was not one of the charges levied against Crouse.

Judge Grabau wrapped up his comments by diverting from legal issues to statements on the unfortunate, decrepit condition of the thirty-year-old courthouse and the fact that everything in it was past its useful life. He spoke of the poor air quality and that the chillers responsible for controlling the temperature "were shot." The temperature in the courtroom was approximately 80 degrees, and it wasn't likely it would get any cooler for the duration of the trial.

Adrienne and John Baccari briefly spoke with the jurors and explained what lay ahead on the bus trip. They each talked for a few minutes about the purpose of the bus ride and the stops along the way and what they could and couldn't expect during the viewings. They explained that they would point out and comment on numerous places, views, and items that did not seem important at the time. However, they were all relevant to the case and asked them to imbed the information into their memory banks. They told them the relevance of why they wanted them to either look at something or to stand in a spot and take a 360-view for future proceedings. Jurors couldn't question them or seek clarification; they could only listen and look. They assured them that as the trial progressed and the evidence presented, everything they witnessed at the locations would have meaning and relevancy to the case.

The session ended, and the jurors filed out of the courtroom and returned to their room to gather their belongings and head out to the back elevator and down to the bus that awaited them. Judge Grabau, the attorneys, and the necessary court personnel joined them there. Tommy

Crouse wasn't going along for the ride. The judge denied the defense motion requesting he make the trip, and he went back upstairs to the jail and lunch with his tier mates.

The bus driver navigated the narrow streets of Cambridge and in half an hour pulled into the parking lot of the Malden Mills Condos. Everyone piled off the bus and gathered in a tight group to listen to a few introductory remarks before they walked together through the front door and into the building's foyer.

Adrienne led the "walk about" inside where she would point out a dozen or so areas of importance. She escorted them upstairs so they could see the view from a tenant's bedroom window out to the parking lot, the taxi company across the street, and the Mobil station on the main street. She walked them down a corridor noting Crouse's condominium as they passed. They travelled to the basement where she pointed out Crouse's designated storage area. Baccari spoke to the jurors as well, and like Adrienne, he asked them to note certain points of reference that he might discuss with witnesses during the trial.

They entered the function room. It was clean and bright and smelled of summer flowers. There was comfortable-looking furniture and an expansive eating area where guests at birthday parties could enjoy pizza, beer, and birthday cake. They made their observations, listened to the attorney's words, and walked out of the room and up the stairway to the exit and the bus. Within twenty-four hours, they would learn they'd stood in the exact same place where a fourteen-year-old girl was brutally raped and murdered. The smell of the smoke or flood of water could not reach them on the view, but once they listened to the firefighter's description of that morning, their impressions of that room would forever be altered: forever dirty and darkened by soot and the acrid taste of raw gasoline.

Likewise, they would remember their trip to the industrial park in Hookset, NH, and the walk they took off the side of the road into a sandy open area with trees and bushes and the sounds of a running brook that was swirling several feet below. But in a week or so, they would hear police and crime scene technicians from New Hampshire describe the grizzly scene they found the day they were summoned to the same location. Their recall of that bucolic New Hampshire sandpit setting with the bubbling brook and the small depression in the terrain would then bring about thoughts of one man's inhumanity to another.

In both instances, they would see videos and photographs supporting the testimony. It would bring out the importance of the view and the experience of observing the locations in person. The alternative would have the jurors creating mental images and making decisions after viewing a series of 8x10 photographs, which can be difficult to orient to and absorb.

As they headed to their homes that evening, they could not yet realize or appreciate the impact the excursion would have on them in the coming days. Soon, a heavy dose of reality would hit them that would leave an indelible, life-altering mark. To borrow a phrase from Don Henley, this was, indeed, the end of the innocence.

The stark, unambiguous reality that the crimes committed were the work of a cruel, heartless brute, and that he may very well be the man sitting a few feet away at the end of the defense table—the guy dressed in a nice business suit with a smile on his face—a person they would pass in front of several times a day.

CHAPTER 14

The Trial: Day Four
Opening Statements

On Thursday morning at five a.m., Adrienne was awake and preparing for the day. Reading over her sketched-out opening argument for the umpteenth time and working on the tempo and voice articulation, she would soon be getting ready to head into the office.

The fifteen jurors began arriving in the jury room around eight thirty. Judge Grabau's comments about respect and decorum for the Court had made a clear impact, as all of the jurors came outfitted in comfortable business attire. At a few minutes before nine, they ended their conversations, discarded their coffee cups, and lined up by the door. After a swift head count, they walked down the short back corridor, through the entry door to the courtroom, and directly to the jury box and their assigned seats. Their path led them within a few feet of the defense table and the defendant, Tommy Crouse. Once seated, some of the jurors stared stone-faced, while others looked around and smiled or nodded to people in the courtroom.

For the next two-plus weeks, they would follow a similar routine with limited interruptions or distractions: in by nine and out at four with a one-hour lunch break from one to two and short morning and afternoon stoppages to stretch, get a drink, and use the bathroom.

Although the proceedings officially opened on Wednesday morning when they completed the swearing in, this would be the day where the prosecution and defense attorneys would reveal their game plans through opening statements. Everything the judge told them the day before would "start to make sense and have meaning."

They had already heard a brief overview of the case and listened to the introductory comments by the judge and the members of the legal teams representing the Commonwealth and the defendant. They had a feel for the case after touring the areas where the alleged crimes took place, but they had no idea of the depth and complexities of the case. They didn't yet know how the prosecutor would present her case or how the defense would represent Crouse and attack the prosecution's theories of the case against their client.

To be successful in a case that was mostly circumstantial, Adrienne Lynch would methodically have to connect testimonial evidence to physical evidence to expert testimony. She would need to create an extensive and clear picture, leaving no reasonable doubt that anyone but Tommy Crouse could have killed Kelly Hancock and set fire to the function room at the Malden Mills Condo Complex: the place he called home.

Judge Grabau began by welcoming the jurors before slipping right into a few standard questions he would ask every day about whether they had read, seen, or heard anything about this case in the media. There was no response, so he moved on and commented on the rules for note taking. He said he would allow it for the sole purpose of refreshing the juror's memory as the trial progressed. He added that their notes were of a personal nature and they were not to share or use them in their deliberations. He cautioned that everyone had their own style and reason for recording notes and suggested that just because a juror wrote more didn't mean their memory or opinion meant more or was the correct one. He finished by restating the importance of looking at and observing the demeanor of the witnesses during their testimony and advised that if a juror was trying to write down every question and answer they would miss out on this important component of the trial. He then declared, "The Commonwealth will begin its case in chief with its opening."

Adrienne put her hands onto the arms of her chair and slowly rose from her seat. She picked up her manila folder with an outline of her remarks sitting atop a yellow notepad filled with handwritten notes, and with her head up and her eyes scanning the jurors; she approached the podium set in front of them. She walked in a way the jurors would come to realize was the manner she would approach all aspects of this case: slow and deliberate but always moving forward in a cadence and stride that was easy to follow, and most importantly, simple for them to join in and stay in step. As the trial progressed and the jurors adapted to her style and her mannerisms, they would grow accustomed to the way she presented information. She thought out, planned, and presented everything in a clear and persuasive manner. She paced her questions in a way that allowed the jury to understand and absorb the answers and their relevance without any difficulty. No witness of hers would take the stand ill-prepared or lacking focus. When she asked a question, she already knew the answer. She also knew the follow-up questions and answers, because she had composed those days or months ahead but only after she had spoken with the witness on one or more occasions and covered every topic she would ask, based on their participation and their level of professional knowledge about the case.

Standing in front of the jurors, Adrienne took a few subtle deep breaths to reduce any natural anxiety. Simultaneously, she scanned the group, making eye contact with each of them and locking them in for the difficult ride ahead. Then, in an effortless and composed voice, she opened the Commonwealth's case against the defendant with a clear and simple statement.

"Thomas Crouse thought Kelly Hancock was invisible. He thought she was a troubled kid, that no one would really notice that she was gone, and that no one would really care." She offered similar comments about Crouse and how he thought he was both invisible and invincible, never thinking that his movements, captured on video, and his credit cards and phone calls, tracked and recorded, would surface and that certain people whom he once considered friends were now his adversaries.

For the next thirty-nine minutes, Adrienne commanded their attention as she talked of Kelly Hancock and her troubled and tumultuous young life, as well as her run-ins with the law as a CHIN. She spoke of how Kelly had fled from DYS custody one summer afternoon and, while walking alone on the streets of Malden later that night, Tommy Crouse lured her into his trap. He promised her a temporary safe harbor at the Malden Mills Condo Complex where he lived, and she bought it. Adrienne went on to tell them what happened in the hours after they entered the building's function room and described how what started as a welcome encounter turned extremely violent, how Tommy mauled and sexually assaulted Kelly, and how she put up a heroic fight for her life. She explained how Kelly's struggle to escape came to a horrific end when Crouse plunged a knife into her chest and her life's blood gushed onto the floor and furniture and smeared the walls as she careened about before collapsing dead onto the function room floor.

It is not a legal requirement that the prosecution provides the jury with a motive or reason for a killing, but it certainly helps to clear up any questions or thoughts a juror may have as to why the homicide occurred.

Adrienne chose to address her theory with a straightforward comment, "Crouse was on probation for a prior rape conviction, and he couldn't risk going back to prison—he couldn't leave a fourteen-year-old witness." She told them that after he killed Kelly, he packaged her up and drove her to New Hampshire to dispose of her body.

It *is* a legal requirement that in the prosecution's opening statement they must address every element of every crime charged. The prosecution has the obligation not only to mention the elements but also to instruct on how they intend to prove them through the presentation of evidence. If they fail, the defense can request a "required finding" on the charges and have the case dismissed. It rarely happens, but every prosecutor is heedful of the rule.

Adrienne was well prepared to cover all bases, and over the next several minutes, she constructed a chronology of events from the initial meeting of Kelly and Crouse through the discovery of her body nine months later in and around a shallow grave in Hookset, NH. She went into detail, explaining how the human remains were unearthed and devoured by small woodland creatures that left behind only scattered skeletal pieces of bone and one very thick hank of reddish auburn hair held together with a kid's yellow scrunchie. She described the process of determining cause and manner of death and talked of how the New Hampshire's medical examiner and Maine's forensic anthropologist collaborated to reach the conclusion that the remains were those of a young female homicide victim killed by a single stab wound to the chest.

She explained how the state and Malden police investigators knew they had a confirmed homicide but still needed to identify the victim. She spoke of how they went public with their information and showed pictures of the victim's hair and clothing, as well as how a response to their plea for assistance led them down a pathway to Kelly Hancock's father's front door. Ultimately, the evidence led to a determination, through dental and DNA records, that the human remains discovered in Hookset, NH, belonged to the same person whose blood they found on the floor and walls of the function room in the Malden Mills Condo Complex in Malden, MA—and that person was Kelly Hancock.

In an opening statement by the defense, the usual strategy is to sow seeds of uncertainty and skepticism about the prosecution's statements and theories. They want to raise questions and plant doubt into the minds of the jurors with a wish that at least one or two of them take root, grow, and spread like entangled weeds.

Moments after Adrienne finished, John Baccari stood at the same podium, stared at the jurors for a quick moment, and then came out punching, strongly advocating for his client. His opening comment to the jury was straight to the point.

"Tommy Crouse and Kelly Hancock never crossed paths on the night of her death." His statement was a little less dramatic than Adrienne's, but his message was clear—and he hoped it was convincing. He showed the jurors he was digging his heels in and spoiling for a confrontation. Rather than speak to the facts as Adrienne had done, he addressed the jurors with a collection of bullet points for their early consideration:

- The reason Crouse paid for the gas with cash was that he had left his wallet and credit card at home that morning.

- Crouse never had a key to the function room.

- The witness from the jail was a heroin addict with a history of testifying for the prosecution to cut himself a deal for a lighter sentence.

- The cops spoke with Crouse that night and a day later, and they never observed any scratches on him, but neighbors say they saw cuts and scratches two days later.

- A knife or other murder weapon was never located.

- They did not find Crouse's DNA at either the crime scene or the burial location.

- The police found two shovels in proximity to the burial scene but could not connect them to Crouse through either fingerprints or DNA.

- Crouse had a gas can in the back of his truck because a day before the fire he had helped his mother move and had placed a lawnmower, snow blower, and gas can into the rear of his truck.

- Crouse and his girlfriend were completely cooperative with the police when they came to New Hampshire and even let the police investigate the back of his truck.

Baccari threw his comments at the jury like darts at a corkboard, trusting that a few of them stuck and stayed. None landed in the bullseye and a few clanged off the metal bracing and fell to the floor, but a few penetrated and held. If he scored some points, those numbers might add up in Crouse's favor at the end. At least for the time being, Baccari's remarks didn't need to be perfect—or even true. If he could only get each member of the jury to stop and consider the facts through a different prism, then his opening remarks were a success. It may not have been a masterful speech but certainly one that provided plenty of opportunities for jurors to question whether they might find reasonable doubt and acquit Crouse.

Baccari closed out his comments with an inexplicable and baffling statement. "There will be testimony of his sexual proclivities," he said, "but not one live witness will testify." This was a clear reference to Crouse's earlier conviction and incarceration for a rape and the potential that there may be testimony referencing the event. The reason the victim wouldn't appear was not that she refused to; it was because she was dead. She had taken her own life. Her mother held the strong belief that Crouse mentally destroyed her from the vicious rape and battery that he inflicted on her and she was never able to recover and lead a normal life again. This reference to the victim was a gamble Baccari chose to take. The callousness of his comment could come back to bite him in the ass depending on how Adrienne addressed Crouse's past criminal history and presented it to the jury.

CHAPTER 15

The Trial: Day Four Afternoon Testimony Begins

After a short recess to allow the jury to stretch their legs, grab a drink of water, and use the bathroom, Adrienne called the Commonwealth's first witness.

"Your Honor, the prosecution calls Edward Trimble to the stand."

Edward Trimble, the captain from the Malden FD, told the Court that he was the supervisor on the first responding engine crew to the fire at the Malden Mills Condo. With almost three decades of experience fighting all types of fires, it was safe to say he was an expert in how to approach, diagnose, and suppress a fire. He described their response from the moment the alarm sounded at Fire Headquarters through their entry into the smoke-filled room and the search for possible victims. He spoke of the ear-piercing alarms and the light on the fire alarm signal board that directed them to the basement. He described their tactical entry and his initial observations, and he said that he ordered his firefighters to vent the room of smoke and water but also to treat the area as a crime scene and not to touch or disturb anything. His training and experience told him that an internal scene that reeked of a gasoline odor, pushed out thick black smoke, and exhibited disarray were all strong indications of arson.

Trimble identified a to-scale diagram of the function room and several photographs of the fire scene's aftermath. His testimony laid the base for the admission of those documents into evidence and for viewing by the jury.

He was a great opening witness. He spoke firsthand about what had happened. He had been there. He had seen, smelled, felt, heard, and literally tasted the fire scene. In the few minutes it took to recall his sensory description of that morning, he changed the jurors' memory of the pristine function room they had stood in a day ago, to a dark, black, ear-splitting, flooded crime scene. He was setting the scene for the witnesses who followed.

On cross-examination, Baccari questioned him about the exact time the alarm had sounded and the response time of the fire trucks. He also asked a few questions about the ventilation of the room. None of the queries changed or affected the facts as laid out by Trimble on direct examination, but for Baccari, they were the opening of his defense and the precise times of events were going to be very important.

Trimble was well prepared and spoke clearly and with authority. His responses were short and to the point. The identification process of the diagram and photos was seamless. Baccari, on the other hand, wasn't as fortunate. He stumbled trying to enter fire department records because he didn't follow the established rules for authenticating documents. His missteps resulted in objections and sidebar conferences. His copies contained handwritten notes and were unacceptable for identification purposes. Adrienne produced clean copies for the Court, which helped Baccari enter the documents into evidence. It was subtle at first, but as the trial progressed, it would become more obvious that Adrienne was prepared, knowledgeable, and engaged at every step of the trial.

Daniel Thoman, the "nozzle man" on Engine 1 and, with Trimble, one of the first men through the door that morning supported Trimble's account and he added information about the function room door closest to the fire. The fire investigator's notes reflected that the door closest to the fire was unlocked when they arrived. Thoman cleared up the question on direct examination when he said that the door had been locked from the outside but he had opened it from the inside, thinking it may have been a closet and he was searching for possible victims. He said he opened the door before the captain ordered them to treat the area as a crime scene. Not a big deal, but it cleared up the potential muddy waters with a plausible explanation of how the door was locked upon arrival and unlocked by the first responders.

On cross-examination, Baccari asked Thoman if he activated his hose at any time, and he replied that they fully charged the hose but the sprinkler system had already repressed the fire.

Patrick Silva, the trooper from the state Fire Marshall's office was up next. He was the first investigator from the Fire Marshall's office to respond to the call for assistance from Malden. Prior to joining the state police, he had been a firefighter for several years in the city of Salem, MA. In an effort to qualify Silva as an expert witness, Adrienne asked about his experience as a fire investigator, and he told the jury he had investigated more than five hundred fires and was a certified fire investigator in the Commonwealth of Massachusetts.

Silva spoke about his training on how to conduct a cause and origin investigation.

"Observations, interviews, and physical evidence allow you to trace the fire back to the source," he said, "from the exterior to the interior— from the point of least damage to the area of most damage. That," he explained, "is the origin of the fire, and it is then scrutinized for the heat sources to determine the cause of it. It could be smoking materials, electrical malfunction of an appliance or electrical cord, accelerants, etc." He spoke of arson situations where gasoline or other accelerants are used and pour patterns remain once the accelerants burn off. He described the patterns he had observed on the rug and furniture once the water had subsided. He also spoke about the discovery of apparent blood spatter and staining on the rug, walls, and pieces of furniture.

Silva then explained in painstaking detail every area where there had appeared to be accelerant or blood evidence and how they had documented, preserved, and collected that evidence for later testing at the state police crime lab. He also mentioned he had requested John Drugan, a state police chemist who specialized in arson cases, come to the scene to assist.

Adrienne turned Silva's attention to the sprinkler system setup in the room. He said there were six sprinkler heads in that section of the room but only the four in direct proximity to the fire had activated. He said the company purposely designed the system that way.

Silva moved beyond the crime scene and spoke of assisting officers with the canvassing of residents before going to two area gas stations and the taxi company across the street from the fire to gather fuel samples potentially to match them with any accelerants recovered in the function room.

Silva's testimony provided a good overview of the scene and the evidence but just as importantly, he also created a foundation for Adrienne to build on with further expert testimony from the state crime lab and privately retained experts.

On cross-examination, Baccari questioned Silva about the placement of the sprinkler heads in the function room and their activation after the fire began. He also asked a few questions about gasoline samples Silva took from two gas stations that were never tested.

The senior chemist in the Arson and Explosive Unit was to be the last witness of the day. John Drugan had been with the department for eighteen years and had worked on eight thousand fire and explosion cases, 75 percent of which were determined to be arsons. After a series of questions to establish his comprehensive background, Adrienne turned to the morning of July 18, 2000, and Drugan's involvement in the fire investigation at Malden Mills. Like those before him, Drugan described the strong odor of gasoline, the partially burned furniture, and a glass table blanketed in soot. He mentioned seeing red stains on the carpet and the cloth covering the furniture, the glass table, and the walls. He said the stains were all field-tested by him and showed positive for blood. He placed numbered placards or pieces of tape next to each sample before photographing, documenting, and packaging them for further analysis at the crime lab. At four o'clock, Judge Grabau paused Drugan's testimony until the following day. Moments after Drugan left the courtroom through the main entrance the jurors put down their pens and notebooks and filed out together to return to the jury room.

The prosecution was off to a good start. Adrienne had mentally brought the jurors back to the function room but this time with a different view. She opened their eyes to the shock and disbelief the first responders had faced upon entry and how their professional observations and experiences had caused them to call for a criminal investigation. In addition, they viewed forty photographs and documents from the crime scene that Judge Grabau deemed relevant evidentiary materials.

The importance of the introduction isn't always initially obvious, but it is a building block in the case's foundation and sets the stage for later witness testimony by medical doctors, chemists, and DNA and arson experts. It is a tedious, repetitive, and somewhat boring part of any trial but a necessary process mandated by the Commonwealth's rules of evidence. If witnesses testify under oath as to what they saw and collected, they have to preface it with a plausible explanation before the Court will authenticate and allow it into evidence.

CHAPTER 16

The Trial: Day Five
Second Day of Testimony

The second day began where the first ended, with John Drugan back on the witness stand. He forged ahead; describing the size of the bloodstains he had tested. He also mentioned that he had found a small packet of what appeared to be crack cocaine under a seat cushion, but after testing at the crime lab, was revealed not to be a controlled substance but rather pure sucrose.

He transitioned to a detailed tutorial on the collection and testing of suspected accelerants and the procedures chemists follow to identify samples with certainty. His testimony was technical and probably best suited for specialists in the field rather than folks with limited knowledge of the sciences. Adrienne did her best to frame the questions in a way that allowed Drugan to respond with short, precise and understandable answers. The prosecution's case would be laden with scientific and medical testimony. All of the information was relevant and necessary to prove Crouse's guilt. She had to make sure that when a witness walked out of the courtroom, the jury understood the importance and meaning of their testimony.

Beyond the evidence removed from the function room, Drugan spoke of the samples he later removed from Crouse's truck in furtherance of the directive in the October search warrant. In closing, Adrienne asked about his prior work with Lucy, the accelerant-sniffing canine. He said that he had worked several cases with her and "found her nose and instincts to be accurate 85 to 90 percent of the time."

Attorney Baccari asked a few questions about testing and comparing samples from various gas stations and if the samples had differed. Drugan said samples of gasoline could differ from moment to moment, as new shipments of the product were added from a different tanker and mixed it with the gas already in the tank.

Pounding the jury with technical data is necessary but best offered in small doses. If it isn't, the attorney runs the risk of losing their attention as well as the point and relevancy of the testimony. Adrienne transitioned away from the science to focus on eyewitness testimony.

Tony DeLuca was the first of several witnesses without a public safety or science background. He was the resident who saw Crouse on the morning of July 18. He told the Court that shortly after six, as he walked toward the parking lot from the building's main entrance, he saw Crouse walking from his truck toward the building, pulling a kid's plastic wagon. He recalled it was red with tan sides and appeared empty. He said he knew Crouse by name and thought he had a wife or girlfriend and children and that they lived on the first floor. He added that he never spoke with or socialized with Crouse and they never acknowledged each other that morning. He remembered that Crouse's truck was not in its assigned parking space but in a designated visitor slot much closer to the building. He said at the time he thought little of what he saw, and he continued on to his workplace in Cambridge.

DeLuca said he first learned of the fire when he took a call from his roommate and fiancé an hour after he arrived at work. He said when he returned home around two that afternoon; he looked into the basement area before going about his business. He recalled speaking with two of the investigators later that afternoon, and when asked if he saw anything out of the ordinary that morning, he mentioned seeing Crouse pulling the red wagon.

Dev Kumar, a former clerk at the Mobil station was the second to testify that he saw Crouse on the morning of the fire. He said he worked at the combination gas station and convenience store from Monday through Friday and on the morning of July 18, 2000 he unlocked the door and opened the store at six.

Adrienne asked about security cameras at the business, and he described a simple four-camera system that recorded the front door, the clerk and cash register, and two outside views of the gas pump area. She produced a videotape and asked him if he could identify it. He said that he believed it to be the same tape he had turned over to a state trooper after speaking with him on July 19. She queued it up on a video machine that transferred the images onto a video screen for the jury to watch. She had Kumar explain how the system worked and had him point out an important discrepancy between the date and time on the screen and the actual time. He said it was one day, one hour, and a few minutes ahead of the actual time.

Over the next few minutes, Kumar watched as the video played in slow motion, and he stopped it for clarity at several stages. He pointed out his first customer of the day and remembered that the buyer paid five dollars in cash for gas on Pump Number 7. To verify his testimony, he indicated on the screen image where the camera records the date, time, and cash transaction.

Adrienne capitalized on the relevance and importance of the video-tape. The original, but with enhanced images, clearly showed someone resembling Crouse making the purchase moments before the arson in the building next door. It also showed him pumping the gas into a container in the rear of his Blazer and not into the gas tank of his vehicle.

To expound on the value and importance of the tape and to hammer home her points, Adrienne called Paul Melaragni, a member of the District Attorney's media relations staff with specialized training in video enhancement to the stand. His training, education, and experience allowed for expert testimony regarding state-of-the-art software and hardware specifically created to enhance and enrich videotape images. For the next hour, he explained in minute detail how a typical video security camera system functions and the impossibility of discerning every image clearly with the naked eye. He talked of the advanced training he received at the FBI Computer Training Center in Quantico, VA, specific to video enhancement for forensic purposes. He said he received certification in the use of both hardware and software developed by the Avid Corporation, which had allowed him to enhance and clarify the video from the Malden Mobil gas station.

He talked of how the gas station security system recorded forty hours of video on a quad screen and crammed it onto a two-hour tape. As a result, the quality of the resolution on the tape diminished greatly. By feeding a copy of the original tape into the Avid system, he was able to slow the images to show thirty frames or pictures per second. When viewed as individual frames the result was greatly improved pictures with the images more distinguishable and sharper. Melaragni spoke of another feature of the forensic software. He said that he was able to adjust the borders of the video to view more of the original image and see bits that were not visible in the conventional viewing.

This enhancement refined the images of Crouse paying for the gas. The difference in the quality of the camera shot of the counter transaction went from "that looks like him" to "that's definitely him." Similarly, and equally important, the images from the outside video camera went from "he's gassing up the truck" to "he's putting the gas into a container in the rear of his truck." The difference was spectacular. Melaragni incorporated the computer-generated images onto a PowerPoint display, and at Adrienne's direction, he showed them to the jury on the video monitor.

There was no cross-examination because Attorney Baccari told the judge at sidebar that he couldn't understand PowerPoint and wasn't able to look at the disc of evidence that was sent to him by Adrienne. He had argued against showing the presentation to the jury because he didn't think the scientific community had accepted the software as accurate. Thankfully, Judge Grabau disagreed with him.

After lunch, Adrienne brought forward a series of five witnesses tied to either Crouse or the Malden Mills complex. Each was brief and presented small, important pieces for the foundation she was building to support and sustain the more damning testimony she would present against Crouse the following week.

The first was Sue Ellen Hyde, the day dispatcher for Malden Transportation. She said her shift began at five in the morning. Adrienne presented her with an enlarged aerial photograph showing the area around her office building that included both the Malden Mills Complex and the Mobil gas station. She said she recognized the area in the photo, which allowed its admittance for identification purposes. Adrienne placed the photo onto a tripod facing the jury so the dispatcher, with the help of a pointer, could highlight the points of interest.

Adrienne asked if she knew Tommy Crouse, she said that she did, and that he came into the office several times a week to visit with his stepfather. She believed he worked for a construction company involved in the Big Dig Project and that he lived with his girlfriend, Esther, and two children across the street in a condo owned by Morovitz. She identified Crouse's blue Blazer in a photograph. Adrienne narrowed her questions to the morning of July 18 and asked if she had made any observations regarding Crouse's Blazer. She replied that she saw his vehicle leaving the Malden Mills parking lot around five thirty, going in the direction of the Mobil station. She said she couldn't see if anyone else was in the truck. A few minutes later, the truck returned to the parking lot, but left again approximately ten minutes later. She further recalled that fire trucks pulled into the Malden Mills parking lot twenty to thirty minutes later. She said she could not be sure of the exact time. She closed out her testimony saying Crouse never came into the office that day, nor did she answer any calls from him looking to speak with Morovitz.

The next witness was a tenant who lived on the second floor of the complex. The jury had visited his unit during the view and had looked out his living room window onto the parking lot and the taxi business across the street. The Mobil gas station was also within view. His testimony would highlight the importance of the second building canvass days after the recovery of Kelly's remains.

He spoke of the morning of the eighteenth and how he looked out his living room window to check the weather as he did every morning. He saw a vehicle that he recognized as belonging to a resident of the complex driving out of the parking lot and onto Eastern Avenue at an accelerated rate of speed and taking a wide turn. He couldn't be exact about the time, but said he went into the shower and about ten minutes later the fire alarms sounded throughout the building. When asked if he knew the owner of the truck, he replied he had spoken with him briefly several times. He didn't know his name but knew he lived with a woman and two children on the first floor. Adrienne asked if he recognized that person in court, and he pointed directly at Crouse sitting at the defense table.

As important and effective as the testimony was, it was not without a glitch and Adrienne wanted to point it out to the jury before the defense could address his initial lack of candor. He had been interviewed during the initial canvass on the day of the fire, and he did not mention seeing Crouse's truck or anything out of the ordinary. When interviewed the second time, he was more forthcoming. He testified that he changed his statement in the second interview because he learned of the "seriousness of the situation, and I just thought it would be important to let them know everything I knew." He also admitted to having a key to the function room that he had never returned after hosting a party. He said he had turned the key over to a police officer at the end of the second interview. Not good to hear, but far from fatal, and Adrienne was able to address it in a positive way.

As expected, defense counsel tore into him on cross-examination for lying to the police in the first meeting. Baccari hammered him for saying he had seen nothing that morning and that he told the police he did not have a key to the function room. Baccari also made the point that months went by and he could have corrected his original statement but never did.

On redirect examination Adrienne asked what made him think things were more serious in May of 2001. He responded, "I found out that it was a young girl who was murdered, and that made it more serious. And just the thought of it and talking to other people and I realized that it was very serious."

Adrienne's foresight and planning allowed her to take a negative and turn it to a positive. She turned her witness from a chump to a champ in the eyes of the jurors.

The next person to testify lived in a basement level condo a few feet away from the function room. He said that on the morning of the eighteenth he was awake, dressed, and preparing to leave for a doctor's appointment when the fire alarm went off. He said he walked toward the room, noticed water running out from under the door, and saw smoke billowing inside through the door's window. He returned to his unit, woke his girlfriend, and told her to leave the building. She was a trustee with a key for the function room, and she gave it to him as she left. He said that as he headed back to unlock the door, the firefighters entered the building. He escorted them to the function room, unlocked it for them, and then he also left the building.

Another condo resident took the stand and told the jurors he had rented the function room for a small birthday celebration on the Saturday night before the fire. He spoke of how spotless the room was at the time of the party and how he and friends had returned on Sunday to clean up after themselves. He mentioned that on Monday, the day before the fire, he noticed the door was unlocked and open and he peeked in and saw that the people from the cleaning company were inside and tidying up the room. He added he was given a key as part of the rental agreement but returned it to the office after the cleanup was finished.

Her last witness of the day was the property manager for the building. He testified his primary office was in Boston and he only stopped by once a month to check on things. He handled the financial business and oversaw the contracts and work of the vendors including the cleaning company. He said the function room remained locked unless a resident rented it for a special occasion. He added there were only five keys to the function room: three assigned to the building trustees and one each to the cleaning and management companies. He said he couldn't be sure if any of the keys had been replicated, adding that the keys were not the type that were stamped "do not duplicate."

Adrienne asked if he knew Thomas Crouse, and he said their paths had crossed a couple of times and that Crouse had rented the room for his child's christening or baptism in April of 2000. He recalled they had cleaned up the room after the gathering, and he thought that Crouse had returned the key.

Attorney Baccari offered no cross-examination. Once the witness left the stand and cleared the courtroom, Judge Grabau brought the day and the first week of the trial to a close, adjourning until the following Monday morning.

• • • •

The first week went as well as we could expect from Adrienne's point of view. She was pleased with the jury selection process and the fifteen people who sat in the jury box. She was setting the scene for the jury and making a small dent in her witness list. Those who she called to the stand never strayed off point, fumbled through, or surprised her with their answers. Her preparation with each of them was clearly time well spent. The pieces of the puzzle were falling into position and locking into place.

Monday would come too soon, and she had a busy weekend of witness preparation in front of her. There would be no time for a Friday social hour or a glass of wine. Before they could close the curtain on the past week and start to prepare for the next, she and Nat met in Johnny McEvoy's office, as they did at the end of each day, to discuss the day's testimony and events and to go over the game plan for the coming days.

CHAPTER 17

The Trial: Day Six
Third Day of Testimony

Jurors may not have taken notice on the first or second day of the trial, but by Monday of the second week, it was evident that the middle-aged man and woman sitting together in the first row of spectators were Kelly Hancock's parents. Mark watched and listened intently as each witness took the stand. He never left his seat when court was in session, and he heeded Adrienne's cautionary warnings about facial expressions or disruptive behavior. Jackie was at his side unless she was needed across the hall in the DA's waiting room to attend to the needs of their three youngest kids.

From the moment of Crouse's arraignment, the couple committed to each other and to Adrienne that they wanted and needed to be at all of the court proceedings as Kelly's representatives. Their journey began with appearances at the motion hearings listening to countless legal arguments about the admittance of evidence and expected witness testimony. They asked questions of Adrienne, Anne, and Nat and did their best to understand and absorb the complexities of the legal process. Their early preparations readied them for the main event.

As emotional, and at times overwhelming, as the testimony would be to hear, "We knew from the first day that we needed to be there regardless of costs, or work commitments, or anything else," Mark said. "We paid the household bills ahead of time, filled the fridge and pantry with food, adjusted our work schedules and other responsibilities, and when possible, we found adults to care for the little ones."

They left their home in Walpole very early each morning to be there on time and in their seats when the jury entered the courtroom. Adrienne or Nat spoke with them every day, and Anne was usually sitting next to them in the courtroom. They knew the witness schedule in advance and decided the only time they would stay away was when the medical doctors testified about her autopsy and the New Hampshire troopers explained how they had exhumed her remains.

• • • •

Karol Setalsingh was the first witness on Monday morning. The jury was fresh from their weekend break, and his testimony would once again be somewhat scientific and technical, requiring their full attention and focus. He was a good choice to start the week off.

Setalsingh was the trooper from the Crime Scene Services Section who responded to Malden Mills and played a pivotal role in processing the scene for potential evidence. He took the photos of the fire scene and could identify and authenticate them for the record. He could discuss the list of physical evidence he located, documented, and preserved for further testing at the crime lab. Furthermore, he processed the area for latent fingerprints and, as an expert witness, could explain the forensic testing he did, as well as the results of the tests. He would also reveal a gem of damning evidence that would shine a bright light directly onto Crouse. It wouldn't convict him, but it added to the foundation Adrienne was building, and it was significant.

Karol provided the jury with an overview of his responsibilities, adding an estimation that he had processed hundreds of crime scenes and conducted thousands of fingerprint comparisons with several hundred hits.

Adrienne had him describe the term "latent prints" and explain the role they can play in an investigation. He said that latent prints come from ridges or raised portions of the skin on hands, fingers, and soles of feet. They form patterns made of loops and whorls and arches and because the pores in human skin are constantly secreting perspiration, they can leave an impression or reproduction on an object.

He explained that prints are mostly invisible to the naked eye, but with different light sources and treated with fingerprint powder or a chemical to enhance them they become observable. Fingerprints are reliable because they are permanent and unique and no two prints are perfectly alike. Comparisons are made by placing the latent print next to an inked impression of a known subject and using a magnifying glass to seek out significant similarities to either match them or not. He said that locating and collecting prints is not always possible, adding that smooth surfaces are best and that rough or porous surfaces are more difficult and that some people do not perspire much and are less likely to leave a print.

Shifting to his work at Malden Mills, Adrienne inquired what his initial observations were and how he had processed the scene. He answered that he had arrived around one thirty on the eighteenth and took photos and videos but the area was soaking wet and covered in soot so it hampered his work. He said he couldn't attempt to raise any latent prints because the powder he relied on would clump and not be effective wet. He did notice several areas on a floor-to-ceiling column, the floor, the walls, the furniture, and a door that appeared stained with red blood. He tested them by spraying the surface with a chemical known as Leucocrystal Violet (LCV). He said the results are immediate, and if the stains turn purplish, it is a positive sign of blood.

Adrienne had been using an overhead projector known as an ELMO to project images and photographs onto two large white screens for the jurors to see during witness explanations or identifications of particular items or locations. She placed sixteen photos of positive-tested samples onto the screen, and Setalsingh identified them all. He also spoke of his observations of a tipped over broken glass table with a metal base and stained, damaged furniture, including seat cushions, in the same area. And he noted that the glass had specks of brown-reddish stains and a strand of hair attached to them. Adrienne produced photos of those areas on the overhead, and he identified them as well.

Adrienne asked about the thoroughness of his processing that afternoon, and he replied that he only remained for a half hour due to the wet condition of the scene but returned two days later and met with Troopers Forster and Donoghue and completed his work. The items he had wanted to process needed to dry out before he could search for latent prints. He added that, because it appeared at that time to be only a crime scene for an arson and not a homicide, Malden PD took custody of the broken table.

Baccari raised an evidentiary issue that required a sidebar conference with the judge. He said the prosecution was poised to offer a pair of underpants found tucked into the frame of a couch as evidence, and he objected because there was no offer of proof that they belonged to the victim. Adrienne disagreed and countered they were relevant by saying they were part of the crime scene and there would be testimonial evidence that Crouse used the room to bring "broads" there. Judge Grabau allowed the underpants as evidence because prior testimony indicated that the cleaners had thoroughly cleaned on Sunday and Monday and found no pants.

The testimony continued, and Adrienne asked Setalsingh whether he was able to locate any latent prints on the second day. He answered that he did a thorough analysis of the area of the room where the fire took place to include the furniture, floor, walls, and doors with negative results. However, while looking through the rest of the L-shaped room with Eddie and Duke, they located what he described as "a men's magazine" on the top shelf of a cabinet over the kitchen sink. He had removed it and bagged it for further analysis at the lab. He mentioned there had also been two kid's plastic golf clubs in the room: the same ones that Moccio referred to seeing when he was cleaning up after his party the previous weekend. He processed them, and there were no latent prints found on either.

Focusing in on the men's magazine, Adrienne asked Setalsingh to describe what he did to process it for latent prints. He said the surface of the magazine was smooth and glossy and was a perfect surface to retain a print. He continued with a precise and detailed account of the "fuming" method he used to identify a print. He said he had rinsed soot from the cover and then placed the magazine into a box the size of a small fish tank, put a small amount of superglue onto the surface of an electric coffee cup warmer, laid that into the tank aside the magazine, sealed the top of the tank, and plugged in the warmer. He explained that once the superglue vaporized, the vapors adhered to the moisture in a fingerprint and essentially sealed it into place.

He said once the fuming was complete he had made a visual check of the magazine and thought there might be a print on the lower left side of the front cover in the area of the bar code. He dusted it with a fine powder, and a latent thumbprint appeared. He said he called one of the investigators and told them of the discovery and they asked to examine the print against a known print card of Thomas Crouse, and when he did, he determined there was a match. "In my opinion," he told the Court, "after examining both the latent and the inked, they were made by the same individual to the exclusion of all others."

Adrienne had Setalsingh stand next to one of the video screens while she showed photo after photo of his work, and he pointed out the side-by-side comparisons of every whorl, loop, and arch. His presentation was tedious at times, but in the end, it was very impactful.

Later testimony would reveal Crouse told investigators on more than one occasion that the only time he had been in that room was more than a year prior for a birthday party for his daughter and that he had never possessed a key to the room. The company published and sold the magazine in November 1999, months before Kelly Hancock's death but also months after the Crouse family birthday party.

Setalsingh finished by telling the jury he was unable to locate any other latent fingerprints in the room and, because of the heavy foot traffic and water damage, it precluded a footprint analysis.

Attorney Baccari aimed his cross-examination criticisms at what investigators did not do versus what they did, suggesting incompleteness of the overall work. He questioned Setalsingh about not processing more areas, including loose change found at the scene, the kid's golf clubs, and the original doorknobs to the function room doors replaced following the fire. He asked for a more thorough explanation of the fuming technique and hanging the magazine vertically and not lying it down to give full advantage to the vapors. He closed by asking Setalsingh if he had examined the entire magazine or settled on the front cover alone after finding just one print. Setalsingh answered he only processed the front and back covers and not the other 146 pages.

• • • •

Lester Morovitz, Crouse's stepfather, took the stand and spoke about the interactions with his stepson on the morning of the fire. Morovitz was a well-liked, stand-up kind of guy with a long history of philanthropy within the Malden community. He told the jurors he owned the taxi company on Eastern Avenue for more than thirty years and was in his office most mornings between four and five o'clock.

Tommy Crouse was not his blood and he did not create him, but he did inherit him along with four daughters through marriage. He funded Tommy's life: from the condo he lived in, to the truck he drove, to the phones he used, and to the credit cards he abused. He also secured and paid for Crouse's trial attorney. He did it because he loved his wife.

He had been cooperative and forthright with the investigation from the beginning, and his testimony would be no different. He said he spoke with Crouse on the telephone at around 5:40 on the morning of the eighteenth, and Crouse told him he was leaving for New Hampshire shortly with his girlfriend, Esther, and her two kids. They were going to her family home in Candia so she could get treatment for a case of poison ivy. Morovitz added that a short while later, he saw the fire trucks across the street and went over for a few minutes to see what was going on. He said when he returned to his office, he called Crouse to tell him the news but he didn't answer the phone.

On cross-examination, Morovitz told the jury that on the day before å machines into the rear of the Chevy Blazer, which could have accounted for the smell of gas. He also mentioned that he rented the function room for his granddaughter's first birthday party that Tommy and Esther hosted for about sixty guests.

Robert Fournier, Esther's father, followed Morovitz to the stand. He said he was a structural engineer with his own consulting business in Hooksett, NH, and had worked in the past at the General Electric Plant on Industrial Park Road, a short distance from where they had found Kelly's remains. Adrienne called him as her witness to explain the timeline of events from when he and his wife had found out when Crouse and his family planned to arrive and when they left his house. To be kind, he was a mess of contradictory statements, and Adrienne corrected him several times when his testimony and memory on this day differed radically from statements he had made to investigators and to the Grand Jury regarding the timing of the events. The timeline he recalled not only differed from his earlier statements; it now sided clearly in Crouse's favor.

Adrienne challenged his memory and his statements so often there was a sidebar conference requested by Baccari because her questioning had become confrontational and she was impeaching her own witness. The court allows this form of probing in limited situations, usually when the witness is hostile or purposely evasive to the questioner. Judge Grabau sided with Adrienne and let her continue to question Fournier as though he was being purposefully uncooperative.

Fournier told the jury his testimony changed because several months after talking to police and testifying in the Grand Jury, he had looked at his telephone bills and they refreshed his memory on the critical timing of events. He also offered a comment about talking to Crouse after he and Esther returned from the hospital, although there was no prior indication or conversation that mentioned Esther ever leaving the house and going to the hospital.

Baccari's cross-examination was an attempt to rehabilitate Fournier, but while he looked better prepared for these questions, he continued to bumble his way through his memory bank.

Adrienne then called Esther's mother to the stand to either support or conflict her husband's testimony, but her memory was even more confused and limited. Neither denied the visit on the morning of the eighteenth or the supposed reason for it, but the timing and length of the events was vague, at best, for both of them.

Adrienne asked her a series of questions about the timing of telephone calls between Crouse and the Fourniers, as well as what time the family arrived in Candia, what they talked about and why, when Crouse left to go to the store, when he returned, and what he said when the police arrived. These were all important pieces of the puzzle and ones that could have helped give perspective to the day had she remembered them, but she couldn't. The Fourniers were in the best position to provide truthful explanations, and they failed miserably.

The brilliance of this approach by Adrienne deserved notice. The Fourniers would have been more helpful to Crouse if Baccari called and questioned them as his own witnesses. They should have been his best alibi, but try as they might to help him, they didn't. Placing Crouse at their house, eight miles from the scene of her Kelly's burial site just hours after the murder, was an early advantage for the prosecution. Adrienne essentially nullified their effect with the jury by calling them as her witnesses and not waiting for Baccari to bring them in as his witnesses.

The jury broke for lunch perhaps more confused than settled with the tainted alibi attempts by the Fourniers, but it did explain to them why their bus trip to New Hampshire included a brief stop at the house on Candia Road a few miles from the burial scene.

Testimony regarding the telephone records from Crouse's home and mobile phones highlighted the afternoon session. Although not enthralling, these records were heavy with important information pinpointing the timing and travels of Crouse on the night of the seventeenth and the entire day and night of the eighteenth. The records represented the truth that the Fourniers couldn't or wouldn't provide.

The keeper of the records for AT&T Wireless explained how they kept detailed histories of each call for billing purposes. He talked of how dates, times, and length were recorded, as well as whether they were incoming or outgoing and what telephone number they connected to. Specifically, he testified about the mobile phone number that was associated to Malden Taxi: the one that both Morovitz and Crouse said was in Crouse's possession on July 18, 2000.

A radio frequency engineer for AT&T explained how cell tower sites connect with mobile phones to carry the signal. He said, in turn, the tower signals link with each other so that when a customer moves or drives, there is uninterrupted service. He finished his direct testimony by pointing out the location of the towers that Crouse's cell phone hit on at the time in question.

Having laid the groundwork, Adrienne was ready to show the jurors how telephone records kept in the ordinary course of business aided investigators in tracking Crouse's movements from the evening of July 18 through midnight of the following day. She brought two certified criminal analysts to the stand who worked for the New England State Police Information Network (NESPIN), a federally funded agency created by the Department of Justice (DOJ) to assist federal, state, and local law enforcement agencies in the furtherance of criminal investigations. They trained in the use of software designed to analyze cell phone usage records and create historical roadmaps of where and when the cell phone was in use. That information was broken into visual, explanatory segments and then reproduced on a series of linkage charts, graphs, and spreadsheets projected for the jurors onto the big screen.

The first analyst explained how she compared Crouse's cell phone call records against the cell tower records from Massachusetts and New

Hampshire for July 17 and 18, 2000. The result was a series of diagrams illustrating the specific times and locations when and where the phone signal contacted the cell towers. Adrienne put the images up onto the screen for the jury to see and follow, ultimately entering those images into evidence. They were geographic maps with small icon overlays pointing out cell tower locations and their proximity to other pertinent locations, like the Malden Mills Condos.

With a pointer in her hand, the witness stepped from the stand and stood next to the images on the media screen. She answered Adrienne's questions while indicating the tie-ins on the map for the judge and jury. She directed their attention to the phone usage during the day and night of July 17 and showed that the last call made from Crouse's mobile phone was at 10:43 at night and it "bounced off" a transmitter in the town of Everett. While several of the calls that day appeared to originate in Malden, there were more than a few signals indicating others came from or near at least four other towns that bordered Malden. Moving on to the morning of the eighteenth, one call came from Crouse's phone at 5:39 that bounced off a Malden tower, but the rest of the ones that day were all made from New Hampshire.

Adrienne placed another map onto the monitor, and the witness shifted her attention to the New Hampshire records from July 18. Like the one before it, the cell towers were marked, as were the Fournier home on Candia Road, the Hanover Street Mobil gas station, and the area in the industrial park where they found Kelly's remains. Judge Grabau, over the objection of Attorney Baccari, allowed Adrienne to place a small icon of a human body onto that spot for identification purposes.

The first calls began at 7:13 in the morning, bouncing off a tower just south of Candia, NH. The next series began at 8:01 and filtered through the tower nearest to the Industrial Park in Hooksett where they had discovered Kelly. The records showed nine calls made from the open area of the Industrial Park over the next six hours.

The cross-examination was short, with Baccari only asking a few questions about how she got the information that she had transposed over the maps. She answered, "From Trooper Donoghue."

Her simple, brief explanation of the information revealed in the business records ran headlong into Crouse's alibi statements to police that he was home in his condo with his girlfriend and children during the evening of the seventeenth. It was yet another shot in the gut to his credibility and truthfulness during his questioning by investigators.

The second analyst from NESPIN focused on connecting both outgoing and incoming calls from his home and mobile phone to their destination phones. She, too, had prepared charts and graphs to support her testimony. The substantial number of phone calls tying Crouse with others would be a mind-numbing test of concentration for the jurors. To make for a clearer visual experience, the phone numbers were color coded with blue boxes for outgoing calls from his home phone, yellow boxes for incoming calls to his cell phone, black boxes with white lettering for outgoing phone calls from his cell phone, and peach boxes to denote calls to the Fournier home in Candia.

By any rational standards, Crouse's use of his cell phone was prolific, if not obsessive. Daily calls of fifty or more were the norm, with ninety-to-a-hundred appearing on the telephone records more than once.

Digging into the records, Adrienne asked about telephone calls on the night of the seventeenth, and the witness confirmed there were three outgoing calls. The final one was to his home telephone made at 10:17. There were two incoming phone calls at 10:40 and 10:56 from his home telephone number.

The first call Tommy made on July 18 was to the Malden Taxi company at 5:51 in the morning. Over the next several hours, he made or received more than a dozen and a half calls. The final call to Crouse's cell phone for the day was incoming at 7:50 in the evening.

Adrienne produced a simple frequency bar chart graphically depicting the amount of daily outgoing calls made from Crouse's telephone over a three-month period. Baccari objected to its admission, challenging the accuracy of the number. Judge Grabau told him at sidebar that the time and manner to dispute the numbers was through a motion in limine during the pretrial discovery process. He hadn't done it, so his objection was overruled.

The chart popped up onto the overhead screen, and the witness pointed out that on July 19, 2000, there were 154 outgoing calls made from Crouse's cell phone. The next nearest amount of calls was one hundred on August 7 and ninety-seven on July 13. As the calls on July 19 outdistanced every other day in the three-month period by at least 50 percent they stood out on the chart like Pinocchio's nose.

Adrienne's direct testimony of the witness concluded with references to a series of calls that tied Crouse's phone to those of a half dozen phone numbers registered to witnesses who had yet to testify.

As the clock struck four, Judge Grabau ended the day and almost apologetically told the witness she would have to return on the following day for her cross-examination by Baccari.

CHAPTER 18

The Trial: Day Seven
Fourth Day of Testimony

Adrienne's ability to maintain a jury's focus, even while she adapts and adjusts to an unanticipated change in her game plan, is an understated, refined trait. She doesn't fluster and leaves the impression with the jurors that the sudden swerve off the main road was always part of the original plan. She makes a jog in the park while juggling sharp objects appear perfectly normal. That is why extensive preparation is critical to a successful game plan.

The jury was expecting to start the day with the cross-examination of the NESPIN analyst, but her return was temporarily on hold so the Court could accommodate the schedules of the medical examiner and the forensic anthropologist. This was the only day of the trial period when they were both free of commitments and available to come to Cambridge. They were travelling together and needed to be back at their offices on Wednesday. What they brought to the case necessitated a team presentation. Offering their testimony at this stage of the trial was odd but, done right, workable.

The morning started before the jury entered the courtroom with a sidebar conference on a couple of issues. Adrienne explained the circumstances that caused her to call her witnesses out of order, and Attorney Baccari did not object. He added that he had a forensic anthropologist seated at the defense table to listen and observe the morning's testimony, and Adrienne did not object.

The second issue was more important and concerned Adrienne wanting to show photographs of the victim's remains through and during the doctors' testimony. Section Three of Part Four of the Massachusetts

Rules of Evidence precludes attorneys from presenting evidence that is "more prejudicial than probative." It is common in murder cases for prosecutors to offer photographs of the victim at autopsy, displaying the wounds and general condition of the body to support the medical findings and, in some cases, as an offer of proof regarding the level of violence or extreme atrocity suffered by the victim. It is just as common for the defense to object to their production because the photographs are more prejudicial to the defendant than probative for the prosecution.

While there is no absolute way to deal with every situation, judges usually allow a limited number of photos into evidence but insist they be sanitized (to the best of the prosecution's ability) and cleaned or shaded from blood and gore before being shown. Adrienne had to disclose in advance how she would use the photographs for a specific and necessary reason rather than just to shock the jury's conscience. After listening to both arguments, Judge Grabau allowed for a limited use of the photos, emphasizing they were primarily of bones and were necessary to corroborate the expert witnesses testimony about the condition and identification of the body at the burial scene and at autopsy. This issue would surely rise again when it came to testimony regarding the identification based on dental records and photographs of Kelly's skull and teeth.

Dr. Thomas Andrew took the stand first. Speaking of his medical training and experience, he told the jurors he had performed over twenty-five hundred autopsies. He added that each year in New Hampshire there were one to three sets of skeletal remains recovered that required an autopsy, and he spoke of the technical obstacles they present in determining cause and manner of death. He offered that he had testified in court about his work more than one hundred times.

He explained his primary duty as a medical examiner was to determine the cause and manner of a person's death. He presented a general explanation and overview of the process of conducting an autopsy before delving into the particulars of Kelly's case.

Using short, directed questioning, Adrienne moved in a quick, logical progression causing Dr. Andrews to share how he first became aware of the discovery of human remains in Hookset and how soon after he reported to the scene. He identified a chart and photographs of where the human skull and body parts were located and told how he had supervised the removing of the remains from a shallow grave. He spoke of the facedown positioning of the body in the earthen grave and the thick auburn ponytail tied in a scrunchie lying in the divot where the skull had been before a scavenger had carried it away. He also described the clothes the victim had been wearing.

He imparted that in skeletal remains cases he always consults with Dr. Marcella Sorg, a board-certified forensic anthropologist employed in that role by the state of Maine. He said that there are so few of these type of deaths in New Hampshire there isn't the need for a full-time medical specialist, so New Hampshire contracts for Dr. Sorg's services. He said he called her from the burial scene and explained the circumstances, and she agreed to come to his office on the following day to assist with the autopsy.

Adrienne led him through the general autopsy protocols from beginning to end. He spoke of recording general observations during the outer inspection of the body and x-raying the remains for projectiles or artifacts, followed by the process of charting, sketching, photographing the body, and removing of clothing and cleaning the body of debris before a thorough medical analysis. She continued with questioning particular to this case, the crime scene, the body recovery, and the autopsy. She put photos and sketches tied to his comments onto the overhead projector for him to identify for the jury. It was shocking visual evidence, particularly to the jurors who likely had never been exposed to anything like what they were viewing.

Dr. Andrews talked of how this case differed from most because there were no obvious signs of identification and the extreme level of decomposition made the body physically unrecognizable. He spoke in detail about how he and Dr. Sorg had reconstructed the skeleton anatomically and laid her bones out onto a separate gurney. He mentioned that they had recovered all but a couple of small bones from the burial site. His comments matched the photos that Adrienne had already put into evidence. He explained how her clothing contained significant amounts of dried blood and that they found defects in her clothing. He spoke of the difficulties they had faced in removing the clothing from her body. He described some of the defects as small tears, presumptively created by animals gnawing at the material and the dried blood, but he said one tear on the front of the shirt was more consistent with a rip caused by a sharp object. He said the location of that tear would have been directly over the soft tissue of her abdominal area, which normally protects the vital organs that lie underneath. He emphasized the cut in the shirt would not have been over the rib cage or other bones.

He said that at the completion of the autopsy, he was not positive about the cause and manner of death, so he had listed the case as pending and filed it away until he could learn further information.

Adrienne asked if he could pinpoint Kelly's time of death, and he replied that because of the poor condition of the remains he couldn't be positive. However, he could say the warm weather clothing on her body, coupled with the vast amount of decomposition, indicated at least partial exposure of the body to seasonal changes and of her being buried around the time she went missing in July of 2000.

Adrienne asked about the possibility of additional stab wounds to her body. Referring again to the level of decay, Dr. Andrews said he didn't know if there were wounds made in areas that her clothing did not cover. He did say that according to reports she was in good physical condition before she disappeared and she did not die of natural causes. Similarly, he said there were no weapons or objects found that would indicate an accident or suicide.

Dr. Andrews closed out his testimony referring to developments that had taken place in late April and May of 2000 and what had caused him to change the file from pending to solved, with a final determination that the case was a murder. He cited several reasons. He spoke of a DNA match that the jury had not yet seen as evidence. He told how a private lab matched a sample taken from one of the victim's bones to the blood recovered at the violent crime scene in Malden, MA. He added that they had identified the victim as a young teenage girl from Malden reported missing on the day she was murdered. He said her remains matched the biological profile developed by Dr. Sorg. A subsequent forensic odontology identification matching dental records with the teeth recovered from the victim's jawbone confirmed her to be fourteen-year-old Kelly Hancock. As a result, he determined the cause of death was a stab wound to the abdomen and the manner of death as a homicide.

On cross-examination, Baccari treaded lightly and asked little of the witness. It is a difficult place for attorneys to be in when their defense is that the defendant never met the victim, nor has any knowledge of the events surrounding the homicide. The medical testimony is necessarily gruesome, and the longer the doctor testifies, the more embedded the visions become in the minds of the jurors. Amplifying or prolonging drama that could be detrimental to your case and client is never a good practice.

Dr. Sorg followed Andrews to the stand to corroborate his findings from the slightly different but supportive perspective of a forensic anthropologist. Her educational background, coupled with eighteen years of experience as a board-certified forensic anthropologist, uniquely qualified her as an expert in her field. Her purpose was to explain how her background and training aided in the identification of Kelly's decomposed human remains and how her expertise assisted Dr. Andrews in reaching his conclusions.

She explained to the jury that forensic anthropology is the study of human remains with the express purpose of identifying the deceased and their cause of death if unknown. She defined her advanced specialty within that role as forensic taphonomy, which is the study of postmortem processes or, in layman's terms, discovering how long a person has been dead and placed wherever it was until recovered, based on decomposition, damage to the body, and other factors, such as climate and topography. She added that she also examines the remains to create a biological profile to determine sex, age, physical stature, and other descriptive information that can aid in the identification process.

After Sorg restated Dr. Andrews' testimony about general autopsy procedures, Adrienne turned to the facts of the case, specifically to the shirt Kelly had been wearing. Dr. Sorg said the left side of the front of the shirt was tattered, fabric was missing, and there were irregular tears. She offered an opinion that this is consistent with the work of animals who forage for their food and are attracted to the areas of the injury and the blood that gathers as a result. She then commented that scavenging is a natural activity and part of the circle of life. Insects, animals, and mammals seek out organisms that died for their natural food supply.

She spoke of the missing bones and attributed it to small animals taking the food away from the scene and hiding it for later consumption. She added that bigger animals, like dogs and coyotes, are more likely to remove larger bones, like the skull, for the same reasons.

She mentioned that the tattering of the clothing included sections of the bra, shorts, and underpants as well. Adrienne asked her about the defect or slit in the shirt that Dr. Andrews had referred to during his testimony. She responded that the slit was consistent with a sharp cutting instrument and not the work of a forager.

Adrienne shifted to Dr. Sorg's expertise in forensic taphonomy and asked if she was able to determine how long ago someone had buried the body in that shallow grave. Relying on her research and study of similar situations, Dr. Sorg answered that based on the level of decomposition, skeletal exposure, the amount of soft tissue remaining in the joints and body cavity, and the clothing on the body, the remains appeared typical of a summer death with hot days and one Northeast winter.

Adrienne offered a hypothetical situation consistent with the timing of Kelly's death in Malden, and Dr. Sorg's testimony about the condition of the body when it was first discovered. Then she asked Dr. Sorg if she had an opinion "as to whether or not the condition of the remains was consistent with the death in the time frame of July 18, 2000."

Dr. Sorg nodded and replied, "Yes. On the basis of the case series and my research on postmortem processes in the Northeast, it is very consistent with that postmortem interval."

Adrienne asked if she had been able to create a basic biological profile on the remains, and Dr. Sorg replied that she had viewed and measured the bones and observed the cranium and was able to deliver an expert opinion that the remains were consistent with Kelly Hancock's age, sex, and height.

Adrienne inquired if she had done a microscopic investigation of the bones to determine any exterior injuries. She answered that she had and, while there were a few areas that looked suspicious to the naked eye when she viewed them under a microscope, she found no cut marks.

Adrienne wrapped up by asking the witness if she was able to form an opinion based on her examination of the body coupled with her education, training, and experience as to whether or not the cause of death would be consistent or inconsistent with a stab wound to the abdomen of the person.

Dr. Sorg responded, "Based on the defects on the clothing, it's consistent with sharp force trauma."

On cross-examination, Attorney Baccari asked why there were no shoes found at the scene, and Dr. Sorg answered that scavengers could have dragged them away. He asked about the condition of Kelly's pants, and she said they were zipped shut. He asked about the size of the slit in the shirt, and she replied, "Approximately one inch wide." He asked if they had fingerprinted the skull, and she replied that she had no idea.

His questioning was brief, and he didn't raise any doubt about her testimony, but he did commit one noticeable, wincing blunder. When he spoke about the missing foot bones, he suggested that chipmunks might have taken them away. It may have been an attempt to soften the picture for the jury, but Sorg replied immediately, "rats, squirrels." The Chip and Dale image he hoped for changed into one of Willard and his sidekick Ben, and that raised a stomach-turning visceral response far different from the one he had intended.

It was a disturbing few hours of testimony for the jurors to hear, see, and absorb. It certainly brought the reason they were sitting there in the jury box into better focus. Adrienne had taken very technical and, under the circumstances, unusual and difficult medical testimony and had the doctors explain everything in simple, straightforward, and understandable terms. She never strayed from her points or went off on tangents: just nice, tight, concise explanations that kept the jury fixated on the witnesses and left no room for any doubt about their findings.

Presentations like these don't just happen. They are the result of months of extensive study and preparation. Adrienne had spent many nights and weekends reading medical treatises, as well as the two books and several articles about forensic anthropology and forensic taphonomy written and edited by Marcella Sorg. She had talked and met with both doctors Sorg and Andrews months before, and she had learned from them. She knew the strengths of their findings and the points of emphasis to pursue. She also knew what she might expect from a defense witness and how she could best cross-examine them. During the doctors questioning, Adrienne had yellow pads and three-ringed binders at her fingertips, all overstuffed with handwritten and typed notes from her conversations and research. She also had the complete question-and-answer path she followed, just in case she had a brain cramp.

The traditional ways of lawyering were changing by the day due to the rapid advances in science and technology that were having a big effect on not only investigations but also the way attorneys presented the evidence in a courtroom. Criminal law attorneys needed to constantly educate themselves to the changes and learn how to use them to their advantage in prosecuting or defending a case. If they fell behind, they did so at their own peril and ran the risk of a lawsuit or appeal based on prosecutorial misconduct or ineffective assistance of counsel.

• • • •

Following the doctors' testimony, the witness from NESPIN returned to the stand for her cross-examination about Crouse's telephone records. Attorney Baccari questioned her about the way they entered the records into the computer and how they generated the graphs from that data. In particular, he disputed the extraordinary number of calls recorded for July 19, the day after Kelly's murder and burial. He spent several minutes questioning her about more than a dozen of the telephone calls. She admitted that she only did the analysis and that two data entry women had inputted the data. The main point of his inquiry was how many of the calls actually connected, how many were unanswered, and whether or not the list included incoming messages. He also wanted to know how many of the154 calls might have been counted twice in error. She said she couldn't answer as to how many may have been voicemails and based on his questions, she agreed that three of the entries might be duplicates.

Attorney Baccari then requested a sidebar and asked that the judge strike all of her testimony and exhibits, telling the Court, "This witness doesn't know how to interpret these records. She didn't do the input, and it's incredible." Judge Grabau said her testimony "goes to the weight of the evidence," and he allowed it, but he said Baccari could make his point here, and if he chose, present his own rebuttal witness during his defense of Crouse. The final determination as to the weight of her testimony would occur during the jury's deliberation.

As both sides returned to their positions, Adrienne suddenly wheeled around toward the bench and requested another sidebar conference. "Mr. Crouse is making comments and making faces at me, and quite frankly, I will put up with only a certain amount. This last time when I went back, he made some comment to me…" she said she did not hear what he said. Nat Yeager supported her comment, although he also did not hear exactly what he said either.

Attorney Baccari defended Crouse with comments about Adrienne's behavior. "If I may," he said, "I'm getting complaints from Crouse's family about Miss Lynch's facial remarks—facial expressions. Since this case began, I haven't—I've seen a little of it myself, I'm—"

Judge Grabau quickly ended the conversation with an admonishment of Crouse. "I'm not interested in what the Crouse family has to say. I have not seen Miss Lynch do anything like that. Tell your client: one more facial gesture and I will do something about it. Okay?" The bench conference came to an abrupt end, and Baccari stopped at the defense table for a moment to speak to Crouse before the testimony resumed.

Baccari continued with a line-by-line inquisition of the records, and the witness stood her ground. At the end, there were no significant admissions about improper input or recording of the calls. On redirect, Adrienne took the opportunity to reaffirm that the methodology used for July 19 was the same as it was for every other day.

The final witness to testify about telephone company records was an investigative analyst from Verizon. Adrienne put a document on the screen, and he identified it as subscriber information for a landline previously identified as the one assigned to Crouse's condo but in Lester Morovitz name. Crouse had told the investigators he was home with his family during the entire evening and night of July 17. Reading from a business record, the witness said on that evening at approximately eight thirty there was an incoming call to the home from what appeared to be Crouse's cell phone and someone had answered it. Further, later that evening at 10:17, someone had placed a call from Crouse's home phone to his cell phone. Someone had answered the call as well, and the conversation had lasted for forty-one seconds. The testimony was short but important because it made the connection between Crouse's home phone and his cell phone on the night of July 17.

On cross-examination, Baccari only asked for two points of clarification and no follow-up.

Business record testimony is always tedious, but they contain critical information that the jury needs to digest and understand because they provide the crucial timeline of events. Businesses do not keep records to assist law enforcement in their investigations; they maintain them to keep the company in business. Unlike witnesses whose memories of past events may wither or fade over time, business records never change unless someone tampers with them. They can be advantageous, or they can prove fatal to an alibi or the theory of a prosecutor's case.

• • • •

Eddie Forster was the last witness for the afternoon. Adrienne wanted him to tie some things together and explain a few of the "hows" and "whys" of the investigation. Some of his testimony would answer questions the jury might have at that point in the trial, and some of it would make sense to them later after other witnesses testified.

Thanks, or no thanks, to television and the movies, people have preconceived notions or expectations of police officers that are exaggerated and untrue. They view us as Joe Friday, "Just the facts, ma'am," or Clint Eastwood in *Dirty Harry,* or as a bumbling character from the detective unit in *Barney Miller.* As Eddie Forster entered the courtroom and walked to the witness stand, I would bet not one juror thought he was a homicide detective. He didn't look or fit the stereotype, and that was why he was so good at his job. He was a laid-back, no drama guy with a humble, unpretentious lifestyle. Eddie matter-of-factly introduced himself to the jury and told them he had been a trooper for twenty years, the last fourteen and a half of them as a death investigator assigned to the Middlesex DAO.

Adrienne asked him to describe his activities as they related to the events at Malden Mills on July 18. Eddie said when he arrived, he gathered with Jimmy Connolly, Duke Donoghue, Johnny Rivers, and Steve Ruelle for a briefing with members of the fire department. He had viewed the fire scene, walked around the building and the grounds, and joined the others with a canvass of the building that was already in progress. He noted that a short time later he and a Malden PD sergeant went to a transfer station on the Malden-Everett town line. During the chaos of the morning, a trash truck had slipped in and removed a dumpster from the rear of the condo complex before anyone had the chance to inspect it for possible evidence.

He testified that by the time they got to the transfer station, the trash truck had already emptied the dumpster and comingled the contents with trash from other locations. He said they spent the next few hours working with the employees to identify the dumpster's contents and then sift through the remnants. They were unsuccessful in finding any obvious evidence or a body.

He said he returned to the complex and continued with the canvassing. He mentioned the conversation with Lester Morovitz and the resulting trip to New Hampshire later that same evening.

After pointing out Crouse in the courtroom, Eddie talked about the conversation Sergeant Ruelle and he had with him at the Fournier home that night. He recalled asking Crouse about what he had done the day before and that day. Crouse told them he spent the previous morning working for his stepfather at Malden Taxi before heading to his mother's house in the afternoon to help clean out her garage. He returned to his condo at Malden Mills in the late afternoon and remained there until six o'clock before heading over to the Eagles Club in Malden. Crouse said he left there between eight and eighty thirty before returning home for the rest of the evening. Crouse went on to tell them that he, Esther, and the children woke early and left for her New Hampshire home so Esther could get medical treatment for a rash. He mentioned going to his storage area in the basement level of the condo to get some items for the kids. He said they had headed north around quarter to six. Eddie also asked him about the function room at the complex, and Crouse answered he had only been there twice, once in April for his daughter's birthday and again the following day to clean up.

Eddie said the entire conversation took less than twenty minutes and that Crouse was cooperative but seemed agitated and was "somewhat vague on his times of what he did." For example, he never mentioned buying gas at the Mobil station before he left that morning. Crouse did consent to them taking a general view into the rear of his Blazer, which they did with the aid of a flashlight. He said there was "stuff" in the vehicle but nothing obvious that appeared related to an arson or a homicide.

Adrienne inquired about Crouse's clothing or noticeable injuries, and Eddie replied there was nothing obvious but they didn't ask him to lift or remove any of his clothing.

As the testimony flowed, Eddie talked of returning to the condo complex the next day and continuing to canvass the residents, adding that at one point he drove into Boston and spoke with the people who had cleaned the function room the day before the fire. He also mentioned that a state police cadaver dog had arrived in the late afternoon and searched both the building and the surrounding outside area for a possible victim with negative results.

Eddie referenced being present during the crime scene processing of the function room with Trooper Setalsingh and the recovery of what he referred to as a "dirty book." He added Setalsingh called him a week later and told him of a positive comparison to a print on the magazine's cover to Thomas Crouse. He said he and Ruelle had returned to Malden Mills and spoken to Crouse about the print. He recalled that Crouse denied any knowledge of the magazine and when asked if he could have just picked it up and looked at it while he was down there, he had repeated emphatically that he had never seen the magazine. He then suggested someone could have removed it from his condo and mentioned the name John and said he lived in the building, perhaps on the fourth floor.

With that nugget of damning information on the record, Adrienne moved on to questions about Crouse's telephone usage. Eddie said they had the phone records for his home phone and were in the process of re-questing subscriber information for the numbers that connected to the incoming and outgoing calls. He said during the interview about the magazine they had asked Crouse for his cell phone number, and he had given it to them. Eddie said it was then that they realized the cell number showed the listing to Malden Taxi, not Crouse, and furthermore, the number matched a couple of the incoming and outgoing calls to Crouse's home phone during the evening of July 17. That information turned out to be a blinking red light because it proved Crouse had lied when he told them he was home all night when he was not. The records for both the cell phone and the cell towers it "hit off," showed that when Crouse said he was home, he clearly was miles away.

Adrienne paused for a moment and let the effect of that information settle onto the jurors. She moved forward asking him about the week of April 23, 2001, and in particular, what he had learned about the recovery of skeletal remains in Hookset, NH. Eddie said the other investigators and himself had travelled to New Hampshire and met with the troopers in the Major Crime Unit who were investigating the discovery of human remains in a rural sandpit. He said that after a couple of days of comparing notes and information they believed there were enough similarities to warrant further DNA comparative testing. He spoke of a joint agreement for New Hampshire to send a DNA sample from the recovered bones to BODE Labs in Virginia and that Massachusetts forwarded a sample of blood recovered from the function room as well. Massachusetts had made the request, so they had footed the bill.

Adrienne skipped over the DNA results, saving it for later when she could formally introduce and explain it in-depth through scientific experts. She did ask what they did after they learned the results, and Eddie said the DA made plans for a media event to seek information about the victim's identity. He said they wanted to show pictures of the clothes she was wearing and the ponytail of thick red auburn hair with the scrunchie attached. He said that immediately prior to the press conference a uniformed Malden PD officer looked at the photos and commented that the hair looked like Kelly Hancock's hair. Eddie said that because of those comments they went to the home of Kelly Hancock and spoke with her stepmother about a dentist and dental records. He added that he thought Johnny Rivers followed up on that and found the dentist.

Once again, Adrienne moved on and saved the particulars of the identification for other witnesses. However, she did question him about what he did after the identification was official, and he spoke of talking with her family, friends, and a social worker who had been with Kelly Hancock on the July 2000 afternoon prior to her disappearance. He said the social worker had identified the photos of the clothes as being the same as the ones worn by Kelly when she last saw her.

Adrienne ended her direct examination with a flurry of questions about a search warrant on Crouse's truck in October of 2000, the clarified video of the Mobil gas station, the Mobil credit card statements, and the court-ordered blood samples taken from Crouse and Esther Fournier at the state police detective unit in March 2001.

It may have seemed that Adrienne was bouncing around, but she was extracting as much damning information from Eddie as she could while saving the deeper, connecting details for later witnesses.

Baccari used the cross-examination of Eddie to make a run at casting his client in the best light possible. His questions came across more like statements, and they were on point. He asked about singed hair or burns on Crouse, indicating he was close to a fire. Eddie said he wasn't looking for those signs and didn't see any evidence of them. He inquired if Crouse may have been agitated because of the intrusion and the fact that he had been sleeping when they arrived in Candia. He asked if the fact that Crouse gave them permission to search his truck was indicative of someone who had nothing to hide. He asked about conversations Eddie had with Crouse about the magazine when Crouse told him his apartment had been broken into and property was missing. Eddie said he didn't recall any talk of a break-in mentioned in any of their conversations.

Baccari wrapped up with a series of questions about an unidentified partial fingerprint found on a shovel near the burial site in Hooksett. He ran a series of names past Eddie and inquired whether they attempted to compare the print to any of those people. Eddie answered yes to some and no to others.

When Eddie left the stand, it was closing in on four o'clock and the rest of the Court's work for the day required a hearing to quash a subpoena, a voir dire on a witness, and a motion in limine, all of which was required to be heard outside the presence of the jury, so Judge Grabau dismissed the jurors for the day. As soon as the door closed behind them, he moved on to the discussions.

The questions that required answers centered around three potential prosecution witnesses and information Attorney Baccari was seeking to impeach their credibility.

The first, filed by the Middlesex Sheriff's Office, was in the form of a motion to quash a subpoena duces tecum filed by Attorney Baccari requesting records of all contributions to Louie Barone's canteen fund. The Middlesex County sheriff was concerned about the privacy rights of the individual and requested that in the alternative, the Court should issue an order that would cover the sheriff's department from a lawsuit by the inmate for a violation of his Constitutional rights. Judge Grabau listened to the arguments and promised a decision the following morning.

The second issue was a Constitutional one and had to do with a person's Fifth Amendment protection from self-incrimination. The potential witness was currently serving time for unrelated criminal offenses. He indicated a willingness to testify against Crouse but questioned if the police could charge him with a crime because his statements might incriminate him and cause an issuance of a criminal complaint. He was asking that the Court appoint him an attorney to represent him in discussions with the prosecutor and defense attorney. This is a routine situation in many cases, and always is, as it was here, allowed by judges. The witness would return to the courthouse in the early morning, and his previously appointed counsel would be there to represent his interests.

Last was a motion in limine filed by Baccari to use past criminal convictions of an expected witness, Pete Grey to impeach his credibility. Grey's testimony might be critical to the case, but he came with an awful lot of baggage and a long criminal record for past illegal behavior. The question wasn't about whether it was inadmissible, but rather Adrienne was asking that it be restricted to nothing earlier than 1988, and Baccari wanted to go back even further. Judge Grabau listened to both arguments and said he wanted to review the current case law and he would have an answer for them in the morning.

CHAPTER 19

The Trial: Day Eight
Fifth Day of Testimony

There was an hour delay of the morning session while Judge Grabau dealt with a couple of matters in open court and on the record. He spoke with a juror who raised a concern because he recognized Eddie Forster as someone he met once or twice through a mutual friend several years before. He said he didn't make the connection until Eddie testified, and he was just following the judge's orders to report these situations. He added he that thought he could remain fair and impartial. Neither Adrienne nor Baccari objected and so he allowed the juror to remain. On the other issue, Judge Grabau appointed an attorney to represent Bob Sanders on the question of his right against self-incrimination.

By ten o'clock, with the jury seated, Adrienne called her first witness: a general dentist with a practice on Ferry Street in Malden. He recalled that Kelly Hancock had been his patient in June of 1999, and as part of his general, introductory patient procedures, he took bitewing x-rays of the left and right sides of her mouth. The resulting two film pictures were included in her patient file. He said that sometime in May of 2001, a Malden PD detective came to his office and requested those x-rays in furtherance of an investigation and he had signed them out to the detective. There were no cross-examination questions. The dentist's testimony lasted less than the time it would take to fill a child's cavity.

Dr. Kate Crowley, the forensic odontologist for the Commonwealth of Massachusetts, followed. She testified that in her work for the OCME she consulted on over three hundred cases per year. She described forensic odontology as the application of dental science in the assistance of positively identifying known human remains.

Adrienne geared her questions to educating the jurors without bogging down and losing their attention with long explanations filled with complex terms. Dr. Crowley told them that there was a large dental database to rely on for comparisons because most people had visited a dentist office at least once and, at some point, had x-rays taken and placed into a personal file. She added that teeth are strong calcified structures that are resistant to trauma, fire, and decomposition and that they contain an almost infinite amount of characteristics to refer to for comparison purposes.

Following a general overview of the science and the identification process, Dr. Crowley told the jury how she had travelled to Concord, NH, on Saturday morning, May 26, and met with Dr. Phelan, her counterpart for the state of New Hampshire. Together, they inspected the dental remains and the postmortem x-rays of the body found in Hooksett and compared them to the premortem x-rays of Kelly Hancock. She described their examination process and explained how they found two unique dental characteristics that were immediately apparent, both clinically and radiographically. They were dental restorations to two molars known as tooth number nineteen and tooth number thirty. After comparing the x-rays with the actual teeth, they formed the opinion that they were the same, and that resulted in the positive identification of Kelly Hancock. She added that in their review all of the teeth were intact and in place except for two, which the New Hampshire forensic team discovered during the recovery of her remains. They were able to determine that they had fallen out postmortem because of the clear, open sockets where they should have been.

Adrienne closed out the direct examination by asking Dr. Crowley if she "had an opinion to a reasonable degree of dental medicine as to the identity of the Hooksett remains based on the information you reviewed."

Dr. Crowley answered, "Yes. Kelly Hancock."

On cross-examination, Attorney Baccari brought up the fact that the American Board of Forensic Odontology had not yet certified Dr. Crowley.

She answered that she had already passed the written and practical testing exercises and only had the oral board segment left to complete.

Baccari asked her if Dr. Phelan's opinion was consistent with hers. Adrienne stood and objected to the question. In a sidebar conference, she said Baccari was seeking hearsay evidence about a person's opinion. She said if he thought Phelan's opinion differed he should call him as his witness. The judge sustained her objection and removed the question.

• • • •

For the rest of the day, the emphasis was on testimony from four people who, at best, would describe themselves as acquaintances of Crouse. Two lived together at Malden Mills and the other two had been a couple until recently and had known Crouse for several years and socialized with he and Esther on occasion. Their testimony was important because of their past dealings with, and knowledge of, Crouse. They saw and spoke with him before and after the fire, and based on his comments and actions, they offered insight into his state of mind during that period.

Their observations and remarks were candid and voluntary and did not put Crouse into a favorable light. However, each witness brought their own significant baggage to the stand and gave the defense opportunities to point out everything from blemishes to deep scars in their reputations as law-abiding and truthful citizens.

In homicide cases like this, the witness list is not laden with saints and business executives. The people who raise their right hands and swear to tell the truth aren't well-heeled suburbanites who consider a clogged toilet a catastrophe and are upset when the lawn service people arrive too early in the morning and interfere with their sleep. These are people with difficult, challenging lives. Many battle addictions and health issues. They fight to find and hold on to a job, struggle every day to pay their bills, put food on the table, and keep their families intact. For the most part, they are good, well-meaning people who battle their demons every day, but above all, they are survivors. They also know the difference between right and wrong, and when that line is crossed and a young girl is assaulted and murdered, they feel compelled to stand up and speak for her and not hide from the truth. Only time would tell what the jurors thought, but one thing was sure, by the end of the day they would certainly have a lot to consider.

Before the next witness took the stand, the judge called the attorneys to the sidebar to address the questions posed the previous afternoon. Judge Grabau told Attorney Baccari that on cross-examination he would allow him to inform the jury of Pete Grey's criminal record for the previous fifteen years but not the twenty he had initially requested. Adrienne had requested to have it capped at ten years, so Judge Grabau compromised and split the difference. The judge also brought the attorney he appointed for Bob Sanders to the sidebar and asked about his client's status. He said that Sanders wanted to invoke his Fifth Amendment right but that there were some ongoing negotiations with the DAO that might change his mind and willingness to testify. The judge put the discussion off until later in the day.

Pete Grey was no stranger to the court system, and that was apparent from his demeanor from the moment the bailiff swore him in and he took the stand. Grey was fifty-four years old and had moved to Malden Mills with his girlfriend in 1999. He had been working as a master barber for the past year. He candidly admitted to a twenty-year battle with drug addiction. He said he would "get straight" only to relapse on many occasions. He disclosed that during the summer of 2000 he was a frequent cocaine user.

After the introductory questioning, Adrienne asked about the morning of July 18, 2000, and the fire in the building's function room. Grey said he was sleeping and the fire alarms awakened him, and like the other residents, he fled the building. He recalled speaking briefly with the police either that day or the next.

He said he knew Tommy Crouse for about a year as a neighbor who lived in a condo around the corner of the hallway from him. He said he didn't see him on the day of the fire but did the following day around two in the afternoon. Grey said he was with his girlfriend and they had just returned from a nutrition clinic in Boston with a handcart full of groceries. He heard a voice "like a loud whisper" from behind him calling his name, "Stevie, Stevie, Stevie." He said he walked back toward the voice and saw Crouse standing outside the closed door to his condo with his hand holding the doorknob. He described Crouse as sweaty, nervous, and smelling of alcohol, adding that he thought Crouse was drunk. "Stevie, what's going on? Have you heard anything? Do you know what's going on?" Grey recalled him asking.

Grey said, "I told him, 'I haven't heard nothing. It's a fire, that's all I know.'"

Crouse responded, "All right. Go. Go. Go," and Grey left.

He said he spoke with the police again on July 26. He remembered it was Trooper Forster and a younger trooper. He said they asked him questions about Tommy Crouse, and he told them that he knew him from a few short conversations in the hallways and parking lot. They were friendly but not friends and had never been inside either one's condo. He added that one day during a conversation Crouse introduced himself and mentioned, "He had just gotten out of the joint."

Attorney Baccari went ballistic on Grey's comment, jumping up and demanding a sidebar conference. He told the judge he was insisting on a mistrial because Grey brought up Crouse's past incarceration. He argued that the rules of evidence disallows such comments because they prejudiced the jury against Crouse and that Crouse was not on trial for his past, just this case. The conversation grew heated between him, Adrienne, and the judge and lasted a few minutes. The jurors could not hear, but they could certainly see their animated conversation. Judge Grabau denied the motion but did tell the jury to disregard Grey's answer to the last question.

Adrienne forged ahead with questions about Grey's relationship with Crouse. He said they had spoken maybe ten to fifteen times and that all of their conversations were short and in the open. He said he knew Crouse lived with a woman and a couple of kids but he rarely saw her and they never spoke. He recalled that a month or two before the fire Crouse had asked him if he ever used the function room to party with girls. Grey said he told him that his key didn't fit the door and questioned why he would go there since he had his own condo for that kind of business. Grey added the manager gave him two keys when he moved in. One fit his condo door and the other the outside doors, fitness room, and laundry. The manager informed him at the time that to use the function room you needed permission and had to pay a fee. Crouse told him it was a nice room with a couch.

Adrienne's questioning turned to drug usage and conversations Grey had with Crouse about purchasing cocaine. He said at different times they each asked if the other could get cocaine. Grey said he couldn't but Crouse told him he could get some if Grey needed it. He added that while they talked about drugs, they never did drugs together.

Grey said Crouse moved from the complex a few weeks after the fire. He said he had seen Crouse three times since then but they never spoke. He also recalled one time when he went over to Malden Taxi to speak with Crouse but they never connected. He restated that they never socialized together, nor did they have any disagreements.

Adrienne knew of Grey's lengthy criminal record but thought his information was too important to disregard. She believed the significance of his testimony outweighed concerns that his past behavior would negate his words. Grey knew of his exposure to criticism and was unconcerned about attacks on his reputation and credibility. She took the affirmative step to bring out his past and did not want the jurors to have an impression that she was presenting Grey as an upstanding, law-abiding citizen, nor did she want him vilified without warning by the defense. As she wrapped up her questioning, Adrienne asked, "Have you ever been involved in the criminal justice system?" Grey answered, "Shamefully so," admitting that he had been convicted of a felony more than once in the past twenty years and had done some time.

Before turning the questioning over to defense counsel, and almost as an afterthought, Adrienne asked Grey if he could identify Crouse. He looked at the defense table and pointed directly at him.

Attorney Baccari knew he had some damage control to deal with and needed to destroy or at least badly bruise Grey's credibility. He began by referencing the morning of the fire and asked him what he did after the fire. Grey said he went to the methadone clinic on Frontage Road in Boston. He said he has been receiving the drug for the past ten years and received a daily dose of fifty milligrams. Baccari asked how he got to the clinic, and Grey responded he got a ride from the transportation company that picked him up every morning. Baccari went deeper and asked if he took rides with Malden Taxi, and Grey responded that he once did but now used Cape Ann Taxi.

As they prepared to take the morning break, the testimony grew contentious when Baccari suggested Grey was "cut off" by Malden Taxi because he threatened to stab a driver in the face. Grey shot back, "That's baloney!" Baccari continued and pointed out discrepancies in Grey's previous grand jury testimony, his statements to police, and ones he made in court that morning regarding dates and times. Grey admitted to not being perfect with exact dates and times and said he did not have a great memory anymore.

Once the jurors went on break, Judge Grabau went to his chambers, where he conducted a short "Martin hearing" with Stan Peterson and his court-appointed attorney regarding Peterson's concern about incriminating himself with his testimony against Crouse. He determined Peterson had a legitimate Constitutional concern and told both counsels about his finding. He also acknowledged there were ongoing talks between Peterson and representatives from the DAO to address his concerns.

When the jury returned, the attack on Grey's reputation continued from where it left off. Baccari led by reading thirteen names that he insinuated were aliases Grey had used on prior arrests and/or court appearances. Grey admitted to most, but not all, of them.

Baccari then brought out an incident that occurred in June or July between Crouse and Grey after Grey allegedly "stiffed" a Malden Taxi driver out of a twenty-dollar fare. Grey admitted to a conversation about it and said that afterward he went over to the taxi company, met with the driver, apologized, and paid him the twenty dollars. Baccari insinuated that it was a contentious argument between Crouse and Grey and that Crouse slapped Grey in the head. Grey was somewhere between angry and laughing with his response. "No! Oh, come on. He's got the balls of an ant. Are you kidding me, pal? He slapped me? Come on." The question asked and answered, Baccari moved on, hoping at least one juror would question Grey's believability.

Baccari asked about conversations Crouse said he had with Grey about hypodermic needles and the danger to children who found them. Grey denied that ever happened. Things heated up again when Baccari asked him about a comment he allegedly made to a Malden Taxi driver in the fall of 2000: that police would find a body in New Hampshire. Grey vehemently denied any such meeting or ever making that statement to anyone.

Grey's testimony ended with Baccari producing an inch-thick list of certified court complaints and convictions against Grey, both in his name and under the multitude of aliases he had used when arrested. The charges dated from 1986 through 2012, they were mostly misdemeanors and minor felonies for theft, breaking and entering, and drug-related offenses adjudicated in district courts. Grey had only one charge for assault and didn't deny any of the other charges, but did dispute a few of the outcomes.

At one point, Grey turned toward the jury and responded to Baccari's question by answering, "Just keep reading them, and I'll just say yes to all of them." Judge Grabau interceded and told him he needed to respond to each question. Grey replied, "Well, he's got my record, Your Honor. I'm not the same person I was then anyway…so." As the questioning about his record continued, Grey once again grew antagonistic and snapped, "You can show it to me all day long, sir. I have a terrible record. You going to read everything? Why don't you call my probation officer; I'm done."

The judge said in response, "Just listen, and answer, and we'll get through this."

Grey may not have liked it, but Baccari was well within his rights to impeach him through his prior criminal records. Whether he made any impact with the jurors about Grey's trustworthiness was only for them to decide when they entered into deliberations, but he certainly did his best to muddy the waters.

The jury broke for lunch, and even if they digested nothing, both Adrienne and Baccari gave them a lot to chew on over the next hour.

• • • •

Nancy Cooper, Grey's girlfriend, opened the afternoon's session with testimony that reaffirmed Grey's statements about the morning of the fire as well as seeing Crouse on the following afternoon outside of his condo. Adrienne moved on and asked her about a chance meeting Crouse and she had in the condo lobby in June 2000 and what they had discussed. Cooper said Grey had a severe relapse as a drug addict and was in a rehab center following an arrest and short-term incarceration when he couldn't afford his bail. Crouse was aware of the situation and had previously asked, "How's Stevie doing? I know he is away."

Cooper thought the conversation was a little odd and too personal. He told her he had checked on her with people they both knew who said she was "good people" and that he "should watch my back for me." She went on to say that as he was talking he kept saying he was a "regular guy" and then he reached into his shirt pocket and removed a plastic baggie with a significant amount of white powder that she thought to be cocaine and asked her, "Would you like some of this?" She told the Court she had previously used cocaine but no longer did and when Crouse made the offer, she told him, "No, I don't do that shit."

In response to questions regarding the hours before the fire, Cooper said she had taken her dog out for a walk twice, once after midnight and again around two. She mentioned seeing a male subject she didn't recognize sitting on a cement pylon in the parking lot on her first trip, but he was not there on her second.

On cross-examination, Baccari opened with more questions about the unknown white male she told investigators she saw in the parking lot. Without saying it directly, Baccari was attempting to inject another suspect into the conversation so he could later question why police didn't pursue that information further instead of just focusing on Crouse. He probed more in depth about Grey's time away from her and the condo, and she estimated it to be around three months and described it as a very difficult time. Cooper admitted that like Grey, she was also on methadone and taking the same dosage of 50 milligrams per day.

Baccari made an issue of the state police assisting her with getting a warrant for her arrest dismissed. She answered that the police made her aware of an outstanding warrant in Lowell District Court for failing to appear for jury duty. She added that she told them she had no transportation to get to that court and they had offered to drive her there. She said she went with them to the courthouse and she went in to the court clerk's office and explained her situation, and the clerk removed the warrant and the case dismissed that day. She added that no police officer spoke on her behalf and they only provided the transportation.

Cooper's testimony concluded with Baccari asking her to affirm her criminal record of one count of solicitation for prostitution, one for disorderly conduct, and a third for assault and battery. Although convicted of all three, she never received a jail sentence. She answered yes to all three.

• • • •

Requesting a witness to testify that may have a Fifth Amendment privilege against self-incrimination is common and not particularly difficult to do, but the process has several moving parts that must be followed and can get complicated. Bob Sanders was one of those witnesses. His testimony would be brief, on point, and an important piece to the ever-interlocking puzzle. He was willing to testify as long as the Court wouldn't charge him with a crime based on his testimony. The DAO was willing to stipulate to that, but it had to be in writing and Sanders, through his court-appointed lawyer, had to be part of discussions. They secured the agreement with minor difficulties, but because Sanders was in custody for an unrelated crime, arranging to get him from the house of correction to the Court was logistically difficult. Fortunately, everything came together on Wednesday afternoon, and he took the witness stand.

As soon as the clerk swore Sanders in, Attorney Baccari requested a sidebar conference. He objected to the testimony stating it was not relevant to the charges against Crouse and their value was far more prejudicial than it was probative. Judge Grabau noted his objection but disagreed and allowed the testimony.

Sanders testified that he was currently residing at the Billerica House of Correction, where he was serving a two-year sentence for assault and battery. He said that prior to his conviction he had lived in Everett for seven years and worked for a company that installed websites. He was a technician who ran the cable connections. He said he had known Crouse since 1997. They met through his cousin, who worked as a driver at Malden Taxi. He said his connection with Crouse was sporadic and was more business than friendship.

Adrienne asked about his telephones, and he said he had a company-controlled Nextel phone and a landline phone at his home. He verified the two numbers she asked about and said Crouse had knowledge of both. She produced telephone records tying calls from Crouse's mobile phone to Sanders' Nextel at approximately seven thirty on the evening of July 17, 2000 and asked if he recalled speaking with Crouse that night. He replied that he didn't have a direct memory of that call or eight other calls that she pointed out from that night to both his Nextel and home telephones.

Sanders referred to Crouse as an "acquaintance and then a friend; also someone that I would go out and have beers with every once in a while." Adrienne asked that although he had no direct memory of the telephone calls, if he were to assume Crouse made them, what would be the purpose for his calls. He replied, "To get something for him." When she asked him to elaborate, he simply answered, "Cocaine."

Adrienne closed out Sanders' testimony by entering the agreement into the record between him and the DAO not to prosecute him on his revelation before the Court that he sold drugs. There was no cross-examination by Attorney Baccari.

Adrienne brought the day's testimony to a close with a woman who was a friend of Crouse for many years. Carla McKay lived in Everett, one town over from Malden. She told of a shared friendship she and her live-in boyfriend Stan Peterson had with Crouse and his girlfriend, Esther Fournier. She mentioned that she and Peterson both worked at Malden Taxi for Lester Morovitz. She said they all socialized as a group about once a month. Until her relationship with Peterson ended in August of 2000, she had spoken with Esther almost every day, and she would see and speak with Crouse every couple of days when he would call or drop by to see Peterson.

McKay spoke of being home on the afternoon of Wednesday, July 19, the day after the fire at Malden Mills. She recalled it was a hot day and she had showered in the early afternoon. She said after drying her hair she heard a noise behind her in the kitchen and when she turned around, she saw Tommy Crouse silently standing there and it startled her. She recalled he was dressed in a long woolen sweater and long pants despite the heat of the afternoon. She said she asked him if he wasn't hot dressed as he was, and he didn't answer. She said Crouse began walking through her house but wasn't talking. She told him that Peterson had been looking for him, and Crouse still didn't answer. She thought the entire visit was about fifteen minutes. She also said that he appeared to be distraught and drawn out, and when Adrienne asked her to define what she meant by that comment, she said, "Well, just, he wasn't saying anything. Usually, he's always talking. We're friends so he used to just, you know, sit and talk, but he didn't say anything. For him to just stand there, I felt uncomfortable."

Adrienne fast-forwarded ten days from the visit on the nineteenth and asked McKay about a Saturday dinner she had hosted that included Crouse and Fournier as her guests. She spoke of serving a turkey dinner on a Saturday afternoon. She said her house was extremely hot inside from the oven being on all day and the fact that it was hot outside. She said Crouse was wearing a short sleeve, baseball-style jersey, and at some point, "While sitting at the dining table, he peeled it off and quickly replaced it with a tee shirt." She said she noticed deep red scratches on his chest and neck area, and commented, "Someone had a good night." She added that he didn't respond to her comment.

On cross-examination, Baccari pressed McKay about Crouse's scratches, and she answered there were six in all with three on each side, extending from his neck to his chest. Baccari asked if she was aware that Crouse had done construction work with cement that week, and she replied that she was not.

The day ended at four o'clock. Testimony from Stan Peterson would have to wait for the next morning. Adrienne wanted to close with him and move on to a day of scientific testimony on Thursday, but circumstances being what they were, Peterson would instead be the first witness on the following day. It wasn't the worst of scenarios because the jurors would still be contemplating information about Crouse's friendships, and maybe Peterson's comments would fill in a few gaps.

After five days of testimony, the pieces were linking together as Adrienne had planned, but there was still a lot more to add before she completed and unquestionably revealed the image of Kelly's murderer.

The jury had listened to Adrienne's opening comments, they had heard the statement of the case against Crouse, and they remembered their steps and thoughts during the view. They were now in a position to draw an inference as to where they had discovered Kelly's remains, but how they had found her, positively identified her, and connected her to Malden Mills was still a mystery. There were still a few days of information and testimony ahead of them to round out and solidify the prosecution's case.

As difficult as it is to be an investigator or witness excluded from the courtroom, and left to wonder if the witness testimony was impactful, I have always felt it was more confusing and challenging for the jurors. They sit and listen intently to every word and naturally have thoughts and questions they want to talk about with the other jurors, but they cannot. They spend all of their time together and can talk about the weather, sports, kids, and grandkids. They can exchange recipes, political thoughts, and book reviews but not a word about the information they learn from the witnesses. From a due process perspective, it is necessary to prevent any pre-judgment of the defendant before the presentation of all the testimony, but while understandable, it is still extremely frustrating for all of them.

• • • •

During a trial, there is usually minimal contact between the investigators and the trial team. Not because of a court order, superstition, or lack of care but out of respect. We give them the space they need to concentrate on preparing and delivering the case to the Court and jury. If they have questions or concerns and need us, we will be standing by to assist. Most, but not all, of the contact is indirect, with messages delivered back and forth through the victim witness advocates assigned to the case, an administrative aide, or other ADAs. The exceptions are conversations prior to our testimony or making sure that the witnesses are present and prepared for when the bailiff calls their names. While not forbidden, personal contacts are usually restrained.

So, late on Wednesday afternoon, when Adrienne walked into the office with Nat, it was a bit of a surprise. "Hi, Billy is Pete Sennott around?" she asked.

"No," I replied, "he headed out a little while ago, but he will be at the airport first thing in the morning to meet Charity from BODE Labs when she arrives from DC. He will bring her to the office first and then upstairs to the waiting room so she'll be standing by to testify as soon as you call for her."

"Excellent," she said with a smile, "We are moving right along, just a little out of synch, but generally speaking, the case is going as well as we could expect. I had planned to have her on the witness stand first in the morning, but now I need to put Stan Peterson on first. We ran out of time today. I wanted to compartmentalize things for the jury and fill the day with testimony from all of Crouse's buddies, but we came up short. Once Peterson is done, though, the rest of the week will mostly be science testimony on the DNA, the bloodstain spatter, and the arson."

"How are you guys feeling about the case so far?" I asked.

"Not bad overall," she said. "Other than witnesses coming in out of order, there haven't been any surprises. The jury has been very attentive, and based on their expressions and the occasional nod of the head; I think they understand what we are presenting. They must have a million questions about how we discovered Kelly's remains that, so far, we have not answered. I hope that after Monday's testimony from the New Hampshire State Police Troopers they will finally see how all the pieces fit together and point toward Crouse. It had to be a little weird to hear about the fire one day and the autopsy the next when they haven't heard anything yet about the victim, the crime scene in Malden, or her discovery in Hookset, let alone anything about Kelly as a person."

"How has the defense gone?" I asked.

She gave one of her common shoulder shrugs, winced, and responded, "It is always hard to say, but I don't think they have done significant damage to our witnesses. Pete Grey was a little tough because of his past record, but I hope the jurors recognize that he did the honorable thing because it was a homicide of an innocent kid. I have no idea how Stan Peterson is going to do because he can be a little spacy and guarded in his responses. He is the only one I would say might be reluctant on the stand."

"Jimmy and Duke have been asking if you have made a decision yet on whether or not you are going to use Barone." I inquired. "If you need him, we just want to make sure he is ready and still on board."

"I understand," was her answer, "Nat and I have been talking about it virtually every day. Right now, I think we are leaning in that direction, so you may want to have Duke or Jimmy reach out to him. The earliest we will put him on is late Monday, but we'll need to see how tomorrow and Friday plays out. We are of the mind that his information from conversations with Crouse is very important and outweighs the negatives that come with him being in jail and having an extensive record. Pete Grey was sort of the canary in the coalmine when it comes to people with troubled pasts testifying for the prosecution. I think he was well-received by the jury and survived his cross-examination with minimal damage."

I told her one of us would make the call to the jail in the morning to set things up, and I asked if they would take care of the paperwork and judicial order to bring him in from the House of Correction for Monday afternoon, and she said they would.

"We are getting toward the end, and with any luck, I'll finish our case on Tuesday afternoon or Wednesday morning at the latest," she added, "I'm not sure how long the defense will be, but I won't be surprised if we aren't doing closing arguments next Thursday."

As they headed for the door and the short trip across the hall to Adrienne's office, I asked her if there was anything else they wanted from us right then and she answered, "Only, maybe have Eddie reach out to Lieutenant Forey in New Hampshire to make sure they are all on board for Monday morning. I think they are all coming in a cruiser together. My plan is to have them on first thing, but I can't be positive until we finish up on Friday. The worst that will happen is we'll have a carry-over witness and they'll go on right after him, but you can tell them I'll have them all headed north by day's end.

CHAPTER 20

The Trial: Day Nine
Sixth Day of Testimony

For Adrienne, Thursday started like every other day throughout the trial. She was sitting at her desk by six o'clock with a cup of hot coffee in one hand while she flipped through her notes and questions for her witnesses in the other. She appreciated the peace and quiet of the empty office and the opportunity for a couple of uninterrupted hours to focus and plan that day's courtroom strategy. On this morning, she was also putting together a legal argument requesting a special jury instruction regarding the previous day's cross-examination of Pete Grey. It was a small but significant matter. It showed that her constant attention to even the smallest details had her in a league by herself, and the jury took notice.

As happened on most mornings, the court day began with a sidebar conference. Adrienne addressed her proposed jury instruction by referencing the cross-examination testimony of both Grey and Sanders regarding their past criminal convictions and the sentencing on each charge. She presented Massachusetts case law rulings that stated that although it was admissible to place convictions into evidence, references to sentencing were not allowable. Judge Grabau and Attorney Baccari reviewed her motion for a few minutes, and the judge agreed with her. While Baccari objected to the finding, Judge Grabau told him that if Crouse or any defense witness were to take the stand, he would hold Adrienne to the same standard and not allow any comments about their sentencing.

The jury entered a few moments later. Judge Grabau addressed Adrienne's motion and told them to disregard any testimony from the day before that referenced the witnesses sentencing for their criminal convictions. He was brief but thorough and told them it was solely their decision about how much weight they wanted to give the testimony of each witness, "But with respect to the length of the sentence, that is not relevant, nor material, to your consideration on the issue of credibility of that particular person."

With the judge's comments complete, Adrienne called Stan Peterson as her first witness. After the usual questions to establish his identity, Peterson said that he was currently disabled and suffered from panic attacks and agoraphobia. He said that in July of 2000, he was living with Carla McKay and they were in a relationship but he moved out in August of that year when the relationship dissolved.

He said he met Crouse approximately ten years before and they had been friends ever since, speaking almost every day. He added that they socialized both together and as couples with Carla and Esther.

Adrienne asked about conversations he had with Crouse about women, and he said they talked about women often, "Like, the way I took it, was just like guy talk." Peterson tried to minimize their conversations and the content of them, but Adrienne dug away. She pulled out his testimony from the Grand Jury, and asked him to read what he said when asked the same question. His answer changed to "frequently."

Adrienne pushed back, "Your words were, and your answer was, 'All the time,' wasn't it?" He said she was correct. He admitted that Crouse would talk about "knockout" girls he met in a bar and how he got their numbers, but he said Crouse could never elaborate so, "I never really believed him." Peterson offered that when they would be driving around and saw a girl or a couple of girls; Crouse would always approach them and try to talk with them.

Adrienne asked him to identify a phone number, and he said it was his home number. He explained that he registered it in his four-year-old daughter's name because the phone company shut off their last phone when they were unable to make the monthly payments. Adrienne asked about another telephone number, and he said it belonged to a cell phone that he bought and activated on July 17, 2000. When she asked if he spoke to Crouse at the time of the fire, he couldn't recall exactly when he spoke with him but said he was sure it wasn't on the seventeenth or eighteenth because he had the new phone and hadn't given out the number yet. He did recall that in the midafternoon of the nineteenth Crouse left a frantic message on his home phone telling him he needed to speak with him on a landline because the state police were there and he thought he was in trouble. He said he attempted to return Crouse's call several times from his home later that day, but they all went unanswered. He recalled they didn't connect again for four days and when they did Crouse was calmer and only said he was afraid because he'd had beer cans in his apartment and that was a violation of his probation.

Adrienne asked about the turkey dinner at his apartment a week and a half later. Peterson said it was late on a Saturday afternoon and that it was the first time they had seen each other since the nineteenth. He recalled Crouse was angry about the police investigation and kept saying it was a "witch hunt" and that he was upset because the fire was right under his condo and could have killed his family if they were home at the time.

Adrienne wound down her direct exam with a series of questions about the Crouse kid's wagon and their family vehicle. Peterson recalled the wagon, and he knew the police had done a search warrant on the truck and removed some carpeting because Crouse had pointed it out to him.

During cross-examination, Attorney Baccari returned to July 19, the day after the fire at Malden Mills, and asked about a meeting between Crouse, another man, and himself at the Eagles Club in Malden. Peterson acknowledged they had met outside the club, and he said his friend and he were not members but Crouse was and he was going to sign them up for membership. He remembered they talked and had a beer or two before Crouse left and they stayed behind. It was an hour or so later that Crouse called and asked him to respond from a landline because the police were at his condo.

Baccari asked Peterson if, in the ten years he was friendly with Crouse, he ever saw him in short pants or carrying a knife, and Peterson said no to both questions. He said Crouse always wore "weight-lifter pants" and then stood to demonstrate the term by showing the jurors he was wearing the same type of pants.

Baccari ended the questioning by asking about the turkey dinner and Crouse's attitude that day. Peterson described him as "agitated."

Adrienne couldn't get out of her seat fast enough to question Peterson on redirect. He was initially her witness, but she went at him about his disclosure that he was at the Eagles Club on the afternoon of the nineteenth with Crouse. She questioned why during all of his interactions with Eddie Forster he never once mentioned that meeting, and he could only respond, "I don't recall."

Whitman was a difficult witness for the prosecution because of his reluctance to testify against his best friend. He was on the witness stand because he had to be, not because he wanted to be. He would answer the questions evasively or with a clouded memory, trying to minimize any damage his answers might cause. He was doing his best not to point an accusing finger at Crouse, but only time would tell whether or not the jurors viewed him as lacking candor.

• • • •

Next on the prosecution's agenda was some of the most important testimony of the trial: the indisputable scientific results of the DNA testing conducted by an independent lab: the connective tissue that bonded Kelly Hancock to the scene of her murder and the recovery of her remains. It wouldn't be graphic or emotionally riveting, but it was critical evidence the jurors needed to hear. When the Grand Jury heard the DNA evidence, it completed the puzzle and persuaded them to indict Crouse. For this jury, Adrienne hoped it would be a critical "ah-ha moment" as well. A flash of clarity and understanding that would have them nodding and saying to themselves, "Now it all makes sense." It was a big moment for the prosecution to solidify their case against Crouse.

Getting to that moment would require Adrienne to follow a complex legal process that had to be strictly adhered to and without shortcuts.

Bringing scientific information to a jury always presents challenges. For most jurors, it would be the first time they had to listen to a biology lecture since high school or freshman year in college, and they may not have understood it then. Adrienne had to present questions to the forensic experts using simplified terminology and workable analogies in a way that brought out answers the jury could understand and interpret. The discovery of DNA was not new, but its application as a forensic science was barely a decade old and memories of the complex and confusing presentation in the O.J. Simpson trial a few years previous was still fresh in people's minds. Adrienne studied the science intensely for months leading up to the trial and her new knowledge, coupled with the guidance of her experts equated to confidence in her approach.

A legal requirement in any trial demands the prosecution document the chain of custody of their evidence that assures its authenticity. In other words, through a series of witness presentations, the prosecutor needs to demonstrate that the physical evidence they want to put before the Court is the same evidence seized earlier and that it remained in the technical custody of the person who seized it. In the event it was removed from the evidence locker for testing or other reasons, there needs to be a sign-out sheet with signatures documenting when and why it left, with whom and where it went. If returned, the returnee had to fill out another form with pertinent information and the date and time, readmitting it to the evidence locker. It is sometimes a simple offer of proof through one witness. However, most often, when DNA matches are such a critical part of the prosecution's case and with the prep work and testing done by different laboratories in different states, the standard of proof is more elaborate and the explanation of the chain of continuity doesn't come in one burst of testimony or through one witness.

To meet the standards Adrienne would bring crime scene specialists from Massachusetts, New Hampshire, and Maine to the stand. To prove evidence continuity, they would discuss how and where they found, documented, removed, preserved, and tested biological evidence from the scenes in Malden and Hooksett for DNA analysis. Like running a relay race, each witness grabbed the baton, shared their expertise, the process they followed and their findings before handing off the stick to the next person in line. Ultimately, they would get to the anchor, who would take the journey across the finish line. In this case, the anchor would reveal the DNA results and offer their expert opinion about the findings. However, as happened several times during the trial, they had to reverse the order of witnesses causing this event to run backwards with the anchor leading off with the other runners to follow. Scheduling and travel plans for the key out-of-state witness, meant the results would come first and the explanation of how they extracted the samples and sent them to BODE Labs would come after.

The forensic technical leader for the BODE Labs Technology Group in Springfield, VA, presented the test results from all of the biological samples sent to the lab for comparison testing.

She talked of her professional and educational background and said she had been in her current position at BODE Labs for four years. She mentioned that prior to BODE Labs she worked for the Armed Forces DNA Identification Lab in Maryland, where she assisted with the identification of the skeletal remains of American soldiers who died in combat on foreign soil. She said her primary responsibility at BODE Labs was to supervise and review the DNA casework performed by others at the lab.

She began by describing DNA as "genetic material that's found in every cell of your body, except for red blood cells, and it's described as the blueprint of life, which basically means it coats everything from eye color and hair color to all cellular functions."

She answered general questions about DNA testing as well as more specific inquiries about the type of DNA analysis she performed in this case. She firmly declared, "STR analysis." She continued by pointing out that STR testing was the current, state-of-the-art method used by hundreds of labs throughout the world for DNA typing. Adrienne asked whether the scientific community, of which she was a member, generally accepted the procedure as valid. She simply answered, "Yes." She then spoke of the guidelines they followed for security and quality assurance to support the reliability of the testing results.

Following the very basic introduction to DNA, Adrienne asked about the samples submitted to BODE Labs for testing and comparison. She explained that Maine had shipped five samples: four were human skin and one was from a human vertebra. She said they had used those type of samples in the past and they were quite common, but she added that in this case, the samples were undergoing decomposition, which had badly degraded the DNA. The vertebra sample was difficult, as well, because mold had started to develop, but they were able to extract a partial DNA profile that they were able to work with for comparison matching.

The questioning transitioned to the cotton swab samples submitted from the Massachusetts State Police Crime lab. The witness said they were able to get a complete DNA profile from that material. Once they had both DNA profile samples, they did a scientific comparison and determined they were a match.

She explained that when there is a match between two items of evidence, they conduct a series of statistical calculations to determine the strength of the match. She said the manner the comparison testing was done was, in her field of expertise, "an acceptable manner of calculating the probability of random matches between unrelated people."

Adrienne continued, "Now, with regard to the 'practical probability frequencies' of these, is this data recognized in your field, having been subject to peer review, as a reliable database?" After receiving yes for an answer, she asked her to indicate to the jury the statistical significance of the match between the vertebra DNA and the bloodstain DNA.

As she started to speak, Judge Grabau asked her to "slow down a bit" so the jurors could understand what she was saying. She related the probability of randomly selecting an unrelated individual with their DNA profile by race.

The numbers she disclosed were astronomical, eye popping, and presented in a simplistic manner. Adrienne asked, "Now, given the statistical probability information you've just described and the population of the world, can you say to a reasonable degree of scientific certainty as to whether or not the vertebrae and the blood samples were from one and the same person?"

"Yes," she responded, "because the world population is about six billion individuals, and these numbers are all significantly higher than that, we can say within a reasonable degree of scientific certainty that these two samples came from the same source."

Adrienne closed out her testimony with questions about the dates of the report and that the lab communicated the results of the profiles back to Massachusetts and New Hampshire.

On cross-examination, Attorney Baccari tried to create a little confusion by questioning the dates the witness signed off on her report against her testimony for the initial review of the testing, but she explained that she signed off the same day as her final review was completed. Then he went where he probably shouldn't have by asking her what the statistical numbers really equated. She simply replied, "It might be one in 31.6 trillion." After that response, he ended his questioning and took his seat. The enormity of those probability numbers could only enhance the juror's belief of the DNA match connecting Kelly to the Malden Mills crime scene and the remains found in Hooksett.

Two crime lab chemists from the Massachusetts lab followed to explain their roles in handling the biological evidence and extracting test samples before forwarding them to BODE Labs to be tested. It cleared up any questions or concerns regarding the chain of custody of the evidence during the entire process.

The chemist from the Massachusetts lab who had collected the blood and hair samples from the fire scene and later assisted in the processing of Crouse's truck during the execution of a search warrant went next. He spoke to several issues, but the most important regarded his discovery of six hairs that had adhered into blood on the glass tabletop that was partially lying on the function room floor in the area where the fire and the struggle took place. He said that after a thorough microscopic examination of the hairs, he could see that only one contained a root and may have contained DNA. He described how he packaged and forwarded the hair for further inspection and testing by a specialist in the state police lab.

The chemist who received the hair sample and performed the testing testified next. Adrienne produced an envelope previously admitted into evidence, with a smaller glassine envelope inside, and the chemist identified it as the one containing the hair she had tested.

She said that before attempting to extract DNA from the hair she first looked to see if the root was connected to skin tissue, a good source of DNA. She said the hair had some charring, with soot covering part of it. She also said the testing on the root section revealed a full DNA profile. She said she had compared that profile to the sample from the Maine lab from the recovered vertebra and determined the two were a perfect match. She offered a mathematical probability of a randomly selected, unrelated individual having a matching DNA, which was almost impossible to comprehend.

In response to the forensic chemist's numerical data, Adrienne questioned her about their significance when weighed against the world's population and if she had formed an expert's opinion regarding the source of the hair. She responded, "I determined it to be a match and that it was highly likely that they were from the same source."

Baccari's cross-examination of the chemist was limited to asking if she had been able to exclude both Crouse and Esther Fournier as the source of the hair, and she replied that she had.

Metaphorically speaking, after the DNA chemist left the courtroom, Adrienne walked the jurors out of the science lab and back to the classroom to the heart of the police investigation. She called Duke Donoghue to the stand. Duke's was a name they heard from previous witnesses, but this would be the first time they would see or hear from him. Adrienne intended his testimony to clear up an unanswered question or two while also tying a few pieces of evidence together to bridge a gap or clear up any misunderstandings any juror might have.

The Sixth Amendment to the United States Constitution guarantees a defendant in a criminal case the right to "be confronted with the witnesses against him." The US Supreme Court has defined the phrase as anyone the police questioned who makes a statement against the interest of, or is harmful to the defendant, must appear in court, and offer testimony about their observations and comments or the information will not be allowed as evidence. The police officer who took the statement cannot testify as to what they talked about other than to comment that a meeting and a conversation took place. The simple reasoning is so the defense can cross-examine the person providing the damning information, not the police officer to whom they spoke. A police officer can only speak to what the witness told them and not to the witness's ability to see or hear, the context in which they made their observations, or any biases they might have toward the defendant. The eyewitness testimony of several people in the movie *My Cousin Vinnie* are classic and directly on point. As funny as they may have been to watch, they are great illustrations as to why the witness must by subjected to cross-examination and not the police officer who took their statements.

Because the judge does not explain the Sixth Amendment to the jurors, they are perplexed at times when an officer comments on a meeting but didn't speak to the contents of the conversation. The officer though can testify that the conversation led to other interviews, searches, or inquiries to further the investigation. This would be obvious in Duke's testimony, as it was with Eddie Forster's, and later, with Jimmy Connolly's.

Duke synopsized his involvement during the first day of the investigation. He spoke of the fire scene, the interviews of resident neighbors, and their trip to Candia in the evening hours.

Adrienne led him into the following day's activities. He mentioned that a state police canine, specially trained to locate and follow the scent of decomposing human flesh, had come to the scene to search for a possible victim. Duke had stayed with the dog and handler while they searched the function room and the interior and exterior of the building. He said the dog did not alert on any areas, nor did they see any bloodstains in their journey except for the ones in the function room.

Duke spoke of stopping into the Mobil station next to Malden Mills where he met with Dev Kumar, the store manager. He said Kumar had provided him with a videotape of the previous day's activities inside and outside the store. He recalled the manager telling him the date and time on the tape were off by one day and a few minutes. He said he viewed the tape later on a small television screen, but he couldn't clearly define what he was looking at because there were four separate cameras playing simultaneously on a screen split into quarters. He spoke of Paul Meleragni's involvement as well as Avid technology in enhancing the video and clarifying the images. He said they did not complete the tape enhancement until some point in November of 2000.

Duke recalled that he and Eddie Forster were with Trooper Setalsingh during his second attempt to process the function room. He said that while they were searching the kitchen area he had blindly passed his hand across the top shelf of a cabinet in the kitchen area, felt a magazine, and took it down. He stated it was a Genesis magazine and that Trooper Setalsingh took possession of it and preserved it for a fingerprint analysis.

As his testimony continued, Adrienne focused on two important conversations. The first was a spontaneous meeting Eddie and he had with Crouse on the evening of July 26 as they stood outside of his condo. The second was in early October 2000 prior to the execution of a search warrant on his vehicle.

Duke said in the first instance, they spoke briefly, and he asked Crouse for the second time about previously going into the function room and if he had a key to the door. Crouse again denied having a key to the room and said he had only been in that room earlier in April of that year for his daughter's birthday and the following day to clean up. Adrienne asked Duke if Crouse ever mentioned getting gas at the Mobil station shortly before the fire, and Duke responded they hadn't asked him, but to that point, he never mentioned getting gas to any of the investigators.

Duke made his second point during questioning about the search warrant for Crouse's Chevy Blazer. He said they had received the warrant in the late afternoon and looked for, but couldn't find the vehicle. At nine o'clock that evening, they went to Crouse's new home address in the city of Lynn, a few miles from Malden Mills. Crouse had answered the door, and Duke had handed him a copy of the search warrant. Crouse told them the Blazer was "in the shop" for repairs. He gave the detectives his keys and the phone number of a contact person who could take them to it. Adrienne asked Duke if he had made any observations of Crouse at the time, and he answered that Crouse's "eyes began to well up as they were leaving."

Adrienne asked Duke to identify pictures of the Blazer and if he knew if you could raise the rear window when the hatch was in the "up position." He answered yes to all of her questions.

She questioned him about the extended length of time it took to get cell phone and cell tower records from New Hampshire and whether or not he had attempted to have an evaluation done of Crouse's home and cell phone records. Duke said they were all gathered and taken to NESPIN, where analysts had scrutinized them.

She asked him about the investigators attempts to locate a victim following the fire, and Duke briefly described the overall progression, including narrowing the search when the victim's blood was determined to be from a female. He spoke of the daily scouring of local, state, and national teletype items for missing women and unidentified human remains as well as how the Malden police had sent out teletypes with the limited information, hope for assistance in furthering the case. He mentioned that the Malden detectives spread the word through their community contacts as well.

Duke continued by addressing the complete recanvassing of everyone they had already spoken to after Kelly's remains were located and identified.

Judge Grabau seized the change in direction of the testimony to take the afternoon lunch break. Before the attorney's left the courtroom, he brought them to the sidebar to talk about his final charge to the jury at the conclusion of the trial. It is customary for both sides to have input into the judge's framing of his comments, and they can request the inclusion or exclusion of information that is relevant to their version of the facts and theories of the case. He gave them until the following Monday morning to submit their final requests. Because both sides knew this moment would come, they were already partially prepared with arguments for and against certain topics and comments by the judge. It was one more burdensome task that the attorneys had to deal with over the next few days while still keeping their witnesses and testimony on track.

When court reconvened, Adrienne asked Duke if he knew a Louie Barone. She was now fully in favor of presenting Barone's testimony about his relationship and conversations with Crouse in the Cambridge Jail. She wanted Duke to lay a foundation before Barone made his appearance. She questioned him on how the two became familiar. He told the jurors of a phone call he received from a fellow trooper, and how, as a result, Sergeant Jimmy Connolly and he went to the Woburn District Court and met with Barone. He summarized their meetings from the holding cell in the courthouse through a series of visits at the Billerica House of Correction regarding information he provided about his time in the Cambridge Jail with Crouse.

Attorney Baccari took a somewhat scattered approach in his cross-examination of Duke with a series of short questions on several topics. He asked about the interview with Carla McKay, and Duke said he wasn't there for it. He asked about the search of the cabinets in the function room when they found the magazine, and Duke said there was little if anything else on the shelves or in the drawers. He shifted to the visit to Candia, NH, and asked about what Crouse was wearing, and Duke couldn't recall. He asked about the search of the truck with a Maglite flashlight, and Duke said he gave his light to Eddie Forster but wasn't there for the search. Baccari asked about a search of the storage room at Malden Mills assigned to Crouse's condo. Duke said that, after the condo was sold and Crouse had left, he asked the new owner if they could look into the storage room. The owner agreed. He added that sometime around May or June 2001 they searched the room but only found a pile of paint supplies.

Baccari switched topics and asked Duke about his conversations with Pete Grey and Nancy Cooper. His first questions concerned Cooper telling them about seeing someone in the parking lot the evening before the fire. Duke recalled Cooper saying she saw one person twice in the parking lot that evening when she took her dog for a walk. He said she couldn't identify the person or give a good description and she hadn't seen him again.

Baccari focused in on Pete Grey and the fact he had provided no information to the police during the initial interview but a week later had a lot to say and notes were made of that conversation. Duke could only answer to what he was told by Grey on July 26 and couldn't speculate about Grey's reasons for not sharing information earlier.

Baccari concluded with questions about Crouse's visceral reaction when told about the search warrant for his truck. He first asked if Crouse was wearing glasses, and Duke said he couldn't recall, and then he asked if it was unusual for people to get nervous and have varying responses like tearing up when approached by the police. Duke did say that he has seen people react nervously with varying responses to questions.

Whenever possible, Adrienne extracted damning testimony illustrating Crouse's unbalanced behavior around the time of Kelly's murder. It was her subliminal way of depicting his state of mind at the time of the murder, and she exposed it through his own words and actions, not through mere speculation.

She revealed it in snippets, beginning with the matter-of-fact way he had purchased and poured the gas into a container in the rear of his truck at the Mobil station a short time after killing a fourteen-year-old girl. Then an eyewitness saw him minutes later powering out of the parking lot at a high rate of speed seconds before the fire alarms sounded.

It came out again in the Fourniers' testimony when they described Crouse on the morning of the eighteenth as the "same old Tommy," upbeat and engaging. This was just hours after he murdered Kelly, loaded her remains into the back of his Blazer, and then buckled the kids into the backseat, a mere foot or two from her lifeless body. They talked of him as though he was a good parent going to the store for milk for the kids when his main reason for leaving the house was to bury her in a shallow grave eight miles away.

Adrienne demonstrated his slow unravelling when he returned to Malden Mills the next day. The people he knew there described him as nervous, concerned, questioning, sweating, and drunk. She introduced the extraordinary amount of phone calls he made on the eighteenth and nineteenth of July, and then she had his best friend, Stan Peterson, describe their meeting in the late morning of the nineteenth over a few beers at the Eagles Club. Peterson recalled Crouse was his usual self at that time but later that afternoon he called Peterson's cell phone in a panic, telling him that the police were looking for him and he was nervous because they found beer cans that could affect his probation status.

Duke's comment about seeing Crouse's eyes well up when he learned they were about to search his vehicle was yet another strike. Adrienne added another piece of information to demonstrate further Crouse's state of mind following Kelly's murder so she called Crouse's probation officer to the stand. The questions and answers had to be delicately constructed and limited to the fact that Crouse was on probation. She could not reference any prior Court-proven crimes he committed because that might prejudice the jury toward his guilt in this case.

The probation officer said her responsibilities included insuring that a probationer followed any court-ordered conditions connected to their release. She told the Court that she supervised Crouse on two occasions, once in 1998 and again in November of 2000. She added that the break in their chain occurred when he changed addresses and moved to another jurisdiction. She said they reconnected in November of 2000 when Crouse moved again and returned to the area under her office's authority.

She said they had a standing meeting in her office every two weeks from November of 2000 through June of 2001. Adrienne asked if they ever talked about the fire at Malden Mills, and she remembered speaking of it three or four times when Crouse brought it up. She said that he mentioned it the first time in passing when he asked if she knew about the fire. She said he told her the police were questioning everyone in the building but that he had left about twenty minutes before the fire started and went to New Hampshire with his family.

She said Crouse brought the fire up a second time when he told her the police had obtained a court order for DNA samples from him and his girlfriend, Esther. She recalled asking him if there was a Grand Jury investigation, and he said there had been one but nothing came of it, which prompted her to ask why the police were still pursuing an investigation. She said he mentioned that a police officer had it out for him. He also told her about a videotape the police had that showed him at the gas station before the fire. He said the police said he never told them about going there for gas that morning until the videotape surfaced. Crouse told her he was sure he had told the police earlier about him being at the station. She said he told her he had driven into the station the wrong way, with the gas pump furthest away from the door to the fuel tank. He also told her he had lifted up the hatch in the back but couldn't remember why. She indicated that at another meeting when the gas station issue came up, she said, "I asked him, I said, 'Well, you know, when you went to the gas station and pulled up on the wrong side, it wasn't like you were putting gas into a container or something.'" She added, "He didn't directly answer me but instead said, "I don't know why I lifted the hatch. You know, maybe it was a hot day. Maybe the kids were thirsty and I was getting them something to drink."

Crouse's comments to his probation officer were shy of an admission of guilt, but the last unsolicited answer indicating he couldn't remember why he opened the hatch and maybe to get the kids a drink was an obvious lie because the videotape showed him putting the nozzle inside the Blazer's rear window, and he knew it. Lying to his probation officer was just another piece of the puzzle. It wasn't enough to convict him of arson or murder, but it was a sign to the jury that whenever he was cornered with a damning question, he chose to lie.

While the rules of evidence forbade Adrienne from asking about the nature of Crouse's criminal convictions that resulted in his being on probation, Judge Grabau did allow her to elicit that she was supervising him for a felony.

On cross-examination, Baccari pointed out that Crouse instigated all of the conversations about the fire and that he shared information with her. He really couldn't probe any further without possibly bringing harm to his client by delving into his criminal record.

Given the choice, Adrienne would have preferred to end Thursday's testimony with an exclamation point and return fresh on Friday morning with her next group of witnesses, who were experts in the forensic sciences. However, there were still a few ticks before the clock struck four, and Judge Grabau was adamant about not wasting the court's time, so she had to produce her next witness.

Detective Lieutenant Ken Martin was a twenty-seven-year veteran and the commander of the State Police Crime Scene Services Section. He was a nationally recognized and certified expert on bloodstain pattern analysis and fingerprint identification. He received certifications as an expert witness in both bloodstain pattern analysis and fingerprint identification by judges in five Massachusetts superior courts, as well as the Boston Federal Court.

Adrienne opened by asking him to describe the meaning of blood-stain pattern analysis. He referred to it as a "study of blood in flight." Her goal was to have him instruct the jury on the science by breaking it down into small, connected segments that would allow a nonscientist to absorb what the meaning of his findings meant to the case.

Attorney Baccari quickly stood before Adrienne could ask the next question and requested a sidebar conference. He objected to the admission of this type of evidence by describing it as "junk science" that was not universally accepted into the scientific community. Judge Grabau responded that he was satisfied that the testimony and science would pass legal scrutiny under the Daubert Rule. He added that he had studied both issues in a previous trial where Martin testified as an expert on both fingerprint and blood spatter analysis and was satisfied that Martin's expertise and the science were both legally acceptable under the rules of evidence.

The trial resumed, and Adrienne asked Martin what he looked for during a bloodstain analysis. He explained in some depth about how he looks at the shape and size of a stain as well as the frequency and distribution of stains. He said he could determine factors such as the height the blood fell from and the angle of approach it took before it struck and adhered to an item. He differentiated bloodstains that fell downward with those that indicated they came from an upward rush of blood. He spoke of bloodstains with tails that indicated the direction the blood came from, and he explained the difference between larger bloodstains versus smaller, very fine droplets that form in a tighter pattern. He demonstrated how blood adhered differently depending on the roughness, smoothness, or slickness of a surface.

Adrienne showed several photographs of bloodstains on the overhead projector and asked Martin to explain his comments by pairing them with the pictures. It was an effective way to help clear up any confusion in the juror's minds while assisting them in further understanding the complexity of the process.

Martin went on to describe blood swipes that occur when blood or an item with blood on it is smudged or smeared against another surface creating a secondary or transfer stain. Before moving on to photographs of the crime scene, he pointed out that in conducting a bloodstain spatter analysis the absence of blood is just as important as the presence of blood. He commented that where there is a void in the staining it can mean that blood fell onto an object like a shoe, a garment, a piece of paper, a glass, etc. and that material was removed or carried away from the scene.

Adrienne turned to the series of photographs of the function room previously admitted as evidence and asked Martin to demonstrate how the bloodstains assisted him in reaching his conclusions. He pointed out the heavy red stains on the cushions from the couch, and how when they landed on the carpet, they left a smudge stain. He also showed where the cushion leaned up against a glass tabletop that someone had knocked off its base. He pointed out both direct and swipe stains on one of the walls, the floorboards, and a door, as well as a fourteen-inch wide bloodstain on the rug by the couch and table. He made note of the stains on the round piece of tabletop glass on the floor that had sat atop a metal stand that also had four stains on the legs of the stand. He spoke for more than an hour about each stain he had viewed in the room. He explained how he used special lighting and microscopic analysis of the staining to view the cumulative evidence and make conclusions about his observations.

Judge Grabau allowed Martin's testimony to continue until there was an objection and a request for a sidebar conference. It was a logical break in the questioning and occurred around four fifteen. Attorney Baccari argued that the fire allegedly occurred after the struggle and that could have contaminated the blood evidence, causing all of Martin's findings to be purely speculative. He once again questioned all of Martin's testimony as being the result of "voodoo science." Adrienne responded, "There is actually a methodology recommended when you are testing blood prints, that heat is a source…is a manner of making permanent the bloodstain in order to keep its position."

Judge Grabau overruled Baccari's objection and told him, "That's all good material for cross-examination. You can point to deficiencies, if any, in his methodology." At the close of the sidebar conversation, he excused Martin and the jurors until the following Friday morning at nine o'clock.

CHAPTER 21

The Trial: Day Ten
Seventh Day of Testimony

Before the jury walked into the courtroom on Friday, Judge Grabau conferenced with both attorneys to discuss what he considered a very serious issue: he wanted Adrienne to provide him with an offer of proof as to what opinions she expected Martin to make. He added that he was concerned she would ask about the parts of the body that were the source of the blood.

"Are you going to ask him whether the blood, more likely than not, to a degree of certainty, came from more than one wound?"

She answered, "No. I am going to ask him about his observations of the tabletop, the observation of certain pattern stains, and the opinion that the table was upright. I'm going to ask him about the fact that heat is a fixative of blood on the wall, in terms of his experience dealing with blood print evidence. So that, assuming hypothetically, there was fire and the heat had a preserving effect on the pattern of the stain, that with respect to his testimony concerning the appearance of the stain that has dried, and then was wiped, that a skeletoning of the stain is the appearance. And that with respect to the stains on the wall, there is no indication of skeletoning on the stain."

Judge Grabau expressed further concern that Martin's opinions or testimony would be based on, or piggybacked off Dr. Sorg's opinions and offer that there was more than one wound.

Adrienne addressed his concerns and said, "No. The purpose of this testimony is with respect to the reconstruction of the event itself and not the injury to the victim. As I had indicated earlier, the Commonwealth is proceeding on a theory of extreme atrocity or cruelty, which encompasses in it the victim's conscious degree of pain and suffering. There has been testimony from Dr. Andrew that a penetrating wound to the abdomen would cause considerable pain.

"With respect to the testimony of Lieutenant Martin, concerning the fact that the blood source was at a 90-degree angle from the table and some of the blood fell onto it, the table was upright at the time. The location and distribution of the stains enables the Commonwealth to make appropriate arguments concerning Kelly Hancock's movements and activities in the room at a time when she was bleeding; that all goes to establishing the Commonwealth's burden of proving beyond a reasonable doubt that the defendant acted with extreme atrocity or cruelty in the murder of Kelly Hancock."

She was firing from the hip after being caught a bit off guard by Judge Grabau's questions, but she delivered a succinct, direct response that not only allayed his fears but showed she had a clear, planned path forward.

The jury entered the courtroom, and as they settled into their seats, Detective Lieutenant Martin returned to the stand. Adrienne resumed the questioning by asking about the measures he took "that serve as a fixative for blood on evidence." Martin explained a chemical process using sulfosalicylic acid, as well as a method of using heat, to fix blood to a surface. She produced a series of photographs of bloodstains and blood spatters that he identified, and she offered into evidence. He pointed out a bloodstain that first hit the top of the glass and then bled to the edge and dripped down the side with the pull of gravity. He pointed out another area where there had been hairs on the tabletop, embedded in a bloodstain. He continued by identifying three tabletop impact spatter stains. At this point, he offered his expert opinion that when the blood dropped onto the table, the source of the blood was positioned perpendicular to the table.

Further questioning of Martin revealed that after the tabletop fell over, there were blood samples that adhered to the underside rim of the glass when the tabletop landed onto the bloodstain on the rug. Adrienne ended with a flurry of photographs for Martin to identify, describe, and then offer his expert professional opinion on how the blood scattered onto a series of different surfaces ranging from the walls, to the rug, to pieces of furniture in the area where the blood was contained.

In closing, Adrienne referred to the larger stains on the carpet and asked if Martin had a professional opinion as to whether or not they were consistent with a blood source being in contact with that area for at least some period. Martin opined that it would take a certain period of time for a stain that large to accrue, and that if the wound were smaller it would take even longer than if, it was a serious wound that would bleed from the source much more quickly.

Attorney Baccari offered no cross-examination of Detective Lieutenant Martin's observations or opinions, nor did he question the basis or theories of the "voodoo science" he referenced earlier during sidebar conversations.

As had happened earlier in the trial with the medical examiner and forensic anthropologist, Adrienne had to ask the Court's permission to present a witness out of order. A criminalist from the New Hampshire State Police Forensic Science Laboratory had scheduling conflicts that prevented her from testifying on the coming Monday with the other New Hampshire witnesses. Like those before her, she would offer testimony regarding Kelly's remains before the jury learned of how and where they had surfaced.

Attorney Baccari did not object, and Judge Grabau allowed Adrienne's request. The criminalist testified that at the time of her examination, she worked at the Serology and DNA Section of the Forensic Science Laboratory. She said her involvement in the case began a few days after they had found Kelly's body and following her autopsy. She said that Trooper John Cody, an investigator assigned to the Major Crime Unit had brought clothing and two shovels recovered at the crime scene in Hooksett, NH, to the lab for inspection and analysis.

She identified the two shovels from photographs shown on the over-head projector. She noted rust stains on the metal blades of both and said they resulted from exposure to the elements. She also pointed out pieces of vegetation that had adhered to the backsides of both shovels.

Shifting her attention to the clothing presented by Trooper Cody, Adrienne showed photographs to the criminalist for identification before putting them onto the screen for the jurors to see. She spoke of the denim shorts and long-sleeved, button-down plaid shirt and said they were stiff to the touch because of the heavy presence of "adiopocere." She described adiopocere as a "white waxy-type substance that sometimes forms when a body decomposes in a moist environment and the bacteria works on the fatty acids in our body to form this particular substance."

The criminalist went on to describe "significant" damage to the shirt. She pointed out that a large portion of the left front of the shirt was missing and the area around it was "jagged." She also pointed to the lower right side of the shirt where there was a "slit that was about three-quarters of an inch long," noting that the addition of the adiopocere made the area around the slit nice and firm. She added that the slit was "clean" with "the lines of the fabric all in line with each other," which was indicative of it being made by a sharp object. She said if made through a pull or a tear, the slit would appear "more fluffy."

Adrienne asked if she had tested the clothing for blood, and she responded that she had but due to exposure to the wet soaking elements, as well as the heavy amount of adiopocere bacteria that "breaks everything down," the stains had degraded to such a level that the tests were ineffective and unreliable.

Adrienne presented the criminalist with photographs of a white Gap tee shirt, which she identified as an item she tested. Using a pointer, she indicated where the left side of the shirt was missing and the area around it "jagged" and where the right side had a slit-like puncture that when viewed under a microscope showed a slit similar to the one on the outer shirt.

A woman's bra was the next item identified, and the criminalist indicated that it was whiter than the tee shirt and had some staining, and she noted an area on the left side where material was missing. The pair of denim shorts followed, and like the upper garments, there was a large portion of the left side missing, there was heavy brownish-looking staining, there were several holes in the fabric, and it had a "shredded look going up the left side."

The last item was a pair of underpants, which also had discoloration marks and several areas where "the fabric was shredded and missing." The criminalist said she performed a confirmatory p30 test and a microscopic exam for the presence of spermatozoa in the crotch panel with negative results from both. She added that exposure to the elements, the effects of the water would dilute the proteins, bacteria would break down the proteins over time, and that would result in a negative effect on any test results.

Adrienne wrapped up by asking the criminalist about her taking samples and submitting them to BODE Labs for analysis, and she responded that she had taken cuttings from the dark-stained area of the clothing and forwarded them to BODE Labs.

On cross-examination, Baccari asked about the slits in the fabric and the conditions of the cuts as well as how she took measurements of the cuts. He asked her about whether or not she had examined blood samples from the soil underneath the body, and she answered that she has never tested earth samples for the presence of blood. He asked other questions about the testing of plant roots taken from the scene, and she said that a botanist would have to do that type of testing because she wasn't qualified in that science.

• • • •

The jury took their morning break, and like during an intermission in a play, Adrienne used the moment to change the scenery in preparation for a new act. She had begun the trial with testimony from the firefighters who spoke of their actions and observations from the time they entered the smoke-filled function room at Malden Mills through the completion of their cleanup efforts. They described the "what, when, and where." It was finally time to bring in the fire science experts to explain the "how." It would be for the jury to decide the "who and why" once all of the evidence was presented to them.

Paul Horgan, from the Fire and Explosion Unit of the State Fire Marshal's office and the handler of Lucy, the accelerant-sniffing canine, was next up. Horgan had testified in court more than a hundred times, and he faced and spoke to the jurors with ease and a confident demeanor. He told them he was a trooper for more than ten years and had spent the last seven as a fire investigator. He spoke of his advanced training, the certifications he held, and the requirement for constant additional training to maintain those certifications.

He talked of and for his partner, Lucy, and their six years together investigating fires and seeking the accelerants often used to start and feed the flames. He added that Lucy and he had trained together every day and must pass an annual testing protocol to retain their nationwide certification. Horgan added that he was a nationally certified fire investigator with the International Association of Arson Investigators, as well as by the Commonwealth of Massachusetts. In addition, he instructed on fire investigations to a national audience at the FBI, ATF, and State training facilities.

Horgan said he had examined more than fourteen hundred fire scenes, more than eleven hundred of them with Lucy. He was qualified as an expert witness in origin and cause of fires on twelve occasions in the Massachusetts Superior Courts, and as an accelerant detection canine handler in several of those cases.

Adrienne spent a lot of time questioning Horgan on his education, training, and experience for good reason. She knew that the defense had hired two fire science experts to review the evidence and Baccari had added their names to his witness list. She also knew their qualifications and hands-on experience paled next to Horgan's, and she wanted the jurors to remember that when they were deliberating the case. She would do the same with the witness who followed Horgan.

Horgan explained how the troopers assigned to his unit always collaborated with local police and firefighters to investigate the cause and origin of fires and explosions. He then described the general path investigators had taken that led them to the origin of a fire.

He explained that all certified fire investigators take a systemic approach to each case following the guidelines established by the National Fire Protection Association (NFPA) and codified in the *NFPA 921*. He said they view the entire scene, define the problem areas, and develop a plan of attack. They collect data, preserve evidence, take photographs, and eventually develop a hypothesis or theory as to how the fire started. Then they test the theory against all other potential hypotheses or causes. The result is a final determination as to whether the fire was the result of an accident or intentionally set. "Or on occasion, when we can't figure it out," he continued, "it would be an undetermined-type fire."

When asked about the role that accelerant detection canines play in an investigation, Horgan answered, "They are used to locate and detect traces of ignitable liquids in fire scenes."

With the foundation established, Adrienne began her inquiry about his response to Malden Mills on the morning of the fire. He talked of his initial observations, and Adrienne produced photographs to support his comments. She presented them to the jury on the overhead projector and he identified each one before entering them into evidence. He spoke of burned areas, a bubbled-up carpet, and the strong odor of an accelerant that caused him to prep Lucy to come into the room to see if she would alert to the presence of ignitable liquids.

He explained how accelerant-trained canines react on a food reward system. The handlers bring the dogs into the scene and after a few moments of familiarization tell them to "seek." If the canine finds a likely source, they sit down and look to the handler for their reward. After that, the next command is "show me." The canine puts their nose directly onto the spot of the strongest source of the odor, and that is where the sample is collected. He added that in this instance Lucy immediately alerted in several areas of the room. He said he placed orange cones onto those spots and took photos to document her "finds." Adrienne provided him with photos of the areas he referenced, and he identified them.

Horgan spoke of an oddity in Lucy's behavior that got his attention. It captured the juror's attention as well. He said after alerting on the accelerant sites she continued to sniff and then lapped up the water and licked at the carpet. He said the only time she did that was at fatal fire scenes and in the areas where a body was or had been located.

He added, "For her, that's a kind of food as well, so I notice that kind of behavior. As the water receded, we had noted a pink or red tint in the carpet. As we began to look deeper into the fire scene, we started to observe things a little more closely. For example, the red marks on the wall. And at that point, we thought we had something here that was a little more than just a fire." He said that was when they decided to call the Homicide Unit from the Middlesex DAO.

For the next several minutes, Adrienne had Horgan address every aspect of his examination from the spotting and collection of evidence to the patterns of smoke and soot that are signs or products of combustion. He not only detailed the general damage but also was particular about the position of the chairs, cushions, and the table as well, saying he determined that the chairs were tipped and the table knocked over before the fire because the areas underneath them did not have soot but the areas around them did.

Adrienne transitioned from the fire to the activation of the sprinkler heads to douse the flames and the heat detectors to sound the alarms to the residents and the Malden Fire Department. Horgan described how four of the pendant sprinkler heads had opened and poured a torrent of water onto the floor and furniture below. He described their location and said the fire scene was inside the area covered by the four heads. He added that several other heads throughout the room did not activate and opined that was because they were outside of the fire zone.

She asked Horgan to explain both systems and describe their activation system. He described the sprinkler system as a "wet-type," which means the pipes always contain water. The heads are independent of each other and are set to discharge when the temperature at ceiling height reaches 155 degrees Fahrenheit. The bulb inside the head heats up and fails, thereby causing the retaining cap to let go, releasing the water in the pipes onto the sprinkler head and showering an apron of water over the heated area. Regarding the alarm system, he said, "The fixed rate heat detectors have a setting of 135 degrees. When the heat invades the detector, a plastic disk melts and releases a plunger that drops down and closes the circuit, which sends a signal back to the alarm panel to tell it there's been a failure of the heat detector." Horgan added that when these particular systems fail there is an immediate, audible alarm within the building and a direct notification to the local fire department.

Adrienne asked Horgan about spilled gasoline on a hardwood floor versus a carpet, and he explained that a carpet absorbs the liquid but a floor allows it to spread out.

At this point, Attorney Baccari requested a sidebar to challenge Horgan's qualifications and expertise. He said that those with master's degrees from accredited colleges should present these opinions and findings. Adrienne argued to the contrary, and Judge Grabau agreed with her.

"The issue of qualifications is for me," he said, "I've qualified him before. And we already did a *voir dire* in this case. I'm satisfied he's qualified to give opinions, even in this area."

Horgan continued and explained that a wider pool of liquid allows the vapors to mix better with the air and the heat release rate would be much higher. Adrienne asked about the term "fire load," and Horgan replied it is the "total quantity of combustible contents in a building or a space or a fire room. And it includes such things as furniture, carpeting, the finish, and the wood on the walls: anything that is combustible within the area."

Adrienne asked if he had formed an opinion on the cause and origin of the fire, and Horgan replied that he did.

"My opinion," he said, "is that the origin of the fire was within an area along the east wall and that the cause of the fire was the deliberate arrangement of ignitable liquid poured into several locations in this room: deliberately poured into specific locations and then ignited with an open flame."

He said the ignition source was the open flame, adding that the actual burn damage was minor and not indicative of an intense, high-temperature, fast-moving fire but more suggestive of a slow-generating fire. He determined it was a gasoline fire because of the heavy black smoke and soot, which are the products of that type of combustion.

Judge Grabau interrupted and called for the lunch break and a respite from the important, but complex, scientific testimony.

When court resumed at two o'clock, Adrienne asked Horgan if his experience and training allowed him to tell which of the four sprinkler heads activated first or if there was a sequential activation. He replied that he could not.

Her questioning shifted from the fire scene to Crouse's Chevy Blazer and Horgan's participation in the execution of a search warrant in October 2000. Horgan said that Lucy and he had inspected the vehicle. He explained how he picked her up and as soon as he placed her onto the tailgate, she made a primary alert on a metal grommet in the right-hand corner of the truck bed closest to the tailgate. He told how he preserved the sample and took other comparison samples for lab testing. Horgan also addressed a discoloration or bleached out area on the truck's tailgate. He identified photos Adrienne put in front of him and pointed out areas of concern on the overhead projector.

Adrienne asked him about the laboratory results on the grommet, and he said they were negative. He added the findings were unusual because Lucy's proficiency rate was in the area of 90 to 95 percent. Adrienne asked if he had reviewed the videotape and still photographs from the Mobil station that showed Crouse pouring gas into a container through the rear hatch of his vehicle. He said he had and that Lucy made her primary hit in that area of the Blazer.

Hogan ended by saying the two-month delay between the fire and their inspection of the Blazer might have affected Lucy's ability to find traces of evidence. He added, "It is a proven fact that the canine's ability to detect minute traces of ignitable liquid are more sensitive than the equipment used to test those samples."

On cross-examination, Attorney Baccari challenged Horgan's findings on several fronts, mostly through the creation of hypothetical situations that were different from the facts of the case already in the record. For example, he questioned whether his testimony would change if he knew that Crouse had moved several pieces of gas-powered machines the day before the fire and that was where the odor had come from. Horgan answered that it could if there was evidence that gas had spilled from the machines.

Over the next hour, Baccari contested Horgan on every aspect of the fire, the sprinkler system, the heat alarms, and his expert opinions. He was doing his best to create doubt in a juror's mind regarding the science of fire and combustion by showing how a slight change in variables or circumstances could result in dramatically different test results and opinions. He had no facts to support the hypotheticals he presented, he just asked "What if?" questions and asked Horgan to respond. The creation of hypothetical, alternative situations that might alter the witness opinion is an often-used tactic by attorneys during the questioning of experts. It was also well-established law that this method or approach is acceptable.

Baccari finished by concentrating on the timing of events from the moment the fire was set through the time the ceiling temperature was hot enough to trigger the alarms. He tried to budge him from his opinion of ten minutes to something less, but Horgan stood fast.

Adrienne spent a few moments in her redirect to have Hogan clarify the term "fuel rich" and offer an opinion that if less gasoline was poured onto the rug, the fuel-to-air ratio would have been greater and would have resulted in a more efficient and intense fire.

This was important testimony for the jury to hear because it not only spoke to the fire but also to the time gap between when Crouse left the parking lot with his family and the moment the ear-piercing alarms went off in the building and at Malden Fire Headquarters.

When Horgan stepped down from the witness stand fifteen minutes remained in the day and the week. Adrienne had another fire expert, Thomas Klem, waiting on a bench outside the courtroom. It was clear he would barely start his testimony before the judge would call an end to the day. It was Friday, and the jurors were looking to start their weekend—and not necessarily to adding to what was already an information overload.

The judge allowed Adrienne to bring her witness to the stand but only to introduce and qualify him as an expert. Klem referred to his profession as a consulting fire protection engineer. His resume presented a broad history of education, training, and experience ranging from a master's degree in fire protection engineering, to a twelve-year career as a firefighter, and arson investigator in Prince George's County in Maryland. He said he had investigated well over five hundred cases where he determined the cause and origin of the fire. He mentioned that he was a contributor to the Fire Investigative Manual referred to as the 921, which is the bible for the investigative process for fire and explosions throughout the United States. He finished his statement of qualifications mentioning he was a certified arson investigator through the International Association of Arson Investigators.

With the introduction of Klem complete, Judge Grabau rose from his seat and said, "We'll stop here. This is a good place."

• • • •

After seven days of draining, often complicated testimony, the jurors looked forward to the break. They needed an opportunity to lighten up and let their minds drift elsewhere. A few had told the court officers they were heading to Cape Cod with family for a couple of days of rest and reflection. Serenity was only an hour or so drive from the intensity of the courtroom to the peacefulness of the ocean and the beach. They were off to places where they could walk for miles in the sand, rummage around small village boutiques for after-summer bargains, or just sit and relax with a book, a drink, and their loved ones. The only noises that might interrupt their thoughts that weekend were the gently rolling waves as they broke and hissed along the shore and the laughter of children as they ran in the sand trying to get their kites airborne- a perfect escape. The short respite and recovery would serve them well because the coming week would be one of the most challenging and difficult weeks of their lives.

Before heading out of the courtroom, Adrienne and Nat spent a few moments with Klem. They apologized for needing him to return on Monday before beginning a quick review of his expected testimony, reemphasizing the points they would concentrate on to make the biggest impact on the jury.

Once downstairs, they made the daily stop to see John McEvoy. They talked of how they had successfully addressed the legal challenges that arose. They discussed their proposed jury instructions for Judge Grabau and the framework of Adrienne's closing argument, which could come as early as Wednesday. Their biggest concern was Louie Barone's testimony and the impact both he and his statements would have on the jurors. He certainly came with the heavy baggage of a criminal past and a few years spent in jail, but he also brought some significant information gleaned during his jailhouse conversations with Crouse that the jury needed to hear. If all went as planned, his testimony would begin at the end of the day on Monday.

At a few minutes before five, as we were preparing to close up shop for the weekend, we could hear Adrienne's heels clicking across the cement pathway from her office to ours. We gathered around as she told us where the testimony ended for the day and that Klem would be on the stand first thing Monday morning. "The New Hampshire guys will go on right after him, and with any luck, we will get through their testimony and end the day with Barone." She continued. "I made the request to have him picked up and brought in from Billerica by the late morning. Eddie, I told them that you were going to be his custodian for the trips back and forth. I hope that hasn't changed. Either Nat or I will have a few moments to speak with him at the lunch break before he takes the stand. Do you think he's ready, Duke? No second thoughts or concerns?" she asked.

"None that I know of," Duke answered. "He seemed pretty matter-of-fact about the whole thing when we spoke with him a few days ago. The corrections officers will have their eye on him this weekend to make sure he isn't harassed or threatened. I think we are all set."

"And Eddie," she said, "Are the New Hampshire police officers still planning on being here for the start of the day? If it's not too late, maybe you can let them know they won't be on first, but I promise, they will be back in Concord before the sun sets."

"They know the courtroom game, Adrienne, and that we can't control the timing," Eddie told her, "But I did speak with Lieutenant Forey this afternoon, and she said they would be here on time and ready to go. So I think we should leave it at that and not start making phone calls at the end of the week."

"We are headed down to the mall," he said, "Do you want to come with us and have a beer to end the week?"

"Thank you, Eddie," she said with a nod and sarcastic smile. "But not today, I have so much work in front of me I'll be lucky to stop for a cup of coffee or a bowl of soup this weekend. I'll tell you what, though; if we have a verdict by this time next week we all go out, win, or lose."

"Adrienne," Eddie cringed and shot back, "Don't say that. You never mention losing, so don't start now. We aren't thinking in that direction at all. All of our faith is in you. No pressure though. You have a deal for next Friday, and we're buying."

She walked back across the hall to look for Anne Foley and talk about the Hancocks. Adrienne saw and spoke with Mark and Jackie on each day of the trial. She wanted them to know what to expect from the witnesses and to alert them to the more graphic testimony. Most days, the couple sat quietly together in the courtroom listening to the sometimes infuriating and often gruesome details about their daughter Kelly's final moments. They knew the information overload wouldn't get any better and that the following Monday the investigators from New Hampshire would speak to the jury about the recovery of Kelly's remains. As difficult as each day had been for them, they continued to hold it together. They knew any outburst could cause a mistrial or Judge Grabau could ban them from the courtroom. They continued to express total faith in Adrienne and the entire prosecution team and did not want to do anything to disrupt their momentum.

Mark was on the witness list for Tuesday, and all we could do was hope his sometimes-explosive temper would be under control. Easy to say, but I'm not sure if I were in his shoes that I could restrain mine.

We headed toward the finish line with just a few days of testimony remaining. Tom Klem would be first up on Monday morning. In some ways, his proposed testimony might appear as a duplication of Horgan's, but it wasn't. His expertise had more to do with the timing of events than the technical operation of the heat detectors and sprinkler system. Adrienne anticipated that Baccari's cross-examination would concentrate on getting Klem to shorten the time gap from the start of the fire to the time the sprinklers and heat detectors activated. Previous witness testimony had Crouse peeling out of the driveway several minutes before the alarms sounded. A slow-growing fire would have taken some time before the heat level rose and the fire and heat alarms sounded. If the fire had developed slowly, the timing between the start of the fire and Crouse's exit would coincide perfectly. The defense theory was the exact opposite. They had to convince the jury that the fire grew and spread rapidly with scant moments between the setting of the fire and the sounding of the alarms. If the jury bought into the defense argument, they would have to believe Crouse had cleared the parking lot long before the fires started and the alarms began to sound. A substantially longer time for the alarm to sound would damage that theory. In a circumstantial case, any unexplained gap between events can be fatal, and Adrienne wasn't going to let that happen.

On another front, Adrienne and Nat knew that Louie Barone was the only person who could bring out the personality and mindset of Tommy Crouse to the jury. At this point, they only knew Tommy Crouse as the person sitting next to the defense attorney. While a few witnesses spoke of or pointed him out, there was only limited testimony about a couple of short alibi conversations the police had with him, some reactions from witnesses who knew him, and a damning thumbprint on the cover of a gentleman's magazine. To this point, there hadn't been any direct conversation from Crouse to anyone about the murder and the fire. As an old prosecutor friend of mine used to say about inmates testimony, "You don't find swans in the sewer," but that does not mean you can't find truthful, empathetic people. Adrienne would do her best to display that side of Barone.

The last challenging hurdle for Adrienne was to find a way to bring Kelly to life. She needed to paint a realistic picture of her but do so with understanding and compassion. To do that, she would bring in the police officer who had found her walking the streets in the early morning hours, the social worker whom she had run from (one of the last persons she had spoken with), a friend she loved, and finally, her dad. Kelly may not have been a saint, but she hadn't been a devil either, and the jury needed to know more about her troubled life.

Jimmy Connolly would be the last witness for the prosecution. He was "batting clean up" in her lineup, and would talk about his supervisory role in the investigation, as well as Crouse's arrest, and his initial meetings with Barone.

Adrienne would spend most of the weekend preparing her cross-examination strategy for the defense witnesses. She knew of two defense witnesses who planned to refute the testimony about the fire science. She had their resumes and reports in separate file folders along with page after page of cross-examination questions she would ask. She had spoken with Klem and Horgan about the defense witnesses, and together they had helped her prepare a rebuttal to their testing methods and findings.

Based on Baccari's witness list, she also anticipated he would call two correction officers from the Cambridge Jail to offer contradictory information that they hoped would offset Barone's testimony. She prepared for that eventuality and was waiting to hear from Jimmy Connolly about conversations he'd had with those jail employees.

CHAPTER 22

The Trial: Day Eleven
Eighth Day of Testimony

The third week of trial began with Judge Grabau asking if anyone had read or heard about the case on the weekend or saw anything about it on television. No one answered in the affirmative. The media reporting had been limited and on many days with the exception of the Boston Globe, nonexistent, which all but eliminated concerns of future appeals about subjective press reports compromising or contaminating the thoughts of jurors and witnesses.

Tom Klem returned to his spot on the witness stand, picking up where he left off on Friday. Adrienne asked about the methodology he had used to determine causes and origin of a fire and he, like Horgan before him, gave a similar explanation and referenced to the *NFPA 921* as the primary sourcebook of guidelines adhered to by all certified fire investigators. When she asked about his involvement in this case and whether or not he had visited the site, looked at photographs and diagrams, and spoken with firefighters and investigators who were at the function room on the day of the fire, he answered yes to all of her questions.

"The way I would summarize that is," he said, "you want to take a look at the on-site fire photos or visit the site, if that's possible, to draw upon your experiences and establish plausible scenarios that are precipitants of the physical evidence." He continued, "So you're trying to gain from the fire scene what happened and determine some of the scenarios that make sense and then proceed through other parts of the methodology."

Klem spoke of the fire protection devices in the function room, particularly the heat detectors, and the sprinkler system. He said he reviewed the original blueprints and the installation plan before conducting a full, standard examination of the systems. He said the pendent-type sprinklers were set to activate when the ceiling temperature reached 155 degrees Fahrenheit. He added that the building owners installed the system in 1988 and there had been no servicing or testing of the equipment since then.

He referenced the term Response Time Index (RTI) and its value as a variable used to predict the response of the sprinkler system based on various fire scenarios and the intensity of a fire. He said the RTI is established when the sprinkler head is new and in optimal condition, but since fourteen years had passed and there had been no upkeep to the device, environmental changes such as corrosion or the gathering of dust and lint could have delayed the response time. In this case, the activation was originally set for thirty-seven seconds, and he said he used that number as his testing variable but added it likely took longer than that to operate.

Baccari requested a sidebar, clearly upset with the line of questioning. He argued he never received any information in discovery that referenced the possible variations that Klem was referring to in drawing conclusions as to the reasoning of his opinions. Adrienne countered that the subject matter he was talking about was common knowledge in the fire investigation field and she needn't provide every possible fire science theory as part of discovery. Judge Grabau agreed with her and allowed the line of questioning to continue. Once again, he told Baccari he could best address his concerns during witness cross-examination.

Adrienne segued into the use of computer software to determine outcomes and asked Klem if there was a distinction between post-fire computer modeling and performance-based design computer modeling? He said there was, and when asked to describe or contrast the differences, Baccari again leapt to his feet to object to the question and requested a sidebar conference. He was furious because he felt blindsided and unprepared for the forthcoming testimony. Adrienne responded that she had provided all of the information in advance as required by the rules of discovery. She was candid in admitting she was presenting the information in anticipation of the defense witnesses offering of testimony that would be contrary to Klem's presentation. She added that "at pages forty to forty-three of her discovery documentation the Commonwealth set out exactly what it expected Mr. Klem to testify to. The fire investigation field utilizes computer modeling. Your expert should be aware of the requirements and the assessments. It's a matter of their professional practice."

Judge Grabau allowed the line of questioning to continue. Adrienne repeated her question about the differences in the computer modeling, and Klem responded, "I think it takes, in my opinion, a different mix of skills in order to do the application of computer modeling as if we were designing a building and anticipating ignition scenarios and so forth. Although there is application for computer modeling and post-fire analysis, one needs an additional set of skills, in my view, in order to accurately interpret the physical evidence on a fire scene and apply the appropriate modeling input data."

Then she asked, "As a fire protection engineer and a certified arson investigator, Mr. Klem, would you ever rely upon the result of computer modeling without consideration for the physical evidence and the conditions of the scene?" Baccari's objection to the question was overruled, and Klem responded, "My answer is no."

Klem's answers about computer modeling appeared straightforward and innocent, but they were also a well-placed preemptory strike against the defense's expert witnesses. Adrienne planned to discredit them due to their lack of experience, skill, and certification that Klem referenced as critical to making assumptions and giving an opinion based on the computer modeling results. The jurors didn't need to understand the importance of Klem's comments at that moment, but his words would resurface later when they were listening to the opposing witnesses and deciding on their credibility.

At Adrienne's direction, Klem stepped from the witness stand and went to the media screen that featured Exhibit 164, a photograph of the function room taken on the morning of the fire. She asked about pour patterns and asked him to point out the areas in the room where his analysis indicated there were sources of gasoline collection. He noted four areas that were already marked with small cones, and he said that Paul Horgan had placed them there to represent the spots Lucy had hit on for accelerants. He offered an opinion that the fire began in a pool of gasoline located along the east wall that had "consumed the nap of the carpet." He theorized the fire had moved from that point to the center of the floor where the furniture was located. He noted the damage to the pillow and chair and referred to the damage as "light, indicating a very light exposure to heat." He pointed to the carbon deposits along the ceiling that ran in a conical pattern from the east wall to the center of the ceiling. He spoke of the fire growth and said, "In my view, the ignition took place and there is a ventilation system along the ceiling, close to the east wall, and that's determined by a two-by-two foot ventilation system that significantly influenced the initial growth, development, and spread of the fire. And that would subsequently result in a delay in the activation of the fire alarm devices within the building, including the heat detectors and the automatic sprinklers."

Wrapping up, Adrienne asked if because of his investigation, he had an "opinion to a reasonable degree of scientific certainty within his field, as to the amount of time between the ignition of the initial fire and the activation of the sprinkler systems in this case?"

He answered, "Based on a review of the data, both on-scene and the computer modeling, I believe and have determined that at least five to five and a half minutes were the delay responsible in this particular fire scenario."

She presented him with a hypothetical situation that mimicked the earlier testimony of the resident who lived in a condo close to the function room. The witness said he was awake and dressed, heard the alarm, walked out of his condo toward the exit, and after a few steps, he noticed the water seeping out of from under the function room door. Klem said the timing of the events supported his findings because it showed the water was pouring from the sprinklers for several seconds before the alarms activated.

Klem described the fire damage as minimal and said the singeing of the couch, pillow, and other materials did not contribute to the overall heat release rate. He said the fire was "not robust." Adrienne ended her direct examination by asking if he had ever seen or investigated a 3,500-kilowatt fire and, if so, could he describe the amount of damage associated with that type of fire. He replied that he had and a fire of that temperature and intensity would result in significantly more damage than this one did.

Klem's cross-examination was of monumental importance to the defense. Perhaps the strongest argument for Tommy Crouse was that there were no known witnesses tying him to Kelly Hancock before her disappearance. Close if not equal to that argument was that he could not have started the fire in the function room because he and his family were well on their way to New Hampshire when the alarms sounded. Each side would present experts to offer opinions on the timing and the magnitude of the fire that would differ by a scant three to four minutes: shorter than the time it took Abraham Lincoln to read the Gettysburg Address from the back of an envelope, but important enough to be the difference between life in a prison bunk for Crouse or one in a lounge chair in the living room of his home. With the prosecution's case built completely on circumstantial evidence, damage to any piece of the prosecution's puzzle could have a devastating consequence. It was clear that the defense team recognized the importance of the moment; they had done their homework and were prepared for battle.

The cross-examination began with Klem restating his opinions on where the fire began and how it had spread. Klem held fast in his belief that none of the heat sensors activated during the fire, insisting instead that the sprinkler system sent the message to the control panel that triggered the internal alarms and the messaging to the fire department. He agreed that the fire was hot enough to melt the two plastic-type light coverings in the ceiling that was seven and a half feet from the floor. He also conceded that he never examined or saw any of the sprinkler heads or heat sensors that were in the room during the fire because they were no longer available.

Klem defined the four gas pour areas as the carpet on the east wall, the end table and the pillow, the couch, and lastly, the wingback chair. He said there were no signs of multiple ignition, but it was possible that at one point, when the sprinklers were activating, all four areas were simultaneously on fire.

The topic changed to computer modeling and a discussion about different software programs used in the industry to recreate or explain what occurred during the fire. Klem explained that while each program offered distinct features, they all relied on the same basic science and algorithms to reach their conclusions. The difference was in the "how and how much" data was collected and inputted by the investigator. Baccari questioned Klem about his findings indicating that it took five to five and a half minutes for the alarms to sound. Klem stood his ground, adding that he included the thirty-seven second delay between activation and notification in his analysis and that he considered the time frame a conservative estimate.

Baccari switched to questions about the volume of gasoline poured into the room. Klem replied that he doesn't base his findings on an assumption of how much gas the arsonist used. "I chose that the more accurate way of doing a fair and accurate analysis is not to make an assumption on the gallons used, because I think that is slushy, but to use the area of burn as indicative of the burning area and then relate that back to the spill area. I did that calculation and I'm in the ballpark of what I estimated to be at $1.35 a gallon, five dollars' worth of gas."

After the morning break, Baccari resumed questioning but switched the topic to heat release rates and referenced a Department of Justice

(DOJ) report that provided the calculations that Klem relied on. They spoke of pool fires versus spill fires and the effects of fire on porous versus nonporous surfaces. The jousting continued with Klem repeatedly offering contrary explanations to Baccari's suppositions and hypothetical-based questions.

Baccari questioned Klem about his assumptions regarding the HVAC system and the vent above the fire source. He asked if Klem was aware that the system was in the off position prior to the fire and asked if that would have made a difference to his findings. Klem said he was aware, but it didn't change his opinion because the heat would still rise and pour into the system regardless of whether the system was activated or not.

As the questioning wound down, Baccari tried to make a substantial and damaging accusation that the RTIs of the sprinkler heads Klem relied on were inaccurate. He produced a letter from the manufacturer that contained an RTI number for the sprinkler heads that differed from the one Klem had relied on. Klem took the letter, reviewed it, and said, "These don't reflect the model that was installed in the function room." He pointed out that the company representative gave numbers for both the 3- and 5-millimeter devices, but the ones installed at Malden Mills were 8 millimeters in size and there was a great variation between the RTIs for all three. What initially looked like a haymaker to Klem's jaw turned out to be a miss that came with a counterpunch body blow that Baccari couldn't return.

The cross-examination looked more like an academic exercise, paralleling a student defending his doctoral dissertation during a critical inquiry into his conclusions. In the end, it appeared that the well-prepared Klem had withstood the attack and effectively championed his findings.

Adrienne's redirect was short and to the point. She asked about his judgment that the delay between the start of the fire and the alarms sounding was approximately five to five and one half minutes. He answered that the times given were conservative.

The testimony proffered by Horgan and Klem was comprehensive and exhaustive, burrowing deeply into the chemistry of fire and the mechanics of the sprinkler and heat alarm systems. The jury probably deserved training certificates for the hours of education they received in the courtroom classroom.

• • • •

While the fire science testimony challenged the learning component of their brains, the next witnesses would strike at the emotional element. Adrienne moved to solidify the connection between the function room and the recovery of Kelly's remains in Hooksett with the New Hampshire police officials who had worked on the discovery and recovery of her corpse.

Leslie McDaniel was the Hookset Police patrol supervisor on the overnight shift on April 23, 2001. He spoke of a radio call dispatching him to a place off Industrial Drive to meet a caller who took him a few hundred yards or so down a tree-lined path and pointed out what appeared to be a human skull sitting on the ground on a small plateau area. McDaniel described inspecting it as well as noticing some dried skin and hair fragments still attached, but he stated he did not touch it or remove it from the original spot.

He stood by the viewing screen with a pointer in hand, as Adrienne put four photographs onto the projector and asked him to describe and indicate the path he had taken and where he had located certain objects. The jurors would recall the scene from their walk through two weeks earlier.

He said he had notified the dispatcher and his chief about his findings and asked them to reach out to the State Police Major Crime Unit for assistance.

McDaniel described the area as one of industrial businesses with several commercial buildings setback from the roadway. Adrienne asked him about snow and rain in Hooksett from the date of Kelly's disappearance to the day of her recovery. He simply responded, "I'm sure there was some between those time frames." Before he left the stand, Adrienne offered a copy of the weather charts for the period from late July 2000 through April 23, 2001. The custodian from the National Climatic Center records previously certified them, so the defense did not object to entering them into evidence.

Trooper First Class John Cody of the New Hampshire State Police Major Crime Unit followed. He spoke of his experience as a police officer and paramedic for the previous eight years. He told the jury of his specialized training and experience in the recovery of human and skeletonized remains, stating he had participated in the excavation of six human bodies.

Addressing the morning of April 23, 2000, Cody said he had responded to the recovery scene and met with the Hooksett detectives and how, with the aid of a state police cadaver dog, they had discovered the larger burial site several feet away. As witnesses before him did, he identified photographs of the area that were then used as reference points for the jury to view and link to his testimony.

He said on first glance the area where the canine alerted appeared overgrown and covered in leaves, but upon closer inspection, he saw a small part of a body protruding from the soil, as well as some pieces of clothing.

Cody said he was the designated evidence technician for the case, and in that role, he supervised the unearthing and preservation of the remains. He mentioned that additional officers and Dr. Andrews were at the scene and had assisted in the removal. He described their slow, methodical process of scraping the earth with trowels and brushes to protect the body from further damage. He said that to prevent any potential loss of evidence he had placed all of the dirt and brush into plastic buckets, which were poured onto a portable mesh-sifting screen and shaken vigorously to separate out any small bones or other evidence from the dirt and leaves. He spoke of the meticulous recovery process, and that anything less could result in a tainted or incomplete removal that could complicate the decision-making for the medical examiner in determining the cause and manner of death.

He described the immediate area around the burial site and said he looked over an earthen berm a few steps away and down a ravine to a brook that ran several feet below. He had climbed down the dirt and rocky ledge and, once at the bottom, noted two shovels: one tall and one short. The team had photographed and eventually removed the shovels for further processing and fingerprinting.

Turning his attention to the excavation, Adrienne asked him to describe what he, Dr. Andrews, and the other troopers did to assure they did not damage the remains in the process. He said they had removed all of the leaves, and brushed on and around the burial site by hand and cut down a small sapling to open up their access. Cody continued, "And then, when we got to the dirt area, we would scoop away and brush away the dirt area, layer by layer, until we got down to the skeletonized remains themselves." Using photographs, he pointed out an indentation in the ground that he surmised was where the cranium had originally been located. With photographs, he pointed out a lower jawbone as well as a complete area of human hair with a scrunchie holding it all together both found just outside of the gravesite perimeter and close to the indentation in the ground.

Adrienne provided Cody with a surveyor's diagram of the area and asked him to point out the areas he had referenced in his testimony. She then asked about the chain of custody of the human remains, and Cody described how he took them from the scene in the major crime evidence van to his office in Concord, secured them in the garage overnight, and then brought them to Concord Hospital the following morning for the autopsy.

Turning his attention to April 24, Cody said he had attended the autopsy at the OCME and assisted in the process by fully documenting the procedures and taking custody of any potential evidence that would require further examination and testing at the state police laboratory.

Cody said he subsequently took evidence to the lab for further processing and later returned to the OCME on the twenty-sixth and signed out certain items consisting of vertebrae, skin, hair, and the clothing that had been on the body. He added that he took those items to the crime lab and turned them over to Kim Rumrill for testing and safekeeping.

Adrienne closed out her questioning by asking Cody about the shovels. He spoke of a tall and short one and the fact that one had a rounded blade and the other a square one. He added that at the burial scene there were shovel markings in the dirt and they were "absolutely consistent" with the blades of the shovels located next to the brook.

On cross-examination, Attorney Baccari focused on the location and type of shovels found at the bottom of the ravine. He didn't ask any questions about the human remains or their removal. He used the moment to deflect the juror's attention from the gore and the emotion of Cody's testimony to the inanimate shovels. He perceived them as a weakness in the prosecution's case, and he planned to address and exploit it more thoroughly later in the day.

Susan Forey, recently promoted to the rank of lieutenant on the New Hampshire State Police, was a sergeant in the Major Crime Unit at the time of the discovery of the body, and was the case supervisor. She talked about the depth of their investigation and their attempts to identify the human remains. She said troopers in her office spoke with more than ninety people and the case file was more than two inches thick. She described the nationwide teletype messages they sent to PDs regarding the recovery of a body and the possibility they located a person reported missing in their jurisdiction. Their messages described the basic profile of a teenaged female, the hair coloring, and the clothing she was wearing when they found her. She estimated they had received responses from dozens of PDs from ten to fifteen states, as well as an inquiry from Trooper Ed Forster from Massachusetts. Forey's testimony was short but reinforced the bridge linking the Malden discovery to Kelly's recovery.

Adrienne knew there were two potentially identifiable fingerprints on one of the shovels, and she wanted to put this information before the jury. She chose to present the exculpatory evidence and not leave it to the defense to bring it up and give the jurors the impression that the prosecution was hiding or holding back potentially critical information that might exonerate Crouse.

A latent fingerprint specialist from the New Hampshire State Police Crime lab explained the four progressive steps he took in his efforts to locate fingerprints. He said he began with a visual inspection, moved to the use of special colored lenses with an alternate light source, before applying a chemical agent to the handles and shaft, and finally performed a process involving super glue and a heat source. He said he had attempted all four options on both shovels and found no prints on the taller, square bottom shovel, but through the super glue process, he had located two prints on the plastic handle of the shorter, rounded bottom shovel. He explained how he identified them as coming from the left index and middle fingers because of their placement on the shovel.

Adrienne asked about the use of comparison or exclusionary fingerprints to match them to the ones he had located on the handle. He stated he looked at an exhaustive comparison group, ranging from all of the personnel who responded to the crime scene, Thomas Crouse, Esther Fournier, and to a series of other names and print cards connected to Crouse. He said all of the comparisons resulted in negative results.

The fingerprint expert continued, saying he also scanned the prints into the Automated Fingerprint Identification System (AFIS) database for New Hampshire, Maine, and Vermont with negative results. He explained how the database had the prints of all arrestees from the tristate area. Adrienne asked if his search ended there, and he replied that he forwarded the prints for entry into the FBI's national integrated AFIS database, which included more than forty-two million fingerprint cards. The results of that search were also negative. He said he then forwarded blown up copies of the fingerprints to both the Massachusetts State Police and the Boston Police AFIS sections for a comparison with their databases, and he later learned that they did not match any prints already in those databases.

Adrienne asked general questions about the effect weather might have on fingerprint preservation in the outdoor New Hampshire-type environment. He explained how the weather could have a great negative effect, particularly with moisture from rain and snow, adding that heat can also "bake" the surface and evaporate the moisture. Adrienne spoke about the fluctuation in temperature and precipitation in Hooksett from the summer of 2000 through the spring of 2001 and the physical position of the shovel when discovered in the ravine, and then she called on his expertise to offer an opinion regarding the survival of any fingerprint. He said that under those hypothetical circumstances, he wouldn't expect a print to survive, adding that he would describe the condition of the two prints he recovered as poor and that may be the reason there were no hits from any of the AFIS databases.

Adrienne made her points. The fact that the prints did not connect to anyone was not a blemish or failure in the investigation. In fact, it pointed to the thoroughness and exhaustive steps taken by the police, the crime scene techs, and the prosecutors. It was, however, a point or opening for Baccari to pursue. Being able to establish that the prints did not belong to Crouse or Fournier was certainly a positive break for him. The question for the jury to decide was if the shovels connected to the burial site at all or if someone simply left or threw them there in an unconnected coincidence.

Attorney Baccari went over the fingerprint expert's direct examination but didn't raise any new or different issues. He did ask about a few fibers found on the shovels as well as one on a beer bottle found near the gravesite. He replied that he had packaged the fibers in individual envelopes for potential testing by other scientists at a later point.

In the little time remaining in the court day, Adrienne brought Louie Barone to the witness stand. She wanted to introduce him for the record, get him comfortable sitting in the courtroom in front of Crouse, and prime the jurors for his in-depth testimony, which would follow the next morning.

Adrienne's opening questions allowed Barone to explain his current incarceration and how he had met, and spent time in the Cambridge Jail with Tommy Crouse. He told the jurors he was currently serving an eighteen-month sentence at the Billerica House of Correction for a probation violation tied to a restraining order that he violated. He said he was initially committed to the Cambridge Jail while awaiting a hearing on the probation violation and stayed there from February 17 until April 16 of 2002. He added that he still had a series of six open cases in Woburn Court on charges ranging from larceny to forgery.

Directing his attention to the time spent at the Cambridge Jail, Barone said his assignment was the G Tier, which was a Protective Custody Unit. He said he had a bunk in a corridor outside of the jail cells due to an overflow issue. He mentioned that he hadn't recognized or known anyone when he arrived, but on the first evening, he met Tommy Crouse. He recalled that Crouse was sitting on top of a bunk, watching television and yelling at someone. He said they had a "small, minor chitchat conversation," adding that Crouse's cell assignment was almost directly across from his bed. He said they developed "as good as any relationship you can have in an environment like that," saying they spoke several times a day.

Adrienne asked if he spent time in Crouse's jail cell, and he answered, "For an extended period of time, no. To run in, run out: yes." He added that because of the living environment, Crouse spent more time in the open overflow area than he did inside the privacy of his cell. She asked if during that time, Crouse shared any discovery documents with him, and he said only once, when he showed him a report from the Fire Marshall's office, "He was all fired up about it because nothing was on the same page. He was enraged about something." Following up on the question, Adrienne asked if he ever helped Crouse or reviewed paperwork in connection with the case. Barone answered, "Absolutely not."

Continuing, Adrienne asked whether they had talked about Crouse's case during the nine weeks they spent together on G Tier. Crouse responded, "You couldn't have a conversation without it coming up." He added that he had never heard about the fire or the murder, and Crouse was "surprised and shocked he hadn't heard of it."

The conversation shifted as Adrienne asked what Crouse told him about the murder scene. Barone responded that Crouse said he was living in the building with his girlfriend and two kids and that there was a common area and that he had acquired a key to it. Crouse told him he used "this room to do cocaine, party with girls, whores, things like this." Crouse said he met the girls through escort services and bars.

Adrienne asked if Crouse ever talked about the victim, and Barone replied, "He told me she was a homeless, troubled young girl." He later said Crouse described his victim as a "little bit of a thing."

Purposefully avoiding direct questioning about the murder for the moment, Adrienne asked about any conversations Barone and Crouse had shared about New Hampshire. "He said that she had some family or someone that lived up there, near there," was the response, adding, "She was found in New Hampshire, and he felt that would throw any kind of heat on whoever lived near this place."

"Now," Adrienne asked, "did Mr. Crouse ever talk to you about what happened during the crime?"

It was impossible to know which rose faster: the jury's attentiveness, Crouse's blood pressure, or Attorney Baccari jumping up from his seat to object and request a sidebar conference.

Judge Grabau brought the attorneys to his sidebar, and before they could speak, he addressed Baccari. "I just saw Mr. Crouse make a sign to his forehead signaling something. I don't know if it was to the witness. He's not to communicate with the witness." Baccari responded, "I'll speak to him. I obviously can't see him."

The reason for the objection and sidebar was an attempt to preempt any questions or answers that might come up concerning Kelly's alleged rape. Baccari argued that since there was no evidence of a sexual assault presented to the Grand Jury then they should not allow evidence regarding the claim at trial. He said the rape claim needed corroboration by something or someone, but Judge Grabau saw it differently, quoting from established case law. He told Baccari the fact that a cooperating witness presented the information covered that requirement.

Adrienne also presented case law from a trial with similar facts where the judge allowed statements because they went to the defendant's motive for killing the victim. "They found that the...that evidence was sufficiently corroborated by the circumstantial evidence of the crime, itself, which I would suggest is present here."

Judge Grabau added, "We discussed the blood in the function room, his accessibility to the function room, the key, and that he lived on the premises, some of the statements he made to other people. All of that is circumstantial, and it goes to that issue of corroboration."

Rather than keep the jury sitting and wondering about the sidebar discussion, Judge Grabau dismissed them for the day, assuring them the trial was on track and not behind schedule. Once the jurors cleared the courtroom, the sidebar conference continued with added discussion on a couple more legal issues.

CHAPTER 23

The Trial: Day Twelve
Ninth Day of Testimony

Tuesday began where Monday left off, with a lengthy sidebar meeting about trial tactics. Referring to yesterday's legal discussion about the admission of information about the sexual assault, Judge Grabau told them the overall issue was not something he could completely resolve at this point, but he was going to allow Adrienne to proceed. "I will permit the Commonwealth to continue in its prosecution at this point under the felony murder theory. I don't know what I'll do at the required finding stage, but at this point, I'm not making a ruling that they can't continue."

Baccari broached a follow-up concern about Barone's testimony, "He cannot mention his conversations with Crouse and any admissions he may have made to a previous conviction for a similar rape offense." Adrienne said she already addressed it with Barone and told him she would not bring up the subject and he could not bring it up either. Judge Grabau added that he would tell Barone again, when he took the stand, "I just don't want that mistake." Simple errors in speech or topic that conflict with a judge's orders could have a catastrophic prejudicial effect on fairness and result in a mistrial that would immediately end the case without a verdict. At this late point in the trial, neither side wanted that to happen.

Judge Grabau finalized the discussion by commenting he would allow the defense to bring up any of Barone's prior convictions during cross-examination but only to the extent that Baccari could read the charges and not the body of the complaint or facts of the cases.

Judge Grabau next addressed a motion in limine that Bacarri filed regarding whether or not to allow Kelly's family members to testify. He stated there is clear case law that allows for family testimony. He went further by referencing a case that stated, "The photograph of a victim prior to death may be introduced to tell the jury something of a person whose life has been lost in order to humanize proceedings."

However, he did inform Adrienne she was limited to one family member. She said Kelly's father, Mark, would be testifying about Kelly's life but added that he would also be adding other information about her behavior in the year that preceded her death.

The guard brought Barone into the courtroom for a quick voir dire prior to his testimony. Judge Grabau told him that he could not refer to Mr. Crouse's prior conviction for rape. He told the judge that he understood and that there would be no "slipups." Judge Grabau then asked about the background to a collection of criminal charges that were brought against him in Essex County where he had been charged with rape, kidnapping, armed robbery, and assault and battery. Barone answered that the charges brought in the Peabody District Court were nolle processed and dismissed by the prosecution. He added that the dismissal of the charges had nothing to do with his offer to testify in this or any other case.

With those issues discussed and decided, Judge Grabau called for the jury.

Once they were in their seats, Adrienne stood and began, "Now, where we left off, Mr. Barone, I was asking whether or not the defendant ever talked to you about what happened during the course of the crime?

"Frequently," he responded.

"Can you tell the Court and the members of the jury what Mr. Crouse said happened?"

With that simple, open-ended question, Adrienne opened the floodgates for the most damning, incriminating testimony any witness would proffer against Crouse.

"He was partying with this girl and things got out of hand."

"Did he say where it happened?"

"It happened in the common area of this Malden Mills, I guess this common room."

"And did he say what this partying consisted of?"

"There was cocaine involved, booze involved, sex involved."

"What specifically did he say about the sex?"

"He specifically said that he tore her ass up."

"Did he say anything else about that?"

"He said that things got out of hand. He penetrated her, I think."

"As best you can recall, can you tell the jury, in Mr. Crouse's exact words, what he did?"

"He fucked her in the pussy; he fucked her in the ass."

Judge Grabau allowed the testimony to continue over several objections by Attorney Baccari.

"Did he indicate where in the common room it happened?"

"Couch."

"Well, did he describe for you what happened after the sex?"

"He said he stabbed her."

"Did Crouse describe for you any evidence in the room or the condition of the room as a result of that?"

"Blood all over the walls. He ended up burning up a couch."

"Now, with regard to that particular event, did he indicate what he did after he stabbed her?"

"He panicked. Went and got some gasoline."

"Did he say where he got it and how much he got?"

"He said he got it at a gas station that was fairly close to there. And he bought about…it was either 2.38 or 2.83 gallons of gas. Something like that, 2.5 gallons roughly. He said it should have been enough to eliminate whatever was left in the room."

Barone continued, addressing more of his conversations with Crouse, including the trip to New Hampshire after the fire was set. He mentioned comments Crouse made about his relationship with Esther, describing them as "rocky, unstable" and that he was worried about what she may do or say. "He wanted to marry her while he was in the jail."

Adrienne questioned him further about the disposal of Kelly's body, and he replied Crouse said he put her into the back of his vehicle and brought her to Hooksett, NH. He recalled Crouse saying he buried her there and he had no worries about DNA because of the amount of time she had been "out there." He said they found her head on a jogging path, "Straight up, not like an animal dragged it out there."

Barone said Crouse told him on the morning of the fire he had run into someone, and at the time, he (Crouse) was "stoned, drunk, high, and sweating."

Adrienne asked if Crouse ever talked about the shovels he used for the burial. Barone replied that Crouse did tell him they recovered the shovels and "there was no way they were going to find prints on it, because 'gloves were involved.'"

Adrienne asked if Crouse was ever concerned about having his fingerprints found on evidence in the case, and Barone replied, "There were two places he was concerned about fingerprints. One was on a glass table that had got smashed by the time it got to the laboratory, and the other one was on an adult magazine that was in the room."

Barone also responded to questions about Crouse's comments about his arrest. He said there were two stories. One was the police came to his door and arrested him, but the other was more involved. He said, "...He was driving down the road in his Blazer, and the police swooped down on him with helicopters and black vehicles, and he jumped out of the Blazer, crouched down, and pulled out his .40 caliber and was ready to take you on like you're either the mob or the police; he wasn't sure which you were."

Adrienne closed out his testimony with a series of questions about the timing of his talking to the state police, his prior record, how he received all of the information about the case, and the reason he came forward with the information. He answered that he waited to share the information with the police until after his sentencing to the house of correction and before he left the Woburn Courthouse on April 16, 2002. He added that he hadn't and couldn't talk to anyone about the case until after he knew he wouldn't be returning to the Cambridge Jail. He said it wasn't until he met Crouse that he knew anything about a fire or murder at Malden Mills. He also mentioned that they had a couple of disagreements during the time they spent together, but he didn't elaborate. Finally, and in answer to why he came forward, Barone said, "I came forward because of my conscience."

Adrienne closed by asking Barone to acknowledge a signed agreement between the Middlesex DAO and himself that for his truthful testimony he would receive suspended sentences for the remaining open cases in Woburn Court. He did.

His impactful testimony was the only direct window into Crouse's thoughts, concerns, and reasons for the murder of Kelly and the arson in the function room. Some of it logical and some of it not, but it was the best evidence we had to make any sense of Crouse's actions and motivations.

• • • •

Baccari's cross-examination was critical. He needed to surgically eviscerate and expose any and all of Barone's weaknesses and flaws and put his criminal past and any agreements made with the DAO center stage. And, for the next hour or so, he attempted to do just that. He began by asking Barone to describe the layout of G Tier and explain how Crouse changed his living arrangement from a cell to the overflow corridor, choosing the bunk next to his.

Baccari stopped and switched gears completely. He asked Barone if the two of them had ever spoken before. Barone said they had not, even though Baccari had made the attempt. When asked why he wouldn't speak with Baccari, Barone replied, "Because I had been personally threatened."

He continued, asking Barone if he asked for help with his cases in trade for the information and whether or not the state police made promises to him if he would speak with them. He answered, "Did they tell me they couldn't make me any promises? Absolutely." Baccari then asked about the agreed-upon plea deal, and Barone responded that he still had additional jail time from non-Middlesex county cases.

Baccari brought Michael "Mucko" McDermott into the conversation and asked Barone if he knew of him before he arrived at the jail. He said he never heard of him before he got to the jail and only knew who he was now because they were together on G Tier. Baccari spent considerable time asking about McDermott and if Barone was trying to get a confession out of him for the police, and further, if he had attempted to sabotage his insanity defense for killing his seven coworkers. Barone denied the question and said McDermott talked to anyone who would listen about what he had done. It was no secret.

Baccari tried to pigeonhole him to particular dates and times of the conversations with Crouse about Kelly Hancock, but Barone could not be definite. He said, "In jail, dates and days of the week didn't matter, nor did time of the day." He added that Crouse talked of the case and his legal strategies constantly.

The questioning turned to the legal paperwork, Grand Jury testimony, and police reports that Crouse had accumulated and kept filed in a box. Barone said Crouse didn't share them with him, nor did he read or look through them. He also denied Baccari's claim that he was a "jailhouse lawyer."

He said Crouse talked of various escort services that he called on, and Barone acknowledged that he used escort services in the past as well.

Baccari was struggling to find small cracks and inconsistencies in the answers and comments, but he came up short. He hammered away, asking how Barone obtained his information, continually suggesting it was through his access to police reports and Grand Jury testimony in Crouse's box of files. He questioned him about his comments that Crouse said he moved the body, but Barone said he knew nothing more about the why or where because Crouse only said he did it but didn't expand on the why or where of it.

After Barone stone walled Baccari's attempts to have him change or alter his testimony, Baccari turned his attention to attacking Barone's character and credibility. He insinuated that Barone was a "gun for hire" who gathered information from inmates about their cases and turned them into an advantage for himself.

Baccari attempted to "throw some shade" onto the investigative team with a series of questions about an unnamed member having a "huge gambling debt" and that Lester Morovitz bailed him out with a loan to save his home. He added that because of that relationship, the person was providing information to Morovitz that allegedly came from the discussions at the weekly meetings in the state police office. Barone said Crouse mentioned that and told him that was how he was getting some of his information and that because of it Morovitz told him, "Shut the fuck up," because his own words were getting him in trouble. Baccari continued to push the point with questions aimed at exposing the officer, but Barone responded over and over that he had no idea who it might be because Crouse never said who the someone was, nor was he specific that it was a police officer. Try as he might, Baccari came up empty on his approach. It was a pure attempt at a character assassination with no named person connected to a loan from Morovitz.

Baccari then questioned Barone about a series of names of inmates and asked if he ever asked them for financial help in getting him bailed out. He denied every one of them. Next, Baccari asked whether he spoke to Crouse about getting OxyContin snuck into the jail. He denied that as well. Then he asked Barone about his request of Baccari to sneak contraband to him from his jail cell into Woburn Court. Barone initially denied it but changed his comment when Baccari referenced a request he made for a pack of cigarettes, not allowed in the jail area. Barone answered, "I asked you for one, not a pack."

Baccari turned his attention to two previous instances where Barone contacted and cooperated with police by providing incriminating information about a fellow inmate. The first instance was a murder-for-hire scenario that developed in the Suffolk County House of Correction where an inmate sought to have three people killed in Boston. Barone said he did so because "the guy was dangerous and the request was real."

The second instance referred to an inmate who, like Crouse, was awaiting trial on a murder charge. He and Barone were in the same dorm area of the eighteenth floor of the Middlesex Jail in October of 1996. During their time together, the inmate made several admissions about the gruesome manner in which he murdered his victim. Barone contacted the Middlesex County authorities about the statements. In this case though, unlike in Crouse's, he didn't wait to share the information until he left Cambridge for the Billerica House of Correction. Barone addressed Baccari's questioning and said, "He wrapped a bicycle chain around a girl's neck and put a piece of pipe in there and cranked it up until she was no longer with us." He added that the inmate talked about it nonstop to anyone who would listen and he "drooled talking about it."

Baccari wanted to know why while he was in the Cambridge Jail he trusted to share information in one case but not in the other two. "Because of who Crouse says he is and who his stepfather is, how he had the power to transfer somebody, how to get them jammed up with an indecent assault and battery in the jail if they did anything to fuck him," Barone replied.

Referring to the second case, Baccari asked, "Did you say you came forward in the Jones case because what he told you was terrorizing you, that you couldn't sleep at night?" Barone answered, "It still bothers me. Any time I hear about violence against a child it bothers me. Yourself?" Judge Grabau stepped in with a quick admonishment to Barone telling him that the defense counsel asks the questions, not the witness.

Baccari's apparent point with this line of questioning was to let the jury know Barone had a history of testifying against others for his possible gain and that he wasn't afraid to bring information to the Cambridge Jail authorities in one case but said he had to wait out of fear on the other two cases until he left Cambridge. He made his points, but in doing so, they gave Barone an opportunity to show he had a conscience and, in the Jones case as well as this one, compassion for the teenage victims.

The cross-examination ended with Baccari reading Barone's criminal record and asking him if the charges and sentences were correct. Barone matter-of-factly agreed to all of them.

On redirect examination, Adrienne took the opportunity to clarify the events brought up by the defense and hoped to erase any tarnish or smear that Baccari did to Barone's character or credibility. In particular, she wanted the jury to know why he came forward with information and what he received in return as far as sentencing.

She asked why he reached out to Deputy Superintendent John Costello in the first instance, and Barone said he knew he had to pass the information on quickly about the murder-for-hire plot but in the other cases he was concerned about his safety if the word circulated that he was talking to the police. He added that during his time in Cambridge, he made observations of many in authority and thought Costello was a man of integrity and "the only guy who didn't bend to Crouse's will." She asked him what, if any, consideration he asked for from the Boston Police or Suffolk DAO for his exchange of information about the murder-for-hire situation. He said he had asked for, "Nothing."

Directing his attention to the case of the brutal homicide of a sixteen-year-old girl, she asked what, if any, consideration he sought or the Middlesex DAO gave him. He replied, "There were no deals whatsoever because I had nothing hanging over my head."

She asked about his state of mind in deciding to wait until sentenced to Billerica and away from Cambridge to talk to the police about Tommy Crouse. He said he was, "Absolutely scared to death. In fact, I am scared at the house of correction. His stepfather is a very close friend of the sheriff." She asked about his observations of interactions between Crouse and people working at the jail. He said based on his "extensive experience in the criminal justice system he found the contact highly unusual." She asked about his present state of mind, and he answered, "It is worse."

Adrienne closed out her redirect with questions about the agreement he had with the Middlesex DAO and his obligations under that agreement.

"My understanding of my obligations is that I'm to be cooperative and truthful."

"What is your understanding of the consequences of your failure to include all relevant information or to omit information?" she asked.

"A lengthy sentence in a prison," he replied.

The final effect Louie Barone's testimony would have on the jurors was unclear at that moment. Their opinions were the only ones that mattered, and they couldn't even share their thoughts with each other until the deliberations began in a few days.

He was firm in his direct testimony and, while a bit testy with Baccari, unwavering on cross-examination. However, he was a convicted felon with a checkered criminal history, and he talked about jailhouse conversations. The damning statements carried a wallop because they weren't comments that Barone overheard in a room full of people. They came during one-on-one talks and happened on numerous occasions when Crouse was seeking Barone's advice and counsel. They were Crouse's own words, and he not only admitted to murdering Kelly, he also described the despicable way he raped the fourteen year old "every which way" before he panicked in the aftermath and took her life to protect himself from being caught.

If the jury believed Barone, Crouse could only blame himself for committing the self-inflicted, fatal wound with his own words. It was the equivalent of setting a fire in a closed room and having the flames consume you.

The prosecution's case was wrapping up, and Adrienne wanted to close with a series of exclamation points and eliminate any question marks. There were still a few small puzzle pieces to plug into the remaining gaps to complete the "big picture." The jurors hadn't yet learned of the circumstances that led up to Kelly's meeting with Crouse on her last night of life, nor anything about her as a person from her friends or family, but that was about to change.

Al Ray, a uniformed Malden PD officer working the overnight shift on July 17, 2000, recalled being on patrol on Route 99 around four fifteen in the morning. He said he was in a conversation with a Saugus police officer at a point where the town lines converged. He said while they were talking, he noticed a very young-looking girl walking southbound along the side of the roadway. "She was very young looking. It was cold… even though it was summertime; it was a very cold, rainy night. And I noticed that she was not appropriately dressed for the weather: no jacket or anything like that." He said he called her over, and she walked to him. He did not recognize her but later learned her name was Kelly Hancock.

Adrienne asked him what Kelly was wearing, and he replied, "I believe she was wearing what is referred to as a baby t-shirt. It would be like a dress t-shirt that you would wear. It was wet and damp out, and she was shivering. I had her sit down in the back of the cruiser."

Ray added that they talked for a few minutes, and he ran a routine warrant check and found that she had a warrant for her arrest as a CHIN. As a result, he took her into custody and brought her to the Malden Police Station. He said he never saw her again after that morning.

• • • •

In July 2000, Laura O'Reilly was a social worker for the Massachusetts DSS and assigned to the Malden office and the caseworker for Kelly Hancock and her family. She recalled Kelly was an eighth grade student at a Malden Middle School when they first met.

She spoke of her interactions with Kelly's family as well as the "collateral" people in her life, such as teachers, doctors, and police and how they worked to develop a plan for her care and treatment. She added that she worked with Kelly's parents to arrange supervised visits and to discuss Kelly's behaviors. She said they met often but added that Kelly was a frequent "runner" who often fled from foster home placements as well as her family home. She explained that Kelly had run from DSS custody on July 12 of 2000 and that the Malden PD arrested her on a CHINS warrant on July 17.

O'Reilly said on the morning of July 17 she was contacted by the juvenile probation office at the Cambridge Courthouse and told that Kelly had been arrested a few hours earlier and was being held for a hearing later that morning. She added that as Kelly's caseworker she was required to attend the hearing and testify if requested. She said at the conclusion of the hearing the judge ordered her to take Kelly under her care and find a placement in a children's facility or foster home. She said they left together and drove to her office in Malden, arriving around twelve thirty. She said that Kelly was very quiet and withdrawn during the ride but she smiled frequently.

O'Reilly said they were sitting in the office awaiting a return call about a placement when Kelly asked to use the bathroom. She said she walked Kelly out of the office and into a common area where the bathrooms were located. O'Reilly said she returned to the office and after Kelly didn't come back after five minutes, she went looking for her, and she was gone. O'Reilly continued and described how she and a couple of her coworkers searched the building as well as a few places in the neighborhood where young teenage kids gathered, all to no avail. She called in to her main office, explained what happened, and requested the issuance of another CHINS warrant. She said later in the day she went to the Malden Police Station and filled out a missing person's report.

She recalled that Kelly was wearing a white tee shirt and jean shorts with sneakers when she last saw her. She added that her hair was in a ponytail, secured with a yellow scrunchie. She recalled that after Kelly's remains were located, the state police showed her photos of clothing and a scrunchie and that she identified them as the ones Kelly was wearing when she was last was with her.

Attorney Baccari offered no cross-examination.

Tracy Heffernan followed O'ReillyMeagher and told the jurors she knew Kelly Hancock for two years before her disappearance. She described Kelly as her son's former girlfriend. Heffernan said she also worked for Lester Morovitz at Malden Transportation and for the past nine years lived in a home by the Town Line Motel and Lounge Complex on Broadway in Malden. She said she last saw Kelly walking alone in the Town Line parking lot in the late afternoon of Monday, July 17. She described the clothing Kelly was wearing and said she had a comb in her back pocket and had a hair scrunchie around her wrist like a bracelet.

She remembered speaking with Kelly for a few minutes and, before they parted ways, Heffernan gave her six one-dollar bills. Kelly walked away and toward the Town Line Bowling Alley.

In an effort to thwart any thought or suggestion that Heffernan's son, might be involved in Kelly's death, Adrienne inquired about his whereabouts during the summer of 2000. Heffernan answered that her son's father lived in Louisiana, and in May, she took him out of school and sent him there for the summer. She said he didn't return to Malden until the late summer, in time to return to school.

Heffernan said that Kelly stayed with her on two occasions and she believed with another friend at other times and, beyond that, she thought Kelly "basically slept on the streets." Her testimony closed with her talking of meeting with investigators sometime after May 2001 and identifying photographs of clothing similar to what Kelly was wearing the last time she saw her, including a "western-style over shirt."

On cross-examination, Attorney Baccari asked about her conversation with Kelly and if she had mentioned where she was going. Heffernan said Kelly told her that she was waiting for a ride.

Kelly Hancock's closest friend took the stand and talked about their friendship and Kelly's troubled, vagabond lifestyle. She was clearly anxious and nervous as Adrienne began her questioning. She told the jury that Kelly and she were eighth grade classmates at the Malden Middle School in the spring of 2000. She said that around the time of April vacation Kelly showed up at her house one night and asked if she could stay with her family. She said her father said it would be okay, adding that Kelly then stayed with them for the next three months, although she disappeared for a couple of weeks at a time and never announced why she was leaving or where she had been when she returned. She mentioned that during the months Kelly stayed at her home her family purchased some clothes for Kelly.

She recalled how the two of them spent a lot of time together and with a small group of friends who usually got together every day and "hung out" at the Town Line Bowling Alley or the cemetery on Salem Street. She recited a list of names, including Tracy's son.

Wanting to add context to the conversation, Adrienne put a map of the area surrounding the Malden Mills Condos onto the overhead projector and asked her to point out the proximity from her house to the condo complex. She noted her family home was one street or a few hundred yards away from the complex and that Kelly and she would often cut through the parking lot to go to the convenience store at the Mobil gas station to buy "some food or Pepsi for my house" but they never talked about anyone they knew living there.

In answer to Adrienne's questions about travelling to New Hampshire, she talked of a family vacation at a campground during Memorial Day Weekend of 2000 and that Kelly went with them. Adrienne asked her to identify a photo she took of Kelly during the trip. She did and commented on Kelly's hairstyle, saying she always "had it up in a ponytail like a half bun-type thing."

She said that at the end of the school year other members of her family and she moved to California for the summer. Kelly told her that when the family left, she was going to stay at another friend's home. She said she last saw Kelly the day before she went to the airport and the last time they spoke was around July 4, when they talked on the telephone. As her testimony continued, she became increasingly emotional and was red-faced and sobbing but able to continue.

Adrienne ended the questioning by asking her to look at photographs of some clothing to see if she was able to identify them. She said she recognized the clothing as being similar to what Kelly wore when she was living with her family.

Attorney Baccari chose not to cross-examine the witness but did comment at sidebar that he wanted it noted in the record that the witness was "crying and sobbing" during her testimony.

As difficult as the testimony of Kelly's best friend had been to hear and watch, it wouldn't get any easier as the bailiff called Mark Hancock to the stand.

More than two years after her murder he still fought the demons every day as he struggled to come to grips with the loss of his firstborn child and the way she had met her death. We had seen demonstrations of his explosive temper when he was angered with the social services system that he felt wrongfully interceded in their lives and took her from him. We had heard and felt his distrust of the entire social services system and his initial lack of faith in our ability to bring justice for his little girl.

As time went on, however, we also witnessed a kinder, more compassionate man who was struggling, but finally succeeding, in keeping his family together. He almost bragged about his tumultuous and violent history and that he was no stranger to the defendant's seat in a courtroom. He would tell you he wasn't proud of his past but he felt he did what he had to do to for his wife and family.

Jackie Shepard knew best how to reign him in during his emotional mood swings and rants. She was always by his side, usually holding his hand. She truly was the angel sent to guide both Mark and the rest of the family through these exceptionally difficult times. Mark insisted he wanted to testify, and Adrienne, Nat, and Anne Foley had spent considerable time preparing him for this moment. All anyone could hope for was that he stayed focused and on point. He said he was ready and promised he wouldn't let Kelly down.

Mark and Jackie invested completely in the prosecution of Tommy Crouse. They appeared at every court hearing leading up to the trial and locked eyes with him more than once. Angry as they were, they maintained their composure because they knew if either of them was disruptive; the judge would ban them from the courtroom. They wanted and needed to witness and absorb every step of the proceedings as Kelly's representatives.

They met with or called Adrienne or Anne whenever they had questions or concerns. One afternoon, as the trial drew near, they were speaking with Adrienne and candidly admitted they had been skeptical from the beginning and questioned whether the DAO cared enough about Kelly's life and if Adrienne was the right person and tough enough to take the case to trial. Mark told her of a morning months before when the three of them boarded a courthouse elevator to head upstairs for a hearing. He said another attorney stepped on and when the door shut, "You ripped into this guy and 'tore him a new one' because you said he wasn't truthful when he spoke to a judge." Mark said it wasn't a pretty sight, but they smiled at each other with a knowing glance, both thinking that there was the gesture of grit and strength they hoped Adrienne would bring to their daughter's case: the sign from above that they indeed did have the right person fighting for them and for Kelly. As Mark put it, "I don't trust nobody, but when I seen that, I got a warm feeling that we were in good hands. I was scared before that because I needed to do the best for Kelly and this part was out of my hands."

Mark barely made it through the opening question when he lost his composure and his voice, breaking down in tears. Judge Grabau quickly called for a ten-minute recess. When the jury returned, Mark was back on the stand with his emotions in check as best as he could. He told the jurors the family had lived in Malden on Newhall Street for several years but recently moved to a home in Walpole, MA, where they were all together. He identified Jackie Shepard as his current wife and Kelly as his daughter. He mentioned that his first wife, Barbara Johnson, gave birth to Kelly on November 6, 1985. He wasn't exactly sure what grade Kelly was in when she went missing, but he knew she was at the middle school in Malden.

Adrienne asked him about the issues Jackie and he had with Kelly, and he answered, "She started to run on me and whatnot. She never stopped, and she ended up bringing the DSS to my home. And when they came to my home…"

Before he went too far, Adrienne interrupted and asked if, because of the DSS involvement, Kelly went to live in other places. "Yes, she did. Many places, dates, I don't know. But she was in various places, from foster homes to facilities to try to help her and to see why she was running all of the time." Adrienne asked if on April 12, 2000, Kelly returned to his custody, and he answered, "Yes. She came back with me. I went to court and got her released from DSS."

Mark told the jurors that Kelly remained home for only three days before she ran again, and once again, the authorities put her into DSS custody. He said that from that day forward she never again lived in his house. He added that although she was no longer living with his family, he spoke with her by telephone almost daily. He said the last time they were together was in Cambridge Juvenile Court on July 12, 2000, after her arrest on the CHINS warrant. He said that she ran from the courthouse that day and her caseworker issued another CHINS warrant.

Adrienne asked if he ever saw Kelly again, and he said that on Sunday, July 16, she had appeared in his backyard on Newhall Street and he saw her from the window. He said he "let it be known he was coming out," and by the time he got to the back door, she was gone. "She jumped over three fences," he said. He said the last time he spoke with Kelly was by telephone on July 17 between eleven and noon. It would have been when she was still in DSS custody following her appearance in court.

Mark's testimony finished with comments about camping with his family at a campsite he had on Keleif Lake in Derry New Hampshire. He said they went there as often as they could, adding that they also went up to the mountainous area of New Hampshire and along the Kankamangus Highway for the scenery and to hike.

Mr. Baccari offered no cross-examination, as literally nothing he could ask Hancock would benefit Crouse's defense. At moments like this, it is always best to take the high road and allow the witness to walk away in a dignified manner. Baccari understood and respected that long-held philosophy.

As Mark Hancock stepped down from the witness stand, the only sounds in the courtroom were of quiet sobbing, sniffling noses, and the rumpling of tissues as they ran across the bottom of swollen, tear-filled eyelids. With few exceptions, the eyes and the hearts of the people in the courtroom were on, and with, him. What the Hancock family and he had been through was unimaginable and difficult, if not impossible, for those in the courtroom to entirely comprehend.

After nine days of testimony, Adrienne had finally reached the moment when she could introduce Kelly Hancock to the jury. Throughout the trial, the anticipation built; the jurors wanted to know about this young girl. They knew all they wanted to about her killer but virtually nothing about her. She had been dehumanized, and it was time to bring her to life, to learn a bit her about her from those who knew her best.

She presented Kelly as she appeared to others during her short life. Kelly's family and friends were her surrogates in the courtroom. Through their words, the jury now had some measure of understanding about the young and unhinged life of the late Kelly Hancock. Remarkably, she was able to do it in two hours and with only five witnesses. Their testimony was short and succinct, but their descriptions of her lifestyle and the irrational choices she made was like raising a shade and filling the room with light. Until now, the jurors knew Kelly Hancock by her name and a few photos of her skeletonized remains. They knew nothing about who she was and how she had lived her life. They only knew how she lost her life. They heard and learned about her from the remembrances of those who saw and spoke with her every day. They received a small glimpse of who she was and maybe some understanding of the confusing and difficult life she had led. The words of the witnesses detailed Kelly's mixed-up logic and false bravado that unwittingly put her fate into the hands of a stranger she trusted, who took her down the tragic path that ended with her sexual assault, a violent struggle to survive, and heart-breakingly, her death.

• • • •

As her final witness, Adrienne brought in Jimmy Connolly to tie up some loose ends and clear up any confusion possibly created by earlier witnesses. Adrienne had a copy of Baccari's witness list and a good idea from earlier discovery and motion hearings about his defense strategy on behalf of Crouse. She wanted to thwart or offset what she could before Crouse's legal team could go on the offense.

Connolly spoke of his involvement in the case from the first call to the fire scene at Malden Mills through Crouse's arrest in June 2001. He also mentioned the conversations he'd had with Louie Barone in April of 2002.

Primarily, Adrienne wanted his testimony to both rebut the defense's claims that Barone was either spoon-fed information by the investigators or that he learned it by sneaking into the discovery files under Crouse's bed and gleaning information when Crouse was tied up elsewhere.

Crouse told Barone a couple of stories about his arrest, including one where he said he was crouched with his weapon out, contemplating shooting at the state police helicopter hovering over his head. The story was blatantly ego-driven and never happened. Connolly detailed how they had an arrest warrant for Crouse and followed him away from his workplace with a plan to isolate, stop, and arrest him. He said Crouse was driving fast and erratically and they had trouble keeping up with him. They were unfamiliar with the geographic area and, out of concern they would lose him in traffic, they requested support from the state police Air Wing to join them in the surveillance. Connolly said a helicopter was already in the area and did assist with additional "eyes from the sky." Crouse eventually stopped in front of a house in the town of Swampscott, and when he did, they took him into custody without incident and without weapons drawn. No one wrote a police report of the arrest, nor did any media comment on the seizure.

The purpose behind the testimony was less about Crouse's arrest and more about the fact that it took place with little drama and was never reported anywhere. It cut into the defense claim that Barone learned about it by perusing the discovery files and not directly from Crouse.

Adrienne next questioned him about a directive she had given a few weeks earlier asking him to review both the Grand Jury testimony and the entire contents of the discovery papers she had turned over to the defense. Connolly said he received more than a couple of thousand pages of written information. He said they filled five three-ring binders and added that the entire file took him over forty hours to read through.

She asked Connolly several questions about cell phone and cell tower records and whether or not they indicated a series of numbers or had names and locations attached. He replied they were only lists of numbers and didn't have names or addresses. He added that he read no Grand Jury testimony tying any names and numbers together. She also asked if there were any police reports or Grand Jury testimony about Kelly Hancock having any relatives or family members who vacationed in New Hampshire. He answered, "No."

Attorney Baccari wanted to close out the day and the prosecution's case by beginning his defense of Crouse through the cross-examination of Connolly. It was not a new or creative tactic, nor was it a bad way to start. At times, it could be an effective way to transition the jurors' attention away from the prosecutor's stark and damning presentation of the case and into an area where they could maybe find some reason to doubt the facts and theories they had listened to over the past few weeks. His plan included cherry-picking bits of trial testimony and using the information to give the appearance of a misrepresentation of the truth because it was inconsistent with their initial statement to the police, their testimony to the Grand Jury, or with the testimony of other prosecution witnesses.

Baccari opened by questioning Connolly on the testimony of Steven Grey and whether or not he told the Grand Jury that Crouse had told them "his, Crouse's, key fit the door to the function room." Connolly reviewed the page of testimony Baccari referred to and answered, "Yes."

In furtherance of his contention that Barone had accessed the defense discovery files without the knowledge or permission of Crouse, Baccari asked Connolly about several investigative reports and Grand Jury transcripts associated with witnesses who had testified during the trial. Specifically, he wanted to know if the prosecutor had submitted them to the defense prior to the time Barone transferred from the Cambridge Jail to the Billerica House of Correction. Connolly answered that in some instances he could say they were but he could not provide a definitive answer for each one without referring to the books of discovery, which were downstairs in his office. His answers weren't that important; Baccari had made his points.

As Jimmy Connolly exited the courtroom, Adrienne rose from her chair and said, "Your Honor, at this time the Commonwealth rests its case in chief against Thomas Crouse."

It was 3:46 in the afternoon of September 24. Over nine full days, Adrienne had presented fifty-three witnesses who offered seventy hours of testimony and more than two hundred pieces of physical and photographic evidence to prove the murder and arson cases against Thomas

Crouse. The next morning, the defense team's opportunity to do their best to tear apart the puzzle—or at least stain the completed picture—would begin.

Adrienne was prepared to defend her case and the legal questions or challenges ahead. Jimmy was the last piece to the puzzle Adrienne created with all of the circumstantial evidence. He was the anchor piece that pulled everything together and locked it in a tight, understandable picture for the jury to weigh in on in a few days.

CHAPTER 24

The Trial: Day Thirteen
Last Day of Testimony

The moment had arrived for the defense to present another side of
Tommy Crouse to the jury as well as a differing assessment of the
fire scene for their consideration. Based on his witness list, it appeared
Baccari would concentrate his strikes on two particularly strong and
important areas of the prosecution's case. On the list were the names of
three fire experts who would offer testimony disputing the findings of
Tom Klem and Paul Horgan, and a pair of correction officers from the
Cambridge Jail, whom he hoped would present testimony about interactions they observed between Crouse and Barone when they were together
in the protective custody unit.

This would be the last day of testimony, and both sides were primed
and ready for the final skirmish. Judge Grabau's morning comments were
short and instructive: "The Commonwealth rested its case in chief yesterday. Mr. Baccari, on behalf of Thomas Crouse, the defendant, wishes to
present evidence. There's no burden on the defendant to prove anything
in this case. He's presumed innocent, so… if he wishes to, he may present
evidence."

• • • •

Under federal and state rules of evidence an expert may offer an opinion
if they are qualified because of their knowledge, skill, experience, training,
or education in a particular and specific area. They refer to the judge
in these situations as the "gatekeeper" because only they can determine
if there is a need for specialized testimony, and whether the proposed

witness has the background to assist the jury to gain a better understanding of the evidence or determining a fact in issue.

The defense's first two witnesses worked for a national fire protection-engineering firm and assigned to the company's regional office in Warwick, RI. Attorney Baccari hired them to conduct an evaluation of the sprinkler and heat alarm systems to determine the period of time it took from the moment the fire started until the systems activated. The results were critical to refute the earlier testimony of Thomas Klem. If these experts analysis could convince any of the jurors that the system activations were considerably closer to the time the fire was set, the findings would benefit the defense assertion that Crouse was long off the property when the function room fire started.

The first expert said he held a master's degree in fire protection engineering and he designed and/or evaluated fire protection systems for already constructed buildings. He was a member of the NFPA and coedited the *National Fire Alarm Code Handbook* for the previous four years. He said he had previously served as an expert in several civil courts, including in the Boston Federal Court.

He told the jury he visited the Malden Mills Complex on August 5, 2002. While there, he examined what he described as a "conventional system of heat detectors, smoke alarms, manual fire alarm pull stations, and water flow switches, as well as a fire pump that kept the pressure on the sprinkler heads and initiated when the sprinkler heads were activated." He said the building divided into ten zones, and he noted that the heat sensors were set to activate when the ceiling temperature in a zone reached 135 degrees. He also mentioned reviewing the control panel in the building's lobby and said it was wired in such a way that every device would "report any abnormality" to it which, in turn, would activate the outgoing notifications to the fire department and the audible alarms throughout the building.

He offered an opinion on the sequencing of the heat detectors activations. He said he based his opinion on Trooper Silva's report that three of the sensors were set off and it indicated that the heat had travelled rapidly across the ceiling with a high enough temperature to cause them to activate.

Adrienne immediately rose from her seat and requested a sidebar conference. She said that she would object to any testimony that this witness would offer regarding cause and origin because his expertise was limited to the operation of the systems and not the fire. She said that Baccari proffered another witness as a cause and origin expert but not this one. Judge Grabau agreed and allowed her objection to that line of questioning. In laymen's terms, he simply indicated the witness could continue with his testimony but he had to stay in his designated lane and not cross over the double yellow line.

Baccari attempted to expand on his witnesses' expertise and asked how many fire scenes he had responded to, and he answered, "A dozen or so … and that was to review the operation or lack thereof of the fire protection systems on behalf of insurance companies in civil lawsuit-related disputes." He added that he received training in determining cause and origin but he was not a certified expert. Baccari made another run at asking him for an opinion on the origin of the fire and, once again, Adrienne objected and Judge Grabau denied the question and precluded any answer. He did allow the witness to testify that he had viewed photographs of the fire scene and it appeared that there was more fire damage in the "center of the room, where the furniture was piled or tipped over."

The questioning turned to the use of a computer program used to determine detector activation. The witness stated that the program commonly referred to as DETector ACTuation (DETACT), was developed by the National Institute for Standards and Technology (NIST) and was a standard testing tool used by fire protection engineers. He said he inputted information "derived from the facts of the case in terms of the ceiling height, the placement of the detectors, the location, the radial distance from the fire, the ambient temperature of the room and, of course, the detector rating: in this case, 135-degree fixed temperature."

Then he spoke about the fire growth, "which, in this case, was an accelerant-based fire, gasoline fire, so it was going to be a fast or ultrafast fire as described in the literature." He added that the heat sensors in the function room ceiling had a RTI of 179 and that was included in the calculations.

Baccari asked, "Do you have an opinion to a reasonable degree of engineering certainty as to a range of time it took for the first heat detector to respond after the start of the fire?"

He answered, "Yes. I believe we are looking in the range of just under a minute or over a minute in terms of response." He added, "The fire was detected, obviously, at 6:20 a.m. because that is when the alarm was received. Working backward with these numbers then we would conservatively look at anywhere from 6:17 to 6:19 in terms of when the fire was started and when it reached the heat release rate that was large enough to trip the detector."

The issue of cause and origin testimony came up again when Baccari attempted to delve into the operation of the building's HVAC and venting system and the affect it may have had on the spread of the fire. Adrienne again objected. At a sidebar conference, relying on her earlier objection, she asked, "How can you say you can predict the activation of the detection system when you are not in a position to opine concerning where the fire started or the magnitude of the fire based upon an examination of the scene? That is a cause and origin expert's job."

Judge Grabau asked Baccari, "What's the relevance of his opinion when he cannot opine as to the cause and origin?"

Baccari answered, "I think he can."

Grabau responded, "You think he can, but I'm not going to let him testify…that's the problem. He's not qualified to say where it started. So the question's out."

Not a huge victory for Adrienne, but it was another example and testament to how well-prepared she was to anticipate and block prejudicial testimony from a witness who was not court qualified to offer that type of opinion.

It was critical for the defense to show the fire moved in a fast or ultrafast manner with the smoke rising and spreading across the ceiling, melting the acrylic light covers and then setting off the alarms. To accent or prove the point, Baccari again led with questions that required a specialized expertise to determine the cause and origin of the fire. After a series of allowed objections by Adrienne, there was yet another sidebar conference.

A frustrated Baccari argued that the judge should allow him the questions and the jury could use their common sense. "Then you don't need his testimony," replied the judge. "If the jury can use their common sense, you don't need an expert. He is not a cause and origin expert so the question is out. I will let you put in a general term … if you want a general question about dealing with the law of physics of vapors: the fire in Point A, the vapors emanate, and you have gasoline at Point B, will the fire and flames from A, can they ignite Point B, I'll allow that question."

Following the judge's guidelines, Baccari asked a series of questions about gasoline vapors expanding and rising from each pool of gasoline and meeting in the air. The judge permitted testimony that there was evidence of four fires set, but the witness was not to give an opinion as to their sequencing. Baccari closed by asking his witness if he ever heard or read of a slow-burning fire, and he said he had not.

Adrienne began her cross-examination, questioning the witness on his experience with gasoline fires on rugs or other porous surfaces, and he said it was "very limited." She asked if, when he made the calculations on the DETACT testing, he had relied on an assumption that the heat release rates for the carpet surface were comparable to those on a hard floor, and he said that was true.

She questioned him about whether or not he ran the DETACT program a second time after the defense received the reports from the prosecution's expert, Thomas Klem. He said that he did. She also asked if in using the program a second time, he had used the calculations that applied only to a fire that was ultrafast and not for one that was fast, and again he agreed. She asked if in his opinion, "this was an ultrafast, 3,500-megawatts fire?" He agreed.

She probed deeper and asked him if the fire was that large wouldn't the person who set it have "been dead on the floor?" He answered, "If it was an instantaneous fire, yes." She pushed the point about the depth of destruction a fire that hot would have caused by producing Exhibit 24, a slightly burned pillow from one of the chairs in the function room. She asked if he had seen it before, and he answered that he hadn't. She inquired if he ever looked at any of the evidence before making his determinations, and he replied that he had only seen the photographs of the evidence because he thought the crime lab threw out the actual evidence. She continued, "And with respect to this particular pillow, if this pillow was in the midst of a 3,500-megawatts energy release fire, I wouldn't be holding it, would I? It would disintegrate, wouldn't it? With regard to your involvement, you formed an opinion as to the ultrafast rate of growth of this fire, yet you didn't even know this pillow existed, isn't that right?"

"No." He replied, "That was the reason...the reason it didn't is the sprinkler operated very quickly. The sprinklers operated right after the heat detectors."

"But," Adrienne came back, "your opinion is that the heat detectors went off first?"

"The heat detectors went off first," he said, "and shortly thereafter, the sprinklers operated."

Returning to the DETACT reports; Adrienne persisted with questions aimed at disclosing how his conclusions were based on inaccurate or incomplete information. She asked if the DETACT program allowed for data input regarding medium- or slow-moving fires and not just fast and ultrafast, and Moore agreed that all of those are choices.

"It would have helped," she asked, "would it not, to put in the data for the slow- and medium-growth fires in order to come up with a fairer assessment about whether or not the evidence fit the fire situation here?"

"Certainly," he replied. "But I would not have used the slow or the medium because gasoline does not burn that way."

Adrienne made her points about the tests being inaccurate and purposefully constructed to shorten the time between the setting of the fire and the alarms sounding to under three minutes, in opposition to Horgan and Klem's estimation of closer to ten minutes. The witness stood by his analysis and findings, denying that he put in numbers to reach a more favorable result for his client. He added that he used the ultrafast burn numbers in the equation because the DOJ data defines a gasoline fire as an ultrafast fire.

The jurors heard information and variables that, if believed, were in direct conflict to the prosecution's experts and that would be a major issue for them to consider when they deliberated on the evidence. After an hour and forty minutes of arduous, scientific testimony, the judge called the morning break, providing the defense an opportunity to reset for their next expert's testimony.

The second witness for the defense followed his coworker to the stand. While their professional backgrounds and experiences were similar, this one specialized in designing and installing fire suppression and sprinkler systems. He spoke of his academic and experience credentials, adding that while studying for his master's degree he worked on developing a flame spread model used to calculate the effects of flame movement in a room or compartment.

He told the jury he reviewed reports and photos of the fire scene and visited Malden Mills in early August 2002. He said he looked at the fire department connection and control panel, as well as the function room where the fire was contained, the sprinkler system, and the room that housed the water pump that fed the sprinklers.

He defined the fire suppression system as a wet-pipe type with pendulum-style sprinkler heads that hang from a water pipe and, when activated, spray water downward. He said the police and fire reports indicate either three or four sprinkler heads activated, and it was his opinion that the number was four.

Adrienne objected to his opinion and requested a sidebar conference to argue once again that the witness's opinion required an expertise in cause and origin of the fire and he had neither expertise nor certification in that area of fire science. Judge Grabau agreed and told Baccari if he wanted to rely on the reports and testimony of Horgan or Klem as his base of information that he would allow it but he could not offer opinion evidence that he would only allow from a cause and manner expert.

• • • •

Before the witness testimony continued, a court officer approached the judge and informed him that the two corrections officers scheduled to testify for the defense was present outside of the courtroom. Baccari requested an unusual but necessary interruption of his witness testimony to accommodate the officers. The officers were scheduled to appear later in the day, but there was a memorial service for a deceased coworker in the early afternoon that they both wanted to attend. Judge Grabau and Adrienne had been briefed earlier in the morning of this possibility and neither objected. Judge Grabau gave a quick explanation to the jurors without disclosing the reasons, and the trial resumed.

The first witness identified himself as a correction officer/deputy sheriff in charge of the day shift assigned to the tier that housed the SMU, or Protective Custody Unit, at the Cambridge Jail. He provided the jury with an overview of the living conditions, the fact that there were generally more inmates than there were cells, and how there was an overflow of bunk beds in the corridor to accommodate additional inmates. He said there were fourteen cells and generally six or seven inmates living in the overflow area, and that they stowed their property in bins under the bottom beds.

Baccari asked if he knew Thomas Crouse, and he acknowledged that he did and pointed him out in the courtroom. He added that Crouse worked in the unit as a tier cleaner who "swept the floors, picked up the garbage, and helped keep the place clean."

Baccari's goal was to establish a connection between Crouse and Louie Barone, so he asked the officer if he knew Barone. After he said he did, Bacarri asked him about the living arrangements for both of them. Referring to a list of dates and locations from the jail's log sheets, he told the Court that Crouse's cell assignment was directly across from Barone's bed. He noted the records showed Crouse moved out of his cell and settled into the bunk next to Louie Barone. The log sheets reflected that Crouse's initial move was on March 25 and he remained there until April 28, 2002, when he returned to his original cell. He added that Barone had been in overflow during his entire stay, which stretched from February 11 through April 16, 2002.

The officer said he made routine cell checks, and he recalled that Crouse had a box full of manila envelopes full of legal paperwork that he kept in a cardboard water bottle box and stored under his bunk. Without offering a direct reason why Crouse would move out to the overflow area, he mentioned that during meal periods those assigned to cells stayed locked down for the duration while those in overflow were free to roam on the tier. He said Crouse, Barone, and other inmates would often sit at one of the two metal picnic tables on the tier to play cards and watch television, and on at least one occasion, he noticed that Crouse had placed manila folders onto the table.

Adrienne's cross-examination was short and to the point. She asked the witness if he thought Barone and Crouse had formed a friendship and socialized together, and he answered that they were friends. Next, she asked if the rules prohibited an inmate to go through another's personal belongings or paperwork without approval and if it constituted a serious infraction. He replied that it is both forbidden and punishable. He added that he never saw anything that rose to that level of an infraction between the two.

The second officer told the Court that he worked Monday through Friday on the four-to-twelve (second shift) and his assignment had been the SMU for the previous thirteen months. He quickly cleaned up any misperception that he was a relative of the sheriff of Middlesex County by pointing out that their names had different spelling. The distinction was important since Crouse's stepfather was a very close friend of the sheriff and they didn't want to leave an appearance that the witness was showing any favor or deference to Crouse.

Baccari asked him to define the term "shakedown," and he answered that was a period on the shift when the guards would conduct routine, untargeted sweeps or checks of the inmate's living areas for weapons or contraband. He added he had swept through Crouse's property on more than one occasion. He mentioned the cardboard box containing manila envelopes that contained what he believed to be legal documents. He said the officers might look inside the envelopes to make sure there was no hidden contraband but that he never read the papers. He added that he saw what he thought were Grand Jury transcripts and papers with the state police logo at the top of the page.

When asked if he knew of an individual by the name of Louie Barone, he replied Barone was another resident of the SMU. He said he had seen them together on occasion. He also recalled a time when Crouse had the contents of his manila envelopes spread out on one of the metal picnic tables on the tier. He added that Barone was reading the documents but couldn't be sure what exactly Barone was reading and whether or not it pertained to Crouse's case.

Baccari asked the witness if he ever spoke to Crouse about not sharing his legal materials with other inmates, and he answered that he had discussed it with Crouse and other inmates as well. He said it wasn't a jail policy but because of past conflicts, they always recommended to inmates not to share paperwork regarding their cases with others.

Judge Grabau called both parties to his sidebar and asked Baccari what the purpose was of a line of questioning to the witness about a conversation he had with Barone. He answered, "Judge, I asked Mr. Barone if he told this witness that there was no case against Crouse, and he said, "Absolutely not." It was a minor but potentially important point for Baccari to make in regards to Barone's truthfulness and integrity. Judge Grabau allowed him to continue.

Baccari asked his witness, "At some time before Mr. Barone left upstairs and went to Billerica, did he tell you something or anything about the strength of the government's case against Mr. Crouse as he viewed it?'

He answered, "Something to the effect that, I'm paraphrasing here, that he asked me what I thought. I can't remember exactly what I replied, but it was like, 'I don't really give it too much thought,' and he said something to the effect that 'if this is what they have' or 'this is all they have, they don't have anything' or something to that effect. I'm paraphrasing."

Baccari concluded by asking the officer if Barone ever told him that Crouse confessed to him, and he replied that he did not.

Adrienne's cross-examination was short and to the point. She asked him how often Crouse and Barone sat at the picnic table with paperwork spread out. He answered that it was only one time. He added that he knew it was legal paperwork because when he walked by the table, he saw the heading on a paper that said Commonwealth v. Crouse but he couldn't be sure it was related to this case. He said he didn't interrupt their meeting because he didn't want to appear confrontational and upset Barone if he took the comments to Crouse the wrong way. He said he waited until they were not together before he spoke to Crouse and advised him that he shouldn't share information about his case with other inmates. Expanding on those comments, Adrienne asked if it was "unusual for someone with information on another person who was on their tier to wait until they were in another facility, not with that person, to go to law enforcement authorities regarding them?"

He answered, "Out of fear, is that what you are saying? Yes, I would agree."

She finished with a few general questions about whether or not it would be a "friendly thing to characterize someone's case as weak in order to encourage them that they have a good chance of beating the case?" and, once again, he agreed.

Once the second officer cleared the courtroom, the defense expert reentered and returned to the stand. Baccari resumed where he had left off. The jurors had little time to refocus their attention from learning about life in jail and the social life and interactions of inmates back to the technical aspects of sprinkler head sequencing and fire alarm activations.

Baccari asked the witness if he had a professional opinion about the sprinkler activations. He answered that the sprinkler that activated first was the one closest to the initial fire and he thought that was either the one closest to the door or the one in the corner to the room. He based his opinion on the DETACT model results. He went on to talk of the water pressure flowing through a one-inch pipe, and he estimated the water poured through the sprinkler head at approximately 51 gallons per minute.

Baccari then asked, "Do you have an opinion, sir, to a reasonable degree of engineering certainty as to what component of the fire suppression system activated the alarm?" He said he believed it was a heat detector.

Baccari continued, "Now, assume on July 18 at 6:20 a.m. the Malden Fire Department received an alarm signal from a control panel at Malden Mills and assume further that an accelerant was distributed at the fire scene and ignited. Do you have an opinion, sir, to a reasonable degree of engineering certainty as to a range of time it took for the first sprinkler head to respond after the fire started?"

He answered, "Yes, I do, sir. It was on the order of one to three minutes."

The testimony closed with questions about slow-growth fires. He answered that a slow-growth fire would be similar to a smoldering cigarette in a chair and that was not the case in this instance because gasoline was involved.

The lunch break arrived before Adrienne could begin her cross-examination. She used the hour to review her notes, match them to the direct testimony, and then finalize her questions and approach. She wanted to make a clear distinction for the jurors between her experts who investigated arson fires for a living from the defense witnesses who designed fire suppression systems and had minimal histories in post-fire analysis and no experience of testifying in criminal trials.

• • • •

When the trial resumed at two o'clock, Adrienne wasted no time in setting the tone and intention of her questions. She quickly established that the witness was not a certified fire investigator with the International Association of Arson Investigators, nor did he hold certification in any way as an expert in the cause and origin of fires.

"No, Ma'am. I wasn't claiming to be," he answered.

"With regard to your job, you are in the design area and you make determinations as to whether or not, when a building is to be built, what type of sprinkler heads or sprinkler system would be appropriate for the use of the building and make design recommendations to clients in the normal cause of your job?"

"Yes, I do, Ma'am," he replied.

Things got a little testy when Adrienne inquired about his usual experience when he was called to conduct a post-fire analysis. She asked if his primary role was to determine the adequacy of the fire suppression system at the time of the fire.

"That could be one task that could be done," he answered. After some back and forth and evasive answers, she countered with, "In your experience, you have never testified in a case in which the question is, or the issue before the jury is, a murder and an arson, isn't that fair to say?"

"Yes, it is," he answered.

She asked whether he had reviewed the fire scene evidence before he did his computer analysis, and he replied that he had looked at photos but not the evidence itself.

She moved ahead and asked about the creation of a second DETACT evaluation with a completely new set of calculations that was completed and submitted shortly before the trial began. He testified that he did do a second test and he only used the criteria for ultrafast-moving fires because gasoline-infused fires fell into that category.

Adrienne persisted with a series of questions based on a hypothetical that mirrored the testimony of an earlier witness who lived in the condo closest to the function room. He testified that on the morning of the fire he was already up and dressed when he heard the alarm sound. He immediately left his condo and, after walking several feet, saw water seeping through the bottom of the door from the function room. She asked the current witness if the story as presented was inconsistent with his opinion that the heat detector activated first. He said they were consistent.

She retorted, "You are aware, are you not, that there was a thirty-seven second flow switch activation delay from the area between the pump room and the function room?"

"Yes, I am," he answered. Adrienne put up a diagram of the basement level floor plan onto the overhead projector and used a pointer to indicate where the resident witness lived and how he walked toward the function room. "So that if the heat detector went off first and a sprinkler went off second," she said, "the water from the sprinkler would have to hit the floor and fire, then flowed all the way down here in the time that it took the resident to get into the hall."

He answered, "Assuming that no other sprinklers are operating, if the sprinkler near the door operated first, there would probably be quite a bit of water there." She reminded him about his earlier testimony where he said he believed the sprinkler nearest the corner of the room activated first and not the one nearest the door.

"It could have been," he replied.

The cross-examination wound down with Adrienne asking if a rug would absorb liquid until fully saturated versus a nonporous floor that would not. He agreed. She followed, "So that with respect to your time delays, they do not take into account the fact that that carpet would likely absorb water?"

"I don't recall performing that calculation that you're referring to," he answered.

"The point is this," she shot back, "that is a variable that would play into the delay in the water reaching the hall, do you agree?" He agreed with her point.

Adrienne closed with a series of shotgun-style questions, making the point that several possible variables might have affected the final analysis and that neither the witness nor his staff had considered them.

"Now, with regard to your involvement in this case," she asked, "you are testifying that you merely took numbers, put them into a computer program, and printed them out and that formed the basis of your opinion. Is that right?"

He responded, "It was a little more than that."

There were no further questions.

Baccari never produced the third witness on his list: the one he alleged to be the cause and origin expert. He offered no reason, nor was it necessary. Whom he called or didn't call was purely his prerogative. He wrapped up his defense of Crouse with short testimony from three witnesses regarding or clarifying statements from prior witnesses. Adrienne didn't dispute what they offered except to say that none of the testimony was relevant to anything or any evidence offered at any point in the trial.

. . . .

Eddie Forster testified for the prosecution earlier in the trial but, like all witnesses, was subject to recall by either side. Baccari brought him back to the witness stand and questioned him about his interactions with three of the Commonwealth's witnesses: Pete Grey, Nancy Cooper, and Carla McKay. In particular, he wanted to know about transporting them to area courts to clear up warrants or outstanding fines. Forster replied that he had driven Grey to court on two occasions and that on the second trip he had a conversation with the probation officer. He added that he took Nancy Cooper to Lowell Court to square away a warrant for failure to appear for jury duty and the Court dismissed the complaint after she explained to the clerk that she had no transportation on the date she was to appear. Lastly, he addressed Carla McKay and told the Court, he had never taken her to any court but had advised her of an outstanding motor vehicle warrant that needed her attention.

Baccari followed up with questions about two conversations Forster had with McKay about Crouse shortly after the fire and whether or not she ever talked about seeing visible scratches on Crouse's neck. He answered that she hadn't mentioned anything about scratches until a conversation he'd had with her a few weeks ago, when she was being prepped before she offered her trial testimony.

The fifty-ninth and final witness to take the stand was a brother-in-law of Tommy Crouse. He testified that on July 17, 2000, he arrived home from work and found a snow blower, a lawnmower, and a gas can in his driveway.

Before resting his case, Baccari requested a sidebar conference to discuss a couple of Massachusetts Crime lab reports written by an analyst regarding the comparison analysis she did of fibers found on the shovels and a bottle recovered at the New Hampshire burial site. Adrienne stipulated to the results, which allowed for Baccari, with Judge Grabau's permission, to read the findings to the jury without the analyst being present for cross-examination.

Judge Grabau spoke to the jurors and announced what was about to happen and why. Attorney Baccari addressed the jury and read directly from the two reports. The analyst wrote in the first report that she compared a series of fibers submitted to her from the New Hampshire State Police Crime Lab. They recovered them from the shovels, a bottle, Kelly Hancock's clothing, and the carpet and padding taken from the rear of Tommy Crouse's vehicle. She concluded that the blue fibers on the shovel could have a common origin with the victim's blue jeans, that the beige fibers on the spade and bottle could have a common origin with her plaid shirt, and that the gray cotton fibers from the spade and bottle could have a common origin with her plaid shirt. She also concluded that the report on the fiber samples removed from the carpet and padding in Crouse's vehicle did not mention any of the fiber samples submitted from New Hampshire. The second report referenced fibers taken from the carpets at the fire scene and compared to the fibers on the shovels and the bottle at the recovery site in Hookset. She said the fibers found in New Hampshire did not match the fibers that came from Malden Mills.

• • • •

After he read the reports aloud to the jury, Attorney Baccari rested his case. Adrienne offered no rebuttal witnesses. Therefore, after eleven full days of sitting, watching, and listening, the curtain finally lowered. There could be no more testimony from either side. Only the closing arguments remained. Both sides had one hour on Thursday morning to address the jury directly and sum up their cases. It was their last opportunity to highlight the strengths of their presentations while pointing out the weaknesses in the oppositions. It was evident that both Adrienne and Attorney Baccari believed in their "clients" and would make passionate appeals in their closing arguments.

Before dismissing the jurors for the day, Judge Grabau provided an overview of the next day's agenda. He told them to return at nine thirty the next morning and expect a full day. It would begin with the closing arguments, followed by his instructions about the law and the criminal charges they would be deliberating. Afterward, they would retire to the jury room for lunch and to deliberate Thomas Crouse's fate.

CHAPTER 25

The Trial: Day Fourteen
Closing Arguments

After the judge released the jury for the day, Adrienne and Nat waited a few moments for the courtroom to clear. They loaded their cardboard boxes of reports and notes onto a handcart before returning to the second floor for a final strategy meeting in John McEvoy's office. These peer gatherings are standard in all homicide cases. For this case, the three of them, and Martha, Marguerite, and some other folks who could enhance the conversation and the advancement of the prosecution often, joined them.

This particular day's meeting was slightly different. The evidence presentation and witness testimony were complete. There was nothing more for either side to add. In legal terms, they "rested"; in layman's terms, they said, "Folks, that's all we got." All that remained to discuss were the closing arguments and any final recommendations or suggestions to Judge Grabau regarding his instructions to the jurors on the relevant law, burden of proof, the requirement of unanimity in their findings, and a few other housekeeping matters.

Adrienne appeared calm and composed but not overconfident. Each year, there are as many as twenty homicide trials in the Middlesex Superior Courts, and Johnny and Adrienne had each written and delivered dozens of closing arguments. Throughout the trial, Adrienne kept a running list of important and noteworthy evidence and testimony she wanted to make sure had a place in her closing comments. She had put together a bulky rough draft that needed to be refined and prepared for presentation, and she was eager to get it in order. She welcomed suggestions and comments from others, but in this final stage of the trial, the words she wrote and then delivered in her own voice were what would matter.

In reality, she was working on her closing argument long before she wrote her opening statement. We all learned this strategy in law school during trial practice classes. When you start with the ending and work backward, it is easier to build and shape the direction you want the trial to flow throughout the process. It's like sketching out a roadmap to get you from Point A to Point B. You want to travel in the safest and most direct manner, understanding there are places where you can pass through quickly and places you will bog down with a lot of traffic, caution signs, and traffic lights. The purpose is to frame and steer your case so that the jury can follow along and ultimately reach the only logical conclusion: to find in your favor, regardless of which side you represent.

There is no standard, universal, or perfect way to compose and deliver a closing argument. It is pure persuasive techniques. Conventional wisdom is to spend the majority of the time discussing the strengths of your case, then address and discount any perceived weaknesses or negative comments made by your opponent. Be short, succinct, and on point, and then move on. Think of a key phrase or two and weave them into your talk whenever you can. You want those words and the reason behind them to thump with a rhythmic pace repeatedly in the juror's brains as they deliberate.

The meeting was over in less than an hour, and Adrienne went back to her office to hunker down, refine her words, and lay out the presentation in a logical, strongly connected manner that would remove any thoughts or consideration of reasonable doubt from every juror's mind. We knew she wanted to be alone, but one by one, we made the thirty-yard trek across the hall to offer encouragement and to let her know we would all be in the courtroom for her closing statement.

Before the trial began, Judge Grabau invoked a strict sequestration order keeping all potential witnesses out of the courtroom. His order was only in effect during the presentation of witnesses and evidence. Once both sides rested their cases, the doors would open for all witnesses to come in to attend the closing arguments. Generally, all police officers connected to the case appear for the closings.

She spent the next few hours hunched around her desktop computer, her glasses resting halfway down her nose as she sat squinting at the notes on her legal pad. There would be a few moments of quiet followed by the sound of ruffled and shifting pages, then quieter, before a sudden tat-a-tat bursting from the keys as words shot across the computer screen, spelling out her sudden stream of consciousness.

By eight o'clock, she'd had enough. She shut the computer down, turned off the lights, grabbed her bag, and walked out the door to her car in the parking garage down the street. After a quick dinner, she did another reread, made a couple of more edits, and was in bed by midnight.

What she didn't do was phone Marguerite to read the final script and ask for her input. May not sound like much, but she always did. On that night, she did not, partly as a break with tradition or maybe a bit of super-stition, but it definitely was a deliberate decision.

At five o'clock on Thursday morning, her alarm sounded. She was already awake and halfway through her morning routine. Dressed, as always, in a professional-style business suit, she picked up her overflowing tote bag, keys, and was out the door and on the road to Cambridge by six a.m.

Once in the office, she sipped at her coffee and sat reading her closing one last time. This time, it was to get the pacing down, to know when to let her voice raise a bit to emphasize a point or to slow down to hammer a point home. She knew her craft and always excelled in her presentation, and this trial would be no exception.

The next few hours passed painfully slowly. She appreciated the words of encouragement from the umpteen people who popped their heads into her door, but she wanted to get underway. She and Nat were waiting at the courtroom door when the court officer opened it for the session. There were no boxes to wheel along today, just a file with her closing argument typed out in large font and a few copies of Court decisions to support any legal arguments she might need to make if Judge Grabau or Attorney Baccari questioned or challenged the legal precedents behind her words.

We slid in before any spectators to make sure the room was safe and to save spaces for the Hancocks and Anne Foley. As the nine o'clock hour approached, the courtroom filled with spectators. Beside the investigative team, most of the troopers in the office were there, as was Martha Coakley and a large contingent of ADAs who came to watch, learn, and to support Adrienne.

Judge Grabau entered the courtroom exactly at nine and met with both counsels to go over the boilerplate rules of courtroom decorum at this point in a trial. He also wanted any final thoughts they had regarding his charge or instructions to the jury. He wanted to be sure the exhibits were all in order and marked correctly, so they could go into the jury room during deliberations without issue.

At nine thirty, the jurors filed in and walked to their seats. As they passed by Crouse not one of them looked at or acknowledged him sitting there. They stared either at the floor or at the back of the neck of the juror in front of them.

Because meeting the burden of proof is always the responsibility of the prosecution, they make the initial opening statement to present their case. For similar reasons, they make the final closing argument, offering proof that they have shown the defendant's guilt "beyond reasonable doubt."

With a nod from Judge Grabau, Attorney Bacarri approached the podium placed dead center in front of the juror's box. He started with a reference that the law presumes all defendants are innocent and that his client was "cloaked in that innocence until the government tears it from him." He mentioned that it was for the jury to determine what was evidence, and not he or Ms. Lynch and that, "It is their collective memory and decision that counts, not theirs."

He then set out on what appeared to be a scattered and unfocused rant beginning with the fire scene and the potential for evidence neither gathered nor tested that might prove his client's innocence. He talked of the magazine with the fingerprint and suggested it may have been in the room at the time of the birthday party for Crouse's kid and he moved it to the top shelf so children wouldn't see it. He queried why Trooper Setalsingh only tested the cover and not one of the other 177 pages of the magazine. He jumped from the fire to Crouse's cell phone records and suggested the calculations were all wrong and the total amount of incoming and outgoing calls were much lower.

He treaded lightly around the burial scene and mentioned that Dr. Andrews thought it was five inches deep while the trooper said it was eighteen. He found it confusing there was such a disparity in memories. He addressed the autopsy results by questioning the opinion of Dr. Andrews only saying it "makes no sense."

He spoke more about the lack of identifiable fingerprints on the two shovels at the bottom of the ravine than he did about the condition of the body.

He talked about the consensual search of Crouse's Blazer the night of the death and the more detailed one months later when the police had a search warrant, and how, on both occasions, they came away with no evidence of blood, gas, or a murder. He spoke of the bleach stain and asked what pickup truck doesn't have a flatbed full of stains.

As disorganized as Baccari may have appeared, he wasn't. He was trying to sow small seeds of doubt in juror's minds. He only needed a couple to hold out or grasp onto his unanswered questions to get a hung jury. Better yet, if he could get a half dozen or more, Crouse might walk out the door a free man. At a minimum, he might expect that his words would be a cause for a deeper deliberation by the jury.

He turned his focus to the testimony of the government witnesses and started with minor differences in those of Grey and Cooper. He spoke about the fact Cooper said she had seen a suspicious person in the parking lot a couple of times but the police never looked for him because they were only looking at Crouse.

Then he raised the issue of their honesty, insinuating that the prosecution bought their testimony because they both received rides to the courthouse and at another time got a ride to clear up an outstanding warrant.

He spoke about the witness that testified about Crouse's use of cocaine and how he allegedly told people he used it to lure girls into the function room. He questioned the importance of the statement because there was never any indication that Kelly Hancock used cocaine.

He spun back to the fire scene and brought up the prosecution witness Tom Klem, saying, "He jumps all over the place, and he is more confusing than anything else."

He said that although Crouse allegedly stabbed Kelly Hancock to death, the police never found a knife, no one testified that Crouse ever carried a knife, and there were neither knives nor kitchen utensils in the function room cabinets. "So," he said, "did Crouse go up to his condo, fetch a knife, and come back down to kill her?"

Baccari was skimming over topics and making quick comments with no substance or depth before moving onto the next items on his agenda. He continued to try to scatter the seeds that he hoped would sprout as reasonable doubt.

The next person on his list was Louie Barone. Baccari attacked his credibility immediately and said, "Beware of those that wail the tale to keep themselves from jail!" He talked of the deal Barone cut with the DA in return for his testimony. He quotes Barone as saying, "Crouse said he stabbed Hancock in the abdomen." Baccari paused for a second, looked directly at the jurors, and said, "Is that something someone would say? Only Dr. Andrews." He insinuated Barone saw a copy of the death certificate to improve or enhance his memory.

He mentioned that Barone testified in another Middlesex County murder trial a few years previous, and was currently talking to the Boston

Police about someone in the Suffolk Jail trying to hire him to kill people when he was free. The implication being that Barone was a professional informant who would say or do whatever it took to keep himself out of jail.

As his allotted time was expiring, Baccari slowed and narrowed his focus on a few important factors. "Now, look at the fire science evidence. None of that evidence points to Tommy Crouse. Those facts are stubborn. You can't put them, all that evidence, into a little bag. Search your conscience. Are you at ease with the tenant's testimony? How about Pete Grey and all those aliases he uses? Can you sleep with the likes of Louie Barone?"

"The judge is going to instruct you on proof beyond a reasonable doubt. Please—know we all know you are going to follow those instructions. You folks have a difficult, awesome responsibility, but when you look at the hard evidence, there's none. It really boils down to Barone and a little bit of Grey if you want to buy that business about the key."

"Think hard," he finished, "Weigh the testimony. Scrutinize Barone and return a verdict that only makes sense in this case. Don't convict him because he might be a good suspect. Only convict him if the government proves to you beyond a reasonable doubt to a moral certainty that Thomas Crouse and no one else in the world did this Godless act. Otherwise, acquit him."

Overall, Baccari did the best he could with what he had. His job was to spot and accent weaknesses in the prosecution's case, and he did that. Metaphorically, he loaded a shotgun with 20-aught buckshot and sprayed it at the prosecution's case. Even if only some of the pellets hit the intended target, he still could inflict significant damage.

In comparison, for her closing, Adrienne needed to bring a high-powered rifle with a mounted, sighted scope and every round had to be center mass with no margin for error.

• • • •

As Baccari turned away and walked back to his seat, Adrienne rose and moved to the podium with the same purposeful, rocking side-to-side shuffle step she had shown throughout the trial. She opened the manila folder and looked down at her printed thoughts. A few of her scripted words were circled in pen with arrows pointing to the margins and the notes she had added while listening stone-faced to Baccari's comments and attacks on the credibility of her evidence and her witnesses.

She paused, took a few deep breaths, and, like she had done with her opening argument, made eye contact with each juror, insuring she had their undivided attention. For the next hour the floor was hers, and she wasn't about to squander a second.

We all hoped that Adrienne had already persuaded the jurors of Crouse's guilt. However, hope on its own is never a good plan. This was her final persuasive push to support the charges that Crouse committed a murder in the first degree and then started an arson fire to cover his tracks. She had no murder weapon, eyewitnesses, or confession. However, she did put more than fifty witnesses on the stand and offered more than two hundred pieces of evidence to prove her case. It was all circumstantial evidence though, and in sixty minutes, she had to show how everything fit together nice and tightly, leaving no room for even a hint of reasonable doubt.

She had one hour to sketch a portrait for the jury, not with oils or chalk but with dozens and dozens of ragged pieces of a puzzle that she needed to methodically connect and transform into a picture of the murderer that was recognizable and unmistakably that of Thomas Crouse.

"Good morning, ladies and gentlemen of the jury," she began, "On July 18, 2000, Thomas Crouse brought fourteen-year-old runaway Kelly Hancock to the basement function room at the Malden Mills Condo building, and there, he used her for his own selfish purposes, for his sexual gratification. And when he was done with her, as a man on probation out of superior court for a felony, he could not afford to leave a live fourteen-year-old victim.

"Because he could not leave a fourteen-year-old victim, he brutally murdered Kelly Hancock in that room. Not only was Thomas Crouse calculating enough to murder a witness against him, he was calculating enough to set about to conceal his crime, to set fire to the function room. He was calculating enough to destroy all of the evidence against him.

"He thought he could get away with murder. Everything he did that morning, he calculated to cover his butt. He didn't want to go to jail, he didn't want to have a witness to a rape or sexual assault, and so he killed the fourteen-year-old witness so he could avoid prosecution. And then he went about concealing the crime and disposing of her so that he could avoid responsibility."

In her first three paragraphs, she provided the motive and mentioned Kelly's tender age four times. In Massachusetts, the age of consent for sexual relations is sixteen; anything less is statutory rape.

"But Thomas Crouse made mistakes," she suggested. "Thomas Crouse was seen, and Thomas Crouse was heard. What he said and what he did is the evidence that proves beyond a reasonable doubt that Thomas Crouse is a murderer."

With those comments as a backdrop, she set out to support her accusations. "When police showed up on the morning of July 18, they did not know who the victim was, and they did not know where she was. But they continuously worked a thorough, painstaking investigation to gather the evidence that is the pieces of the puzzle, which when, piece by piece, are put together, give you a picture that proves beyond a reasonable doubt that Thomas Crouse is guilty of murder in the first degree and guilty of arson."

She pushed ahead, focusing on the importance of the cell phone records for three reasons. First, they established a timeline of when important things happened. Second, they provided a roadmap pinpointing Crouse's whereabouts during critical times. Lastly, they were a blueprint of his state of mind on the day before, the day of, and the day after the murder.

She tied the cell phone calls to his statements to police about the evening before the fire. "I was home and didn't go out," he had told them. How does that explain a series of calls that included one from his cell to his house phone and a little bit later a call from the house phone to his cell? "Those records alone prove he is a liar." she said, "He's driving around, he's calling people, he's hitting off the cell towers." She connected a couple of the calls to Bob Sanders, an admitted cocaine dealer, and said those calls prove he was out and bought cocaine. It also shows his state of mind at the time.

She referred to statements made by Crouse and the Fourniers about the timing of phone calls and his arrival in New Hampshire, but the records tell a different story and prove deception on all of their parts.

Adrienne addressed a derisive comment in Baccari's closing. "He took a body to New Hampshire with his girlfriend and kids in the car?"

"Well, what were Thomas Crouse's options that morning?" She asked, "He's going to douse the function room and set it on fire so it's the towering inferno obliterating Kelly Hancock's evidence, and he's going to leave them behind so that he can go alone to dump the body? It was a risk that he had to take. He had no other options that morning, and it was a risk he took. And it was one he was able to accomplish: drive up to New Hampshire, drive around, and dump her in a location seven miles away from where he ultimately went."

Still referring to the morning of the eighteenth, she talked about Crouse being seen pulling the little red wagon across the parking lot and him admitting that he was in the basement and removing stuff from his storage bin and putting it into the back of his truck. "He knew he had been seen, so he admitted to that, but he never mentioned his stopping at the gas station and filling up a gas can because he didn't think the police would find that out."

She continued on, transitioning to the following morning when Crouse returned from New Hampshire alone and the conversations he had started with acquaintances. "They all thought he was acting strange that day. He tells them stories and offers untrue excuses. He was worried because he had made mistakes, he had been seen, and the police were on to him." She went on, indicating he later lied to his probation officer about police questioning him about the fire, and she never questioned him or solicited any information about the fire from him. At that point, she hadn't even spoken with police about Crouse.

Returning to the phone calls and the "panic chart," Adrienne pointed out his calls for that day and tells the jurors that regardless of how you want to calculate them, they were way in excess of any other day in a three-month period. She points out the enormity the volume of calls and says they are an indicator of Crouse's state of mind at the time. "He was running scared."

Adrienne continued, suggesting that all the evidence and testimony pointed to only one person, Thomas Crouse. "The police investigation in this case revealed a timeline of evidence that points to one person and one person only," she declared. "If you think about it in this way: there are several things that are absolutely clear about Kelly Hancock's murderer. Kelly Hancock's murderer had access to the Malden Mills. Kelly Hancock's murderer not only had access to the Malden Mills, but he also had access to the function room." She made the claim supported by evidence that Crouse had a key to both locations and bragged to others that he went to the function room late at night to "party with broads."

"We know that whoever killed Kelly Hancock was the only person who had the motive to set fire to the function room. And if it wasn't connected to the function room, they wouldn't need to even take Kelly Hancock's body away.

"What we know about Kelly Hancock's killer is he had to have gone to New Hampshire. He took the body to New Hampshire. And, lo and behold, Thomas Crouse drove to New Hampshire that day."

Adrienne returned to the period before the fire and mentioned the witnesses who put the events into a small, tight time frame. In the same sequence, she talked of the all-important video evidence from the Mobil station that showed Crouse opening the hatch window in the rear of the truck, filling a gas can, and never putting the nozzle near the gas cap leading to the truck's fuel tank. She commented on some furtive movements when he thought someone was watching him and the fact he paid in cash and not with the credit card that he always used—and that Lester Morovitz financed. She insinuated it was because he didn't want to leave a paper trail.

"He brought it back to the building," she said in a slightly louder tone. "He spread it over Kelly Hancock's blood as if he were holding her hand that close to it. Then he sets it on fire without any regard for the lives of the fifty or more people whose apartments were in that building, without regard to their safety, their property, and without any regard for the firefighters for the City of Malden who responded. Selfish purpose, most importing thing was Thomas Crouse getting away with murder."

She concentrated on the fire and the expert testimony explaining how it started, and what suppressed it before it became an inferno. She tells them about State Police Sergeant Paul Horgan who has investigated more than fourteen hundred fires in his career. "He tries to belittle that man," she said, referring to Baccari's comments. "Did he seem squared away? Did he seem candid and forthright? This man's job was to respond to fire scenes and figure out what happened. What does Paul Horgan have to gain by coming up with any scenario but the truth?" She then referenced the defense experts, "This isn't some game like the defense experts seemed to think it was—some intellectual exercise. It's fascinating putting data into the computer and coming up with these academic opinions that have absolutely nothing to do with the day-to-day reality of the work of a Paul Horgan and a Thomas Klem."

Then she turned to the search warrant on Crouse's truck in October and the fact that they found a bleach stain but no evidence of blood or anything else tying him to a murder. She explained that the police didn't have probable cause for a search warrant until three months later, after they had received and scrutinized the phone and credit card records.

Adrienne slowed her pace and with a shrug of her shoulders and slight tilt of her head she asked, "Do you think that in that period of time Thomas Crouse could have figured out how to vacuum out his car and get rid of all kinds of trace evidence of Kelly Hancock? Do you think someone who is calculated enough to murder a fourteen year old, set fire to the room where it happened, and then dump her body in New Hampshire is not going to figure out how to clean out a Blazer?"

After a few words about the persistent efforts of the investigators to find a victim, Adrienne transitioned to finding Kelly's remains in New Hampshire. She began by dispelling the defense allegations about the two shovels in the ravine and the lack of identifiable fingerprints on either. "The shovels are just a diversion. They do not create any doubt. You heard expert testimony about the things that affect fingerprints and that exposure to the elements, submersion in water and snow, would make it likely this print would not survive if left there in July. In that nine-month period of time, Kelly Hancock's body almost completely decomposed, and yet, this fingerprint somehow survived?"

After citing that through dental records they were able positively identify Kelly's remains, Adrienne spoke of the testimony of Drs. Andrews and Sorg and their explanations that the slits in Kelly's clothing that were consistent with a knife wound in the left abdominal area. She then explained how "that is where the scavengers would focus their attention because that was where the opening was and that was where the blood would pool. They tied that to the damage to her clothing made by the rodents that picked away at her shirt and undershirt. It followed that the damage to her pants was consistent and logical with blood dripping onto them from the gaping wound."

"So that while Dr. Andrews can say to a reasonable degree of medical certainty, and you can take it to the bank that it is beyond a reasonable doubt, there was definitely a stab wound to the abdomen. The evidence on the left-hand side of the scavenger activity is consistent with it being attractive to scavengers—leads him and Dr. Sorg to say it is consistent with that area having a wound that the animals were attracted to."

She mentioned how after Kelly was found and identified the police did a second canvass of the residents of Malden Mills and it produced a few changes in people's original statements. She explained the change by saying, "People may withhold what they know when they think it's just a property crime, but that all changes when they learn it was a homicide and the victim is a young girl. Their consciences take over, and they realize their observations may be important to investigators after all."

Turning to the critical testimony from Louie Barone and others, she commented that Crouse was a braggart who loved to talk about what he did. "This guy does things, and he's not smart enough to keep his mouth shut." She mentioned his telling Pete Grey he'd had a key to the room and Stan Peterson how he meets other women and brings them there.

"So what is so incredible about Thomas Crouse saying to Barone, 'Hear about my murder? You hear about my case? They got nothing on me. Yeah, I brought her to the function room. Yeah, we did coke. Yeah, we did it on the couch. Had sex with her every which way.' I'm not going to use the defendant's words, but you heard them."

Addressing Baccari's attack on Barone's credibility and truthfulness, Adrienne said that Barone wasn't some paid informant. He didn't seek a deal for his testimony. He got jail time. He waited to contact the state police until after his sentencing on his probation surrender, and he knew he wouldn't be going back to the Cambridge Jail but on to the house of correction in Billerica.

She walked through the testimony of Barone and the litany of statements that resulted from his conversations with Crouse. "There were facts that would be known only to someone talking to Tom Crouse," she said. "These were not the result of Barone sitting studiously in the cell area reading five volumes of discovery material, as the defense counsel insinuated. He heard it from the horse's mouth."

"The only problem in this case is that the defendant made a mistake in trusting Louie Barone, just as he made a mistake in trusting Bob Sanders, Carla McKay, Stan Peterson, and Pete Grey. He made mistakes."

As her allotted time wound down, Adrienne returned the jurors' attention to the crime scene and went through the gruesome bloodstain evidence, piece by piece—all of the places they had found Kelly's blood in smudges, smears, spray, and small pools throughout the room. Traces were also on the rug, the walls, the chairs, the glass table, and the door. She referenced the chilling testimony of Ken Martin, who had tracked every stain and provided the explanation of how Kelly's final moments of life had unfolded.

"Kelly Hancock was fourteen years of age, and she was a runaway. And for her—all her seeming fearlessness, not being afraid to sleep in a cemetery at night, not being afraid to walk alone on Broadway at four fifteen in the morning, for all of her fourteen-year-old bravado, in those last minutes of Kelly Hancock's life, she knew that she was in over her head. She knew that this was not going to be easy for her to escape. And in those last minutes of Kelly Hancock's life, she looked into the face of her killer, and she saw Thomas Crouse."

In her last few moments at the podium, Adrienne touched on the elements of first-degree murder. She spoke of premeditation, extreme atrocity, cruelty, indifference to Kelly's conscious pain and suffering and how Crouse's cronies described him as his usual cheerful self while he was in New Hampshire a few hours after Kelly's murder. She ended with the arson charge and the willful and malicious way Crouse went about starting the fire.

"Thank goodness he made a mistake. Thank goodness he used too much gasoline. Thank goodness it was a low, slow-burning carpet fire and that the systems in place were sufficient to suppress it because think of the further tragedy that would have been compounded by one man's calculated, selfish quest to get away with murder."

She concluded by saying, "When you look at the evidence, you consider the reasonable inferences to be drawn from that evidence; that's what you do in a circumstantial case. You will hold an abiding conviction of the truth of these charges beyond a reasonable doubt, and you will return from your deliberations, and you will return to the courtroom, and you will, with confidence, announce your verdict in this case that Thomas Crouse is guilty of murder in the first degree and guilty of arson."

You could have heard a pin drop as she turned and returned to her seat. She shot us a glance, and all we could do was nod and smile back. We were encouraged by her closing argument, but we knew the jurors had an awful lot of work in front of them. We hoped none of them had daydreamed at any point and lost the continuity or depth of her argument.

• • • •

After the jury returned from a short morning break, Judge Grabau gave them their final marching orders before they retired to the jury room for lunch and deliberations. For the next hour and a half, he read the mandatory instructions connected to each of the criminal charges against Crouse. He told them once again that they were the "sole and exclusive judges of the facts. You alone determine the weight, the effect, and the value of the evidence and the credibility of the witnesses. And once you make these determinations of fact, it is your duty to apply them to the law as I will give it to you in determining whether the defendant is guilty or not guilty of the charges made against him." He talked about the presumption of innocence and the Commonwealth's burden to prove their allegations beyond a reasonable doubt. He spoke about Crouse not testifying and how it was his right to "remain passive and to insist the Commonwealth prove its case beyond a reasonable doubt without explanation or denial."

He launched into the legal definition of reasonable doubt, explaining, "Reasonable doubt is that state of the case when, after the entire comparison and consideration of all the evidence, the minds of the jurors are left in the condition that they cannot say they feel an abiding conviction to, a moral certainty of, the truth of the charge. It is not enough for the Commonwealth to establish a probability. This is not enough."

He talked of the difference between direct evidence and circumstantial evidence, of expert witnesses and why they can give opinions, of gruesome photographs and how they shouldn't have any effect their decision-making. He spoke of the difference between specific intent and general intent, of making inferences based on witness testimony and evidence.

Then he went through a lengthy, thorough explanation of each element of every charge against Crouse, including the need for unanimity on all of the elements for a finding of guilty.

At the conclusion of the jury charge, the clerk spoke and announced the name of the juror who would act as their foreperson and spokesperson. He placed fourteen small papers with the names of the rest of the jurors into a wooden box and selected three from them; those would be the alternates. They would stay together in a side room during the deliberations and, on the judge's orders, not discuss the case. They would only be part of the decision-making if the judge dismissed one of the twelve deliberating jurors for any reason, and then he would insert one of them in their place. If a backfill became necessary that, too, would be a blind draw.

At ten minutes after two, the jurors headed to the jury room for lunch and deliberations. At ten minutes after four, they returned to the courtroom. Their discussions had begun, but it had been a long day with a lot to absorb, and they wanted to end the day at the regular time and start fresh the following morning.

CHAPTER 26

The Verdict

For everyone, no matter what their connection to the case, regardless of whether they stood for the prosecution or the defense, everything boiled down to the coming moments. It was more than two years since Kelly Hancock went missing and fifteen months after we had arrested Tommy Crouse for her murder when we received the word that the jury had decided his fate and the reading of their verdict was imminent.

They had been deliberating for a day and a half. They had gone through the witness list and discussed each person's testimony. They had reviewed all of the evidence and compared or matched it to the testimony. They had discussed, and undoubtedly debated, the pros and cons of all of the key points and considerations. Only then did they vote. They had filled out their ballots at least once and maybe several times, until they reached a finding that was acceptable to all of them. Each time a vote was called for, the foreperson passed out small pieces of paper to each juror, and they simply wrote "guilty" or "not guilty" on the slip, folded it over, and placed it into a small pile. The foreperson went through each of them, tallied up their votes, and announced the outcome to the jurors. A simple procedure, nothing technical or complicated, carried out the same way juries have voted in every jurisdiction since the jury system began.

In a few minutes, we would have their collective decision. Months and months of investigation, trial preparation, and courtroom presentation came down to one or two words from the mouth of the foreperson: "guilty" or "not guilty."

It doesn't matter how many times I've heard the words, "The jury has a verdict." My reaction is always the same. Intentional or not, the internal switch flips over to autopilot. My senses heighten in one way but constrict in another. Tunnel vision takes over. I can see straight ahead, but things on the periphery are fuzzy or blocked out. Likewise, I can still hear, but the words can become a blur of garbled white noise. Personal feelings like these aren't something teammates talk to each other about, but I have to believe that we all have similar, if not exactly the same reactions.

It mimics the helpless feeling I had sitting in the stands or standing on the sidelines toward the end of my kid's sporting events. You did your job, and you can do nothing more, and the outcome lies in the hands of others. It isn't a feeling I ever like.

You can only hope the jurors listened and absorbed the statements and observations of the witnesses. Hope they found them to be truthful, knowledgeable, and believable and that the evidence and Adrienne's presentation covered all of the bases and answered any of their doubts or questions. Hope Adrienne's game plan was the winning formula. Hope that they saw the same weaknesses in the defense that we did. You cannot replicate the unease and discomfort in words. Will the jury's decision validate all of our collective work, or will it not? We would have our answer in the following few moments, and it couldn't arrive soon enough.

Heartrates elevated, conversation dropped to a minimum, and eye contact was fleeting as we regathered and started to file back into the courtroom and took our seats. The Hancocks went in first, accompanied by Anne Foley. They sat on the same wooden bench they had sat on every day throughout the trial. The rest of us gave them space but sat near them as a gesture of our support and protection. Crouse's crew sat a few benches away, undoubtedly, as the rest of us, lost in their own thoughts and concerns.

When verdicts come down, the courtroom is usually full. Troopers from our office come upstairs in support of the team and so they can be present in the event there is a reaction or outburst following the verdict. Similarly, the DA and other superior court ADA's come up as a show of solidarity and support.

The deputy led Crouse from his holding cell back into the courtroom.

He removed Crouse's handcuffs, and Tommy stood emotionless at the defense table next to his counsel. Adrienne and Nat stood in front of their chairs at the prosecution's table. Adrienne turned to look at everyone in the benches at the back and broke into a subtle, nervous nod and smile, an acknowledgement that everyone was together as one in the courtroom.

With everyone in place, Judge Grabau entered, walked up to his seat, leaned over, and had a quick, quiet conversation with his clerk before straightening up to address everyone in the room. His words were similar to those of all trial judges at this point in the proceedings. He explained how the deliberation process worked and what would occur when the jury returned to the courtroom. Most importantly, he told everyone to maintain courtroom respect and decorum regardless of the jury's findings. He said he wouldn't tolerate outbursts of any nature from either side, and if there were, he would order the court officers to remove them from the courtroom. It is always a stern but necessary message.

The judge nodded to the court officers and instructed them to bring in the jury. Moments later, the twelve deliberating jurors entered in the same single file order that they had for the past three weeks. Next came the three alternate jurors who had remained together but in a separate room. They were not privy to the deliberations or the finding. All of their once cheery and smiling faces were now stern and serious, very serious. Their moment of truth had arrived as well. They had to make a choice that few of us ever want or have to make—to decide whether or not Tommy Crouse would walk out the door a free man or if he would head to jail—and incarceration for the rest of his natural life.

They didn't look at or see us staring at them as they entered and stood in front of their seats; they didn't know we were trying to read their faces and their minds. Did they look at Crouse on their way by or stare away? Did they acknowledge the Hancock family as they passed them by? There is an unproven belief that if a juror won't look at a defendant it's because they have found him guilty. I don't discount the theory, but I have seen a juror or two look at a defendant and smile with, as it turned out, a look of defiance, proud of their decision to convict.

At 3:54 on a warm but dreary Friday afternoon when the court clerk spoke, "Counsel and the defendant are present. I understand we have a verdict." He turned and asked Judge Grabau if he could inquire of the jury. Grabau nodded yes.

"Mr. Foreperson, has your jury reached their verdicts?"

"We have," was the response.

"May I have them please?" The foreperson handed over the paperwork and both the clerk and the judge looked at them, pokerfaced. He returned the verdict slips to the foreperson, and seconds later, the clerk turned to face the foreperson and jury and said, "On indictment number 2001–733, Indictment 001, the Commonwealth of Massachusetts versus Thomas Crouse, charged with the crime of murder, what say you, Mr. Foreperson; is the defendant guilty or not guilty?"

"GUILTY," replied the foreperson.

"Guilty of what, sir?" asked the clerk.

"Of murder in the first degree."

"Under what theory, sir?"

"Deliberate premeditated malice aforethought and extreme atrocity."

The clerk then spoke to all of the jurors at once and asked, "So say you all members of the jury?"

They unanimously responded, "YES."

Because the jury found the defendant guilty of murder on two of the theories of homicide, Judge Grabau asked for a separate polling of the jurors on each count. In one raised voice, the jurors affirmed their guilty findings on both counts.

The clerk again turned to the foreperson and asked, "002, charged with the crime of arson in a dwelling, what say you, Mr. Foreperson, is the defendant guilty or not guilty?"

"GUILTY," came the reply.

"Members of the jury, you will harken to your verdict as recorded by the court, the jurors, upon their oath, do say that the defendant is guilty of arson in a dwelling. So say you, Mr. Foreperson?"

"Yes, Sir."

"So say you all members of the jury?"

Again, they replied with strong voice and in unison, "YES."

"You may be seated, jury. You may be seated, Mr. Crouse."

From the moment, the foreperson uttered the word guilty, audible gasps and sobbing breaths of relief from the spectator's gallery overruled the customary silence of the courtroom. The Hancocks, overcome by the verdict, lost themselves in tears and hugs. They had lived every day with the ache and agony that Kelly would never be physically back in their arms. At least now, they had assurance that for the rest of his life, Tommy Crouse would see the sun rise and set every day filtered through a barbed wire fence affixed to the top of a forty-foot-high wall that surrounded the maximum-security prison that he would forever call home.

Judge Grabau stood and faced the jury and spoke in a calm tone, "Ladies and gentlemen, it's my practice and custom to thank all of the jurors at the end of the case. So, would you kindly wait in your jury deliberation room, all together? I'll be with you shortly."

The total time between the jury entering the courtroom until the time they walked past Crouse and out the door was three minutes. As they passed by him, several looked in his direction but exchanged no words.

First-degree murder in Massachusetts requires an automatic life sentence in the state prison system with no opportunity for parole. However, that didn't mean there wouldn't be an opportunity for both sides to address the Court to argue for sentencing. Specifically, because the jury found Crouse guilty of the arson charge as well, there was a question as to whether Judge Grabau would issue a concurrent or a consecutive sentence, also known as an on-and-after sentence on that charge.

Adrienne was prepared to offer her recommendations regarding sentencing. The Massachusetts Victims Bill of Rights guarantees a victim or, in the case of a homicide, the victim's family the opportunity to express their thoughts and feelings about their loved one and make suggestions about sentencing. Both Jackie and Lisa wanted to address the Court. Mark said he feared what might happen if he made a statement, so he deferred to his wife and daughter.

"They were like a protective wall that kept me from doing something stupid," he said.

Adrienne went first. She drew attention to Crouse's prior conviction for rape and the fact that he had received a ten- to fifteen-year sentence and was out of jail on a suspended sentence when he assaulted and murdered Kelly. More on direct point, Adrienne talked about separating the arson from the murder because the circumstances were different. The fire, she argued, was set to cover the murder, but moreover, it had jeopardized the lives and safety of everyone who was in the building that morning, as well as the fire personnel dispatched to extinguish it.

Judge Grabau welcomed Jackie Shepard to the stand, and after identifying herself for the record, she spoke. She had prepared her words in advance and held them in her hand as she talked. Her voice was soft and a bit shaky, but her words were not. She singled out Adrienne, Eddie, and Duke and praised them for their work on the case. She said the family hoped Crouse would receive the maximum sentence and that they prayed for God to forgive him "for we may never be able to."

She talked of their painful loss and the fact that their Kelly would never have a sweet sixteen party, let alone join them on family camping trips, how Crouse robbed them of seeing her graduate from high school and maybe even college. "She will never have the chance to fall in love, to marry, to have children of her own," she said, before mentioning what each of Kelly's siblings missed most about having Kelly gone from their lives.

She spoke about Kelly and her older brother and younger sister being altar servers at the Immaculate Conception Church and how at her burial, "Father Memis draped her white robe over the casket so that Kelly spiritually served at her own burial mass."

Jackie commented on the nine months from Kelly's conception to her birth and the fact it was the same amount of time from the moment of her murder until the recovery of her remains in New Hampshire. She talked about the days and nights that Mark and she scoured the streets of Malden looking for her, never losing hope until the moment Eddie Forster showed up at their door to deliver the news about the positive dental comparison: their raw finality that Kelly wouldn't be coming home to live with them again.

She mentioned that the entire family remained in the counseling program offered by the Victims of Homicide.

"They say that what doesn't kill you makes you stronger. This may be true, but we wish that we never had to learn this, not by losing Kelly."

She closed her comments by saying, "Not a day goes by that we do not remember Kelly's beautiful smile, her flashing brown eyes, her red hair that was her pride and our joy. Although we cannot actually see Kelly, we know that she can see us, that she watches over her brothers and sisters, and that she will always be in our hearts and in our lives. Thank you."

Lisa was the next to stand before the Court on her sister's behalf. Her comments were short and to the point.

"Your Honor, I came here today to ask the Court to put this man in jail for the rest of his life so he can't hurt anyone else or their families again. This man hurt my sister that I will never see again or talk to again, to ask questions about life and things. When he did all of these things to my sister, it hurt everyone in my family. It was hard for me to deal with. So please, Your Honor, give this man all you can, and don't let him get out of jail ever. Thank you."

It wasn't so much Lisa's words that resonated with everyone; it was the fact that at such a tender age she had the courage to stand ten feet away from the man who took her sister's life and demand justice for Kelly. She was the true voice for her sister, complete with all of her edginess. She didn't go into depth about their relationship. She didn't have to. The fact that she insisted on speaking told us all we needed to know about the two of them. Lisa loved Kelly unconditionally, just as teenage sisters do. She didn't see what other people might have seen in Kelly, like her rebellion and irreverence for authority. She only saw and remembered that they were best friends and that she admired Kelly maybe more than anyone else she knew. It was clear Kelly had made a strong and lasting impression on her little sister.

Lisa bore a strong physical resemblance to her sister, and at fourteen, she was the same age as Kelly when she was murdered. It was impossible to forget that Lisa and Kelly shared and survived a difficult life experience years earlier when they watched helplessly as their mother collapsed and died during a medical seizure. That was horrific enough. Knowing how Kelly was murdered had to be unbearable.

I don't know how her words affected the others in the courtroom, but I do know the strong effect they had on me. As the father of two daughters, and one who continually preaches the importance of family and the need to "have each other's backs" all of the time, Lisa's words put a smile on my face but tore off a small piece of my heart. I couldn't begin to imagine how my girls would go on without each other in their lives. I could only hope they could muster the strength and be there for one another in a time of great tragedy, even if it was postmortem.

Court rules prohibited those in the audience to speak or be demonstrative, but if we could, we would have risen in unity in praise and sustained applause of Jackie and Lisa and the words and efforts they delivered on behalf of their family and Kelly.

John Baccari's one paragraph comment regarding sentencing was simply that "under the totality of the circumstances" to treat the two sentences as one and serve them concurrently.

Judge Grabau wasted no time in making his sentencing pronouncement. On the charge of murder, he applied the mandatory life sentence punishment. On the charge of arson, Adrienne's comments had obviously made some impact because Crouse received an additional seven- to ten-year sentence to serve from and after the life sentence.

The idea of a from-and-after sentence on top of a life sentence may seem foolish or even excessive, but the rationale for it is simple and necessary. A conviction on a first-degree murder charge brings with it an automatic appeal to the Massachusetts Supreme Judicial Court. In the event the Court was to either overturn the conviction or lessen the charge to something that would allow for parole eligibility Crouse would still serve the seven- to ten-year arson punishment after the granting of his parole or the Court would vacate the murder conviction. Simply said, in the unlikely event, that Crouse received parole, he would remain in prison for at least seven more years.

As is custom, when a judge rises to announce his decision on the punishment, the court officers slowly fall into place behind and aside the guilty defendant. Once the judge's comments and sentencing are complete, and assuming there are no complications or outbursts, the court officer gently restrains the defendant's arms and shifts them behind their back. Then an officer pulls a pair of handcuffs from a leather pouch, and the sweetest sound imaginable breaks the silence in the courtroom. In some ways, it is a repetitive sound police officers hear every day and an action they perform with a certain frequency from their first day on the job. However, it sounds distinctively different in these moments. It is the click-click-click sound from the handcuffs as the teeth on the steel swing arm slowly ratchet their way through the pawl and lock into place.

For me, it is the ultimate gratifying sound of confirmation—a final statement that our collective work was thorough, correct, and convincing and that the person responsible for the death of another is about to board a transportation van and head off to a maximum-security prison for the rest of his life.

As soon as the court officers removed Crouse from the courtroom and brought him to a waiting elevator, Judge Grabau was off the bench and headed to meet with the jury. Adrienne and Nat turned around to the audience with looks of joy and relief. They deserved their subdued looks of triumph because they had earned them. They had accomplished all that any of us could have hoped for, and they did it through hard work, expert planning, preparation, and thorough case development and courtroom presentation. They had taken a case that relied completely on circumstantial evidence and information, wove it together seamlessly, and presented it to a jury for their inspection and determination, and they emerged victorious on all counts.

We waited impatiently for them to approach the wooden barrier that separates the spectators from the players. There wasn't a dry eye in the group. We all shared warm, heartfelt embraces and exchanged comments of praise and thanks with the Hancocks, Anne Foley, the investigative team, and others involved in the case. It was amazing to think back to Memorial Day Weekend in 2001, and how what started out as an adversarial meeting full of anger and distrust from the Hancocks would result in such an emotional and genuine sharing of love between all of us: an emotional feeling impossible for any of us to forget.

It took a few minutes for the courtroom to clear and people to head toward the elevator. Adrienne wanted the team to reconvene in the state police office to spend a few minutes to reflect on the outcome before we headed down to a restaurant in the Galleria Mall and a celebratory drink or three.

At precisely five o'clock, the large metal door to the office swung shut and locked. We were still inside discussing the jury deliberations and sharing our thoughts about what we thought had went on inside the jury room. The office phone rang a few minutes later, and the displayed number belonged to Melissa, Adrienne's administrative aide.

"Hi, Billy," she said, "Is Adrienne still there?"

"She sure is, Melissa," I answered. "Do you need her?"

"No, I don't, but could you go to the door. There is someone there who would like to speak with her."

"Will do, is it friend or foe?" I asked.

"You will see," is all she said before hanging up the phone.

I interrupted the conversation.

"Adrienne that was Melissa on the phone, someone is at the door and wants to speak with you. Let's go see what they want."

A few of us walked her to the front of the office and opened the door. What happened next was something none of us expected or had ever experienced.

The jurors were standing together in the hallway, and when they saw Adrienne, they exploded in applause. Their response was incredible, as were their comments that followed. They had endless questions, but most of all, they wanted to express their gratitude. They may have come from different cities and towns, but they were all residents of Middlesex County. One of the women said she was comforted knowing that if something ever happened to her or a member of her family, Adrienne would be on the case and she was sure they would catch the assailant and bring them to justice. Another juror, a sixty-eight-year-old woman, said she hadn't been sure about being a part of the jury; she hadn't seen the purpose. "Now," she said, "I realize sitting on this trial and convicting the defendant was the most important thing I have done in my life."

The congratulatory comments made, their questions all answered, and the handshakes and hugs completed, the jurors slowly drifted away in singles and small groups. Many of them were heading for a drink at a local bar to toast the end of their ordeal and to talk about the bonds they created that led to their newfound friendships. Others just wanted to head home to their families, maybe mow the lawn before it got dark, or stop on the way to shop for groceries, or just do what they usually did on a fall Friday evening. They just wanted to slip back into that familiar groove of normalcy that they once just took for granted.

We went back inside, grabbed our gear, and started to head out like a small wolf pack. While we walked down the small center aisle that separated the workstations on either side, Eddie turned to Adrienne and made one of the most poignant and perfect comments I have ever heard from him or anyone else.

"You know, Adrienne, there are people out there who have no idea that their lives have been saved because Tommy Crouse was convicted today, and if you do nothing else in your entire legal career, you have accomplished more than 99 percent of the people in the world ever will."

Leave it to Eddie to have the last words. And for once, they were absolutely spot on and had us nodding in full agreement.

CHAPTER 27

Epilogue

On some level, it seems that Kelly Hancock went missing a short time ago but, in reality, more than twenty years have passed since the recovery of her remains and the arrest and conviction of Tom Crouse for her murder. Over the years, I have presented this case at dozens of police trainings, both alone and with Adrienne and Duke at the podium. It is not only an emotional and gripping story but a clear and ringing example of "what right looks like" for police and prosecutors. It provides a template of how painstakingly thorough work and dogged persistence by everyone, in a case that at times seems hopeless and back-burner forgettable, can one day prove to be solvable and rewarding. The old saying that "luck is what happens when preparation and opportunity meet" could not have rung truer than it did in this case.

Today, Crouse remains a "guest" of the Massachusetts Correctional System and will remain in their custody for the rest of his life. He, like anyone convicted of first-degree murder in Massachusetts, received an automatic appeal before the full bench of the Massachusetts Supreme Judicial Court. The process usually takes a few years to complete, and often lawyers who specialize in the appeal process rather than trial attorneys present the case. It is a little unnerving for all of us because an assemblage of the best and brightest legal minds in the Commonwealth review and scrutinize every step of the investigation and prosecution looking for errors or constitutional violations that could cause the reversal of part or all of the conviction. They can and should be hypercritical as they pour over the claims or challenges of wrongdoing brought by the defendant. In the end, either the Court approves our work with a thumbs-up or they find constitutional error, or misapplication of the rules of evidence or trial procedure and turn thumbs-down with a crushing opinion that reverses the jury's finding. It doesn't matter that we were sure of our work; we needed to hear it from them before we could box everything up for storage in the archives. All tolled up, Adrienne had accumulated thirty-seven boxes of trial-related materials.

Crouse's attorney for this phase was a highly regarded advocate and appellate litigator appointed by the Court at the expense of the Commonwealth. He raised several issues in his written brief and oral argument regarding Judge Grabau's interpretations of existing case law and trial procedure. He questioned rulings on defense motions made before and during the trial, requesting to include or exclude information and/or evidence from presentation to the jury. He argued that Judge Grabau's decisions were prejudicial to Crouse and the Court should reverse the jury's guilty finding and allow for a new trial. His challenges zeroed in on several points in the trial. He questioned the allowance of testimony about Crouse's behaviors before and after the fire. He challenged the testimony offered by expert witnesses. He disputed some comments made by Adrienne in her opening and closing arguments. Perhaps his most critical argument concerned a denial of a motion by the judge to block the admission of any evidence or testimony about Crouse's past behavior and court convictions for rape and other assault related crimes if he chose to take the stand and testify. It was important, he alleged, because it essentially prevented Crouse from offering testimony that would go to prove his innocence because information about his criminal past might prejudice the jury against him.

Marguerite Grant, with significant discussion and input from Adrienne, Nat, Jim Sahakian, the director of the Appeals Bureau, and Martha Coakley prepared a legal brief answering and rebutting all of his claims. Her brief became the source material for her oral arguments.

In the end, the Court ruled unanimously to uphold Crouse's conviction. They analytically considered and rejected all of the defense's arguments. Admittedly, there were a couple of close calls with nods from them to the discretion allowed to a trial judge, but no critical faults were found to overturn the verdict and Crouse's pleas for a new trial were denied.

The Massachusetts State Police Crime lab built their multifaceted CODIS database to match unknown samples from crime scenes and victims against files of legally collected samples of known sex offenders, incarcerated felons, parolees, and others collected through court orders or search warrants. They activated the system in 2002.

One afternoon, a year or so after Crouse went to prison, Eddie Forster popped his head into my office. "Boss, you got a minute?" he asked. He was clearly anxious and bursting to tell me something important. He was smiling with a broad grin, and the coloring of his face changed in seconds from a greyish-white to bright red. For a second I thought he must have hit the lottery. Without waiting for my answer, he piped up, "I just got off the phone with someone from the crime lab, and they just got a CODIS match on a rape case from Salem that happened back in 1990."

"That's great, Eddie," I answered with a quizzical look, "But why are they calling you with the news? Salem is in Essex County."

"Because," he said with a twinkle in his eye that I hadn't seen from him in a while, "Get ready 'cause you ain't gonna f'n believe it: the hit is on Tommy Crouse. They nailed him on another rape. I'm not surprised, but it is unbelievable, isn't it? I can't wait to tell Adrienne." It was the closest I ever saw Eddie come to dancing as he headed out the door and headed across the hall to hunt down Adrienne and share the news.

In 2003, a detective with the Salem Police Department was at a training seminar learning about the potential uses of DNA in police investigations. A crime lab technician teaching the course suggested when the detectives returned to their stations they should talk with their coworkers and comb through their unsolved crimes, looking for pieces of untested evidence where there may be biological samples containing DNA. He encouraged them to have the evidence tested for DNA at the crime lab so they could enter the results and match them against the

CODIS database. On the drive back to the office, his thoughts were on a vicious assault and rape of a college student in his city thirteen years before. Neither he nor his partner ever gave up trying to solve the heinous case. In the days and months after the reporting of the rape, the detectives did what we did: they haunted the teletype and police information bulletins for news about other sexual assaults and requests for information. They responded to anything that had any resemblance to their case. They wrote extensive reports, interviewed several people, and followed a few hopeful paths that led to dead ends. They stayed in touch with the victim and never abandoned the case. The only evidence they had was a composite sketch of the assailant, a description of a tattoo of a panther on the rapist's thigh, and thankfully, the biological results of a rape examination completed at Salem Hospital on the day of the assault.

They submitted the rape kit to the state crime lab for DNA testing and entry into the CODIS database. The timing was perfect. A few months earlier, following his convictions, the lab entered a sample of Tommy Crouse's DNA into a database of known, convicted felons. Within weeks, the lab confirmed a match between the biological sample removed from the victim and Crouse. To be certain that they had their man, an ADA from the Sexual Assault Unit at the Essex County DAO requested a court order for another DNA sample from Crouse. The judge issued the order, and the second test resulted in the same perfect, confirming match. The detectives reconnected with the victim, now forty and married with children, and broke the news. They showed her a photo of the panther tattoo on Crouse's leg, which she positively identified, and the sketch she provided at the time of her assault bore a decent resemblance to Crouse. She was excited to learn about the DNA match and said she was as ready and committed to testify against her assailant as she was the day of the rape.

A grand jury indicted Crouse for the rape. He fought the charges, but after losing legal challenges to the DNA collection and testing process, he admitted his guilt in return for an agreed upon concurrent sentence of eighteen to twenty years in state prison. His plea came eighteen years to the week of the victim's rape. During sentencing, the judge who presided over the case, said, "At least the victim doesn't have to wonder who this person is, if he is still out there, if he could victimize someone else." He added, "And that wouldn't have happened without the work of the Salem detectives who didn't give up on this case."

With the passing of time, there is always change, and there was no exemption or exception for either the prosecutors or the police. In 2009, an inspection of the courthouse building revealed several structural issues coupled with a heavy coating of asbestos throughout the infrastructure. Extensive renovation required closing the building and, with the exception of the jail, all operations moved thirteen miles north to the city of Woburn. The courtrooms and administrative offices are now set up in a refurbished commercial office building. The DAO and the state police settled into a small office building a mile away. The move broke up the ease and simplicity of the daily routine. There are no longer stops at the coffee shop, or meetings in the cafeteria, or visits from local detectives awaiting their courtroom appearances, or a quick elevator ride to the courtrooms. Most of all, the general closeness with the short walk across the hall to meet, socialize, or strategize on cases has also ended. Now closed and secured doors between the two offices require an identification swipe card to access the offices and even the bathrooms. As with all aspects of life, things beyond your control can change, and you just have to deal with them and soldier on. The environment has changed but not the mission.

• • • •

As I write, the years seem to have passed in the blink of an eye. There have been many personnel changes in the DAO, but there has not been a change in the continuity of operations or in the level of outstanding legal services provided to the people of Middlesex County. Martha

Coakley moved on when she won election as the attorney general of Massachusetts, serving for eight years before joining a private law firm. Marian Ryan, a career prosecutor in the office since 1978, is now the elected DA. Nat Yeager accepted a position in the US Attorney's Office in Boston, where he is the chief of the Health Care Fraud Unit. Recently, Marguerite Grant became an associate justice of the state appellate court, the second highest court in the Commonwealth.

Most of the investigators have moved on as well. Steve Ruelle and John Rivers both retired from policing, although John remains active, working for the United States Marshals Service in the Federal Courthouse in Boston. I stepped away from the office in 2005 to become the director of training for the Division of Investigative Services and then as the commandant of the Training Academy. I retired in 2007 when I accepted a position at the Boston University School of Medicine as an assistant professor in the graduate program in the area of biomedical forensic sciences. Today, I have returned to my professional womb, once again working in the Division of Standards and Training for the state police where I specialize in program development for investigator training initiatives. Jimmy Connolly initially stepped into my position as the detective lieutenant and was subsequently promoted to the rank of major and assigned as the crime lab commanding officer. He retired a few years ago and is now the director of public safety at Suffolk University Police Department in Boston. Eddie Forster rose to the rank of lieutenant and shepherded dozens more homicide cases from crime scene to trial. He woke up one morning, and for no apparent or explained reason said to himself, "I'm done!" He took the ride to General Headquarters and filed his retirement papers. It was a huge surprise on one hand, but on the other, when it came to Eddie's life plans, we always expected the unexpected. I saw him recently, and he has never looked better or seemed happier.

On a very sad note, Attorney John Baccari passed away in January of 2016 at the age of sixty-one. He was still actively litigating criminal and civil cases in both state and federal courts. His passing was not only a huge loss to his wife and four grown children but to the entire legal community in Middlesex County, as well as his friends and members of the civic organizations he belonged to in his hometown of Reading. There may have been legal and procedural disagreements during the trial and the events that led up to it, but they were always professional and never personal. All of us on the prosecution side of the case would agree that John was dignified throughout, represented his client as well as possible, and as we are wont to say, he was "a total class act" throughout.

John McEvoy also passed away unexpectedly at the age of sixty-four. The positive impact he had on the criminal justice system in Middlesex County was monumental. He had the professional respect of everyone from judges, prosecutors, defense attorneys, and police officers. His closing arguments were epic and the benches in the back of the courtroom were always full of both prosecutors and defense attorneys who came to listen and learn. John was a tenacious prosecutor, but more importantly, he was a compassionate and loving son, husband, father, and friend. He is dearly missed.

I can confidently report that the integrity, commitment, and excellence of the DAO remain intact twenty years later, in great part because Adrienne Lynch now directs all homicide investigations, Duke Donoghue is the detective lieutenant in charge of the state police unit, and Anne Foley is the director of the Victim Witness Advocate Program. All three not only continue to "do," they also closely mentor, train, and support the people who represent the future of the office. Collectively, they represent a huge portion of the office's institutional memory, continuing to support and grow the organizational culture that has been so historically successful. The partnership between the prosecutors, troopers, local police, crime labs, and the OCME remains durable and firmly connected. The homicide "solve rate by arrest" for the unit over the past five years is 89 percent; the national rate is 61 percent. Last year, they investigated twenty-one homicides and solved every one of them with an arrest. The conviction rate of those defendants is well over 90 percent, while the national average is 73 percent.

• • • •

In most homicide cases, a bond forms between the prosecution team and the victim's family. The reasons are innumerable and case specific. They come together with a shared goal and a necessary dependence on each other to solve and prove the case. The need for emotional support grows as family members gather their strength to take the stand and maintain their composure. During trial, they sit no more than fifteen feet away from the person who took a life that was dear to them and changed their lives forever. Regardless of how a family tries to steel themselves for those moments, they cannot go it alone, and having a supportive shoulder to lean on or a hand to hold just an arm's-length away is a welcome and appreciated gesture.

The Hancocks were no different, although it certainly didn't appear that way from the start. In police jargon, they were going to be a "hard tow": a reference to recovering a vehicle that had gone off the roadway with severe damage and stuck in a bad place but still needing to be recovered, uprighted, and salvaged as best as possible.

The anger, pain, and anguish that poured out of Mark on our first meeting were completely understandable, although not expected. It took a lot of time and effort by everyone to prove to him that our motives were genuine and we truly empathized with him and were determined to indict and convict Kelly's murderer.

Most of these relationships fade over time as the prosecutors, police, and victim witness advocates move on to other cases and the families refocus and try to inch ahead and put their lives back together. However, the Hancocks are a different story.

They buried Kelly in a cemetery close to their Walpole home, and she doesn't lack for visitors. The site is a common destination for family walks and a place where her siblings go when they want to feel close to her and share a new story or an old memory, much as Kelly did when she sought shelter and intimacy curled up next to her mother's headstone to spend their night together.

In the spring, they spruce up the ground around the stone and plant flowers; in the fall, they decorate it for Halloween; and in December, they honor her with a decked out Christmas tree. Each year on November 6, Jackie, Lisa, and other siblings post on social media in celebration of her birthday. They attach pictures and remembrances about the good times they shared as a family. Mark, Jackie, and Adrienne still talk a few times a year, and on occasion, they visit and bring small, but meaningful, gifts that express their love and respect for the work done by everyone on behalf of Kelly. Adrienne has reciprocated in kind, and it is just as likely that she prompts the conversations, as it is the Hancocks.

In 2004, the Massachusetts Garden of Peace was dedicated on a small patch of land blanketed in the shadows of the state house and two state office buildings. Historically, the area was a tranquil retreat where office workers, college students from nearby Suffolk University, and mothers and nannies with their babies in tow came to sit on benches and read a book, eat lunch, or just close their eyes for a few moments of rest or reflection. Now, the land bisects with a dry streambed containing river stones engraved with the names of homicide victims. Some of the names are of victims of domestic violence, robbery, and gang violence. Some are of police officers or good people who stepped up to protect others and lost their lives in the battle.

A few died in the massacre in Wakefield on the morning after Christmas, and others were victims of terrorism during the attack on the World Trade Center in New York. Some of the names are familiar to all, like Jack and Bobby Kennedy. The display is a visual, moving testament to the need for eliminating violence. This is where families, friends, and the community come to remember and honor the lives of those taken by violence. It is also a symbol of hope for peace and renewal in our lives, our community, and the world.

Adrienne was aware of the garden and had talked with Anne Foley about the special meaning it held for victim's families. She thought it would be a wonderful way to honor and remember Kelly. She spoke about it with the Hancocks, and after securing their permission, filled out the paperwork, and forwarded the request and the engraving fee to the garden overseers. In 2010, a stone bearing Kelly's name was wedged into a prominent place next to that of a young victim of gang violence in Boston. Adrienne called Jackie, shared the news, and invited them to the annual dedication ceremony on the third Thursday of September. Mark, Jackie, and all of Kelly's brothers and sisters arrived as a family. After the speakers were done and the "roll of the fallen" read they joined with other families to seek out their stone. The first viewing was a sentimental and emotional moment for them—one that was hopefully more sweet than bitter.

Since that evening in 2010, every year on the third Thursday in September around five o'clock in the evening, the Hancock family returns to the Garden of Peace. They listen to the speakers, meet with Adrienne and Anne, and mingle with families who collectively share the same pains and bear the same burdens. Before heading out for a family dinner, they meander over to the area by Kelly's rock for a slight nod, a private thought, and maybe a prayer with Kelly. They also leave behind a small votive light and a beautiful flower in her memory. Their annual journey into Boston is a wonderful sign of the enduring love for their daughter and sister that brings them together. I have always thought of a rock as a symbol of strength, stability, and longevity. Now I point to the one marked with her name and celebrate the strength, stability, and longevity of the Hancock family.

I wrote this book because it is the rarest of true crime narratives, one that begins in tragedy and despair and ends in love and devotion. It is a story that literally cried out for sharing. Out of all of the homicide cases I worked, this one doesn't fade or shrink in its memory or importance. I think about Kelly and the Hancocks often. No one can say or know where Kelly would be today if she had survived her attack or never crossed paths with Tommy Crouse. I can see her as a wife, mother, college graduate, and successful woman. Just as likely, though, I can think of her in an opposite and desperate situation. The one thing I do know is that her death brought her family together in a way that may never have otherwise happened.

Like his daughter, Mark Hancock had a difficult childhood and as an adult was no stranger to personal and professional troubles. Jackie Shepard entered his life at the right time and for the right reasons. He wasn't always an easy person to corral or calm down, but she worked hard at changing his behavior. He came to recognize that if he were ever to become the person he wanted to be, it would only be with Jackie as his life partner. Once he determined to work with her and not rebel against change all of their lives started to brighten. Together they found religion, and it helped anchor them. She provided structure to his life, and together they learned to be good parents to their children. They moved away from the city to a suburb far from the snake's nest of bad choices that had gripped Kelly. He gutted and rebuilt his grandfather's house so the kids could grow up in their own home with a nice backyard, where they could go to schools and play sports, with vast choices and options for learning, developing, and succeeding in their own lives.

Today, all of that hard work and determination has paid off. The Hancocks aren't a wealthy family by any monetary gauge, but they are far richer in ways I doubt they had ever thought possible. Losing their Kelly was a tragedy beyond comprehension, but they chose not to wallow in self-pity and misery. Rather, they seized the opportunity to take control of their lives and refocus themselves on what it would take to rebuild their family. They took memories of Kelly and their difficult times together and channeled the negatives into positive energy. They created their own opportunities to regroup, eliminate the bad in their lives, and guide their other children through love, appreciation, and determination.

I spoke with family members as I was putting the finishing touches on their story. Jackie said they have been together for thirty years, and while it hasn't always been easy, they are always able to talk through and resolve their issues. Mark looked at her and smiled, "Well, sometimes we yell a lot, but that is because she is stubborn Irish and I'm stubborn Italian. We always work the problem through though." Jackie added, "In those thirty years, he has raised his voice in anger but never his hands." They know that quitting on each other is not an option; it never has been.

Lisa looked back on her years with Kelly and shared her favorite memories and thoughts about her big sister and best friend.

"Kelly and I were inseparable as kids. We were together when our mother died, when Jackie came into our lives, and as our family grew. She remembered their conversations about running away together. Kelly had all the answers, but Lisa said, "I was the scared one and was afraid to run so I never would."

She remembered how "Kelly was fearless and protective. She would take on the whole school to make sure I wasn't picked on. Kelly didn't shake at the world; the world shook for Kelly. No person, no situation ever scared her, and she loved to be the center of attention. In all of our home videos you can see her making her way into the middle of the picture."

"She loved her family," she continued. "I know that sounds cliché, but she LOVED her family. When Matt was born and Kelly was around it was like there was no one else that mattered. She loved that kid."

"Kelly was my best friend," she smiled, "It was me and her, glued at the hip. We were going to grow up together, go to college; she was going to wait for me. We were going to be bridesmaids in each other's weddings. We planned our whole lives out. When I think of Kelly now, I think of the dance parties in the kitchen, doing Sam and Taylor's hair in the bedroom, and playing basketball with Dad all day long. I love Kelly and think of her every day. I think of how different life would be if she were here. And sometimes I think that she's going to show up one day. That she actually isn't gone."

It is hard to imagine how the murder of a budding fourteen-year-old girl could ultimately result in a story of love and newfound strength and dedication to a family's future in her memory, but that is exactly what happened. A family grew stronger, and a lifetime friendship developed between people who might normally have found themselves on opposite sides of the law and of life. I'm not always sure I know a love story when I see it, but I do know this: Kelly's story is one of the greatest love stories I have ever witnessed.

Acknowledgments

During my many years investigating homicides, I learned that we reached the best outcomes with a multi-disciplinary effort that included prosecutors, investigators, forensic scientists, medical examiners and others trained in related specialties. When I began my research to write this book, I quickly understood it wasn't going to be something I could do alone. I had no idea how time consuming and arduous it would be, nor did I comprehend how many folks I would need to call on to support my efforts. Turns out the parallels between both careers are remarkable.

Like most journeys, the path begins and finishes at home and writing this book was no exception. I needed the buy-in of my family because without it I couldn't have started, let alone completed the work. What I thought would take a year or two took almost six, and my wife Jane and our daughters Meaghan and Caitlin had my back, continuously supporting the effort over the thousands of hours of research, writing, and re-writing. Their personal reviews and critiques along the way certainly played a large role in the shaping and telling of Kelly's story.

The next stop was the Middlesex District Attorney's Office and "the team." Without their approval and backing, my vision for the book would have perished before it took root. District Attorney Marian Ryan enthusiastically supported the idea, as did Adrienne Lynch, and the entire investigative team. We worked together throughout the process. At times, I felt like I was back working for Adrienne as I interviewed, reinterviewed, and researched every detail to be sure I had everything right. Members of "the team" read and offered comments on the first draft, and the second, etc. offering insight from their perspectives, which on occasion, differed from mine.

With the reinforcement of my family and the District Attorney's office, the only major hurdle left was to gain the support of the Hancock family.

While we had met during the investigation and trial, many years had passed, and I didn't know how they might react to the idea of reliving their worst moments and exposing their family lives in a book: an intrusion that would ask much of them. Adrienne and Ann Foley helped me by re-introducing me to the Hancocks at the annual Garden of Peace ceremony in Boston, and by briefing the Hancocks on what I wanted to discuss with them. At our meeting, I explained what I wanted to do, answered their questions and concerns as best I could and by evening's end, they were solidly on board with the project. The assistance and input from Kelly's father, Mark, stepmother, Jackie, and sister, Lisa has added immeasurable depth and content to the story. Their willingness to share their recollections and personal memories of Kelly, and explain how in the aftermath of her death, their resolve to fully commit to each other and to use that bond to strengthen their family during some very difficult times has been nothing short of remarkable and inspirational.

With their reinforcement and support behind me, it was time to learn how to write and tell the story. I had written several articles and stories for state police newspapers and magazines and taken a few writing courses at Emerson College where my wife worked, but writing a book was a whole other story!

I read books and magazine articles to get answers to my questions and concerns about writing and, like everyone these days; I turned to the internet for help. I searched for a personal writing coach and editor who could guide me through the unchartered waters of non-fiction, true crime book writing. I found Cynde Christie a couple of thousand miles from Boston in a rural section of Santa Fe, New Mexico. She has been a godsend. She transformed me from writing standard, information packed police reports, to becoming a creative storyteller who can now narrate with dialogue and descriptive language to bring the story to life. She taught me how to "show not tell."

Before I could begin to write the story, I needed to collect and organize the information, so the storyline would flow in a chronological, historically precise, and flawless manner. At a minimum that required all of the trial transcripts, police reports, media reports, and other supportive documents. For those tasks, I turned to two people with superior organizational skills: Ashley Cunningham from the district attorney's office and Rose Warren from the state police, and they didn't let me down. I am indebted to them both!

I may know my way around a police investigation, but once we make an arrest and the defendant is transported to the jail to await trial, we are somewhat out of the loop. For insight and input about the inner workings and administration at the Middlesex Sheriff's office, I sought and received the assistance of Scott Brazis, the retired Special Sheriff and second-in-command of the Department and John Costello, the superintendent at the Cambridge Jail. They have since retired, but both were in leadership positions at the jail in two-thousand, and provided both historical information and deep insight into the daily administration of the jail, in particular the protective custody unit.

Comparably, while I was a Massachusetts State Trooper for more than thirty years and understood our policies, procedures, and manner of conducting business, I didn't know exactly how the New Hampshire State Police or their Major Crime Unit functioned. For insight, I turned to John Cody, the trooper who supervised the recovery and removal of Kelly from her burial ground in Hooksett. His remembrances and explanations added immensely to the depth and quality of the story. Ironically, when we met, John had retired from the New Hampshire State Police and was working for the Massachusetts Attorney General in Boston. As we closed off our first interview, I signaled John over to his office window and pointed straight down to a clear view of the Garden of Peace and the river rock inscribed with Kelly Hancock's name. It was surreal imagery for both of us.

The first version of this book was cumbersome and a bit clumsy with more than five-hundred pages of text. It needed new and clear sets of eyes to assess and make recommendations for clarity and change. Cynde and

I each chose five beta-readers to scour the manuscript and offer their insights. I am indebted to them for their efforts on my behalf. They were honest and respectful in their criticism and told me things I needed to hear; they offered praise in some areas, but were highly critical in others. A very big Thank You to Cynde's choices who I have never met or spoken with and who have never been involved in the criminal justice system; Sue Gantner, Jack Heinsius, Robert Christie, Tina Olson, and Gretel Underwood.

My beta-readers were closer to home. Adrienne Lynch, Jimmy Conolly, and Duke Donoghue lived it, so they were instrumental in pointing out areas of strength and weakness in the plot. Like the others, they didn't hold back with their comments.

The final two were my brother John and published author Bill Landay. John has been a reporter for the *Boston Globe* for the past fifty years and was the prominent author of a special edition of the *Globe Magazine,* awarded a Pulitzer Prize for national reporting. Bill is a friend and former Middlesex County assistant district attorney and is the author of three best-selling fictional crime drama novels, including *"Defending Jacob"* which was featured in a 2020 Apple TV mini-series. They were both immensely helpful in pointing out when and where I veered off course and floundered as well as how I needed to better develop my role as the narrator and Adrienne's as the story's protagonist. Then they showed me how to fix it and regain control by tightening up the writing, removing information that didn't move the story along so I could recapture or maintain the reader's interest. I didn't always hear what I wanted to hear, but I certainly heard what I needed to hear. It helped that one writes non-fiction and the other fiction so they offered differing perspectives.

Finally, I want to acknowledge the team of professionals that provided the direction and technical expertise to get my efforts into print. Cynde's professional coaching partner and author, Sarah Lovett, offered the "been there, done that," type of suggestions and explanations that answered many of my questions and ultimately led me to make the decision to self-publish. Jack Arnold, an accomplished website designer literally put me on the map and introduced me to the world of book readers with an attractive and beautifully designed website: (www.powersonpolicing.com). Jen Marshall copyedited every page with a meticulous eye for grammar and sentence structure. Christine Woods, a skilled portrait and landscape photographer from my home city of Quincy worked wonders in creating the bio photos for both the book and my website. Nick Zelinger, an amazing, award-winning graphic artist, not only designed the book's front and back covers, but also handled the formatting and layout and the other technical aspects. Veronica Yager, my Amazon expert who guided me through the complex and intricate world of self-publishing, left no stone unturned, or opportunity missed to promote both the book and myself. A very special thank you to my team of professionals.

About the Author

B ill Powers has been active in the Massachusetts law enforcement community since entering the State Police Academy in June of 1974. His early career assignments ranged from patrol to investigations to academy instructor. In the years that followed, he rose through the ranks, gaining experience, and training and ultimately received a promotion to Detective Lieutenant. In that leadership position he was assigned as the Commanding Officer of the State Police Detective Units (SPDU) in both Middlesex and Suffolk Counties, where he had direct oversight of more than one hundred homicides and several hundred more sudden, unattended deaths that were investigated and determined not to be homicides. His State Police career came full circle when he was named Director of Training for the Division of Investigative Services and then to the role of Commandant of the Recruit Training Academy in 2005. He retired as the director of the Media Relations Section.

Bill has an undergraduate degree from Northeastern with a major in Criminal Justice and a Juris Doctorate degree from the New England School of Law. He has been a member in good standing of the Massachusetts Bar since 1985.

After retiring from the State Police in 2007, Bill received an appointment as an Assistant Professor in the graduate program for forensic sciences, at the Boston University School of Medicine (BUSM). For the next seven years, he lectured on criminal investigation and expert testimony to the graduate students. In addition, and as part of his position, he produced several short-term training seminars geared specifically to law enforcement officers. The courses explored subjects as wide-ranging as basic investigation techniques, through more advanced subject matter topics such as Sexual Assault investigations and Medico-Legal Death investigations. Following his tenure at the BUSM, he returned to the law enforcement profession as the Director of Public Safety, at Wentworth Institute in Boston. He is currently a contract employee with the Massachusetts State Police as a Program Development Coordinator in the Division of Standards and Training.

Bill resides South of Boston with his wife Jane. Their two daughters, one a State Trooper and the other a high school teacher and volleyball coach live nearby. His blessings also include five remarkable grandchildren who sparkle like bright stars in the night sky.

To learn more about Bill,
please visit his website at www.powersonpolicing.com

Made in the USA
Middletown, DE
16 September 2023

38506132R00225